DEWEY'S LABORATORY SCHOOL

Lessons for Today

DEWEY'S LABORATORY SCHOOL

Lessons for Today

Laurel N. Tanner

FOREWORD BY PHILIP W. JACKSON

Teachers College, Columbia University
New York and London

Published by Teachers College Press, 1234 Amsterdam Avenue, New York, NY 10027

Library of Congress Cataloging-in-Publication Data

Tanner, Laurel N.
    Dewey's laboratory school : lessons for today / Laurel N. Tanner ; foreword by Philip W. Jackson.
       p.   cm.
    Includes bibliographical references (p.   ) and index.
    ISBN 0-8077-3619-8 (alk. paper). — ISBN 0-8077-3618-X (pbk. : alk. paper)
    1. University of Chicago. University Elementary School—History.
2. Education—Illinois—Chicago—Experimental methods—History.
3. Dewey, John, 1859–1952. I. Title.
LD7501.C428T36 1997
372.9773'11—dc21   96-40141

ISBN 0-8077-3618-X (paper)
ISBN 0-8077-3619-8 (cloth)

Printed on acid-free paper
Manufactured in the United States of America

04 03 02 01 00 99 98 97   8 7 6 5 4 3 2 1

For Ken

Contents

Foreword

HAD LAUREL TANNER WRITTEN THIS BOOK in 1904 instead of today she well might have convinced Dewey to stay put at the University of Chicago instead of hieing off to Columbia University, where he spent the balance of his academic career. At the very least she would have given him food for thought, which is what she offers plenty of for today's readers. She also might have made Dewey blush with embarrassment (shy man that he was) for he could hardly have found a more enthusiastic admirer of his educational accomplishments. Nor could he have been blessed with a clearer expositor of many of his key ideas.

But if Laurel Tanner *had* written this book 90-some years ago instead of today, present readers would have missed out on something that only a retrospective outlook from a fair distance in time can give, which is an illuminating comparison of Then and Now. Fortunately for us, this volume contains much more than a backward look, even though that in itself more than repays the reader's time and energy. Tanner keeps cycling from past to present and back again and almost always with profit. Her book's pages are chock-full of sharp and striking contrasts between practices that characterized the Dewey school and those being carried on in today's schools and classrooms. As one might expect, given the fact that she troubled to chronicle the past so meticulously, the comparisons generally favor the older set of practices. This is not to say that Tanner finds Dewey and his teachers invariably right and today's practitioners correspondingly wrong. But she does make clear that many of today's most talked-about educational ideas and innovations—notions such as the professional autonomy of teachers, multicultural education, character education, and more—pale in comparison when placed beside the way Dewey and his staff handled similar issues almost a century ago. As a result, there is much to be learned in these pages about how to improve even the most up-to-date of our current practices.

Laurel Tanner has been a leader in the broad field of curricular studies for a number of years. The wide readership of the several books on curriculum and on curriculum theory that she has written and co-authored attests to her high standing within the field at large. She also has been a pioneer, as both organizer and contributor, in the rather more specialized study of curricular history. Here too her writings stand as testimony to her scholarly accomplishment. The present book brings together both perspectives—the broad and the narrow—that long have characterized the breadth and the depth of Tanner's intellectual interests and scholarly ambitions. In so doing it reveals the fit and even the necessity of both outlooks. It shows how a close examination of the past can lead to an altered view of the present and a revised conception of the future. Such a demonstration surely would have pleased Dewey, for it was he who said, in *Democracy and Education* (1916):

> The segregation which kills the vitality of history is divorce from present modes and concerns of social life. The past just as past is no longer our affair. If it were wholly gone and done with, there would be only one reasonable attitude toward it. Let the dead bury their dead. But knowledge of the past is the key to the understanding of the present. History deals with the past, but this past is the history of the present. (pp. 250–251)

I cannot help but close this Foreword on a personal note. Laurel undertook much of the research that entered into the writing of this book during the year she spent as a Visiting Scholar at the Benton Center for Curriculum and Instruction at the University of Chicago. She spent much of her time during those months digging through old records and teacher reports from the Dewey school, many of which currently are housed in the archives of the University's Regenstein Library. It became evident as the year wore on that Laurel had come upon a treasure trove of both primary and secondary material and was becoming increasingly eager to begin telling the story of the school's early operations to today's educators. I was Director of the Benton Center at the time and was very pleased to have had a hand in making Laurel's stay there possible. Now that her book is complete I am even more delighted with the outcome of Laurel's visit to the Center than I was back then. For in the pages that follow we have what amounts to near tangible evidence that a host of Dewey's educational ideas (together with those of his teachers and co-administrators) not only have withstood the test of time but remain as forward-looking and as advanced today as they were back then. If the current revival of interest in Dewey's pragmatism among philosophers is one day matched by a corresponding revival of interest in his educational thought among educators (and who among those acquainted with Dewey's educational writings could but wish for such a happy turn of events?) the book you are about to read surely will be credited with having contributed significantly to that end.

—Philip W. Jackson

Preface

As a Dewey biographer has pointed out with obvious glee, Dewey has been rediscovered (Ryan, 1995). But many of us already knew about Dewey and rediscovery was not necessary. What we do need, particularly if we are teachers or teacher educators, is to know more about the workings of his experimental school (1896–1904). That is something I emphatically decided as I read the teachers' reports from a century ago in the marvelous Regenstein Library at the University of Chicago. What those teachers were doing was so current (they could be our colleagues), the problems they were trying to solve so contemporary, and the theoretical basis for the school so remarkable that I had to make these ideas more widely available. There are lessons for today from the school, lessons about child development and learning, school administration and supervision, curriculum development, and character education. The theory behind the Laboratory School—the idea of school as a small cooperative society where children at any stage of development can solve problems, and where "the systematic knowledge of adult consciousness is gradually and systematically worked out" (Dewey, 1897b, p. 364)—is remarkable for it embraces all that we, who as a people demand so much of our schools, could want for our children. So much was accomplished in those 7 short years to develop a consecutive curriculum to match the theory. It really was amazing because Dewey had such a hard time getting his school and the curriculum in shape. We give up too easily but I think there is a reason: We fear that if we stay with a plan we will go down with the ship. The point is that he did not give up; he followed his experimental philosophy and kept on trying until he came up with a form of organization that fit his educational theories. Because of his experimental philosophy the concept of planning was flexible. Without the experimental philosophy his school probably would have failed and closed after 6 months because his first plan of organization did not work out. The school moved to a departmental form of organization but the curriculum was not compartmentalized. How on earth did he do it? There are lessons to be learned from which we can profit.

Dewey's chief interest, like our own, was educational reform. When he established his experimental school, the purpose, as he put it, was "to discover in administration, selection of subject matter, methods of learning, teaching, and discipline, how a school could become a cooperative community while developing in individuals their own capacities and identifying their own needs" (Mayhew & Edwards, 1936, pp. xv–xvi). If ever the term "school restructuring" was appropriate to describe a reform effort, it was in the instance of Dewey's school. A century prior to the recent restructuring movement, Dewey insisted that school administration and curriculum development were organically related activities and should be approached as such. The old autocratic ways of working with teachers would never do.

Dewey and the teachers put into practice some of the ideas that we are trying to implement today: relating the curriculum to children's life and experience, integrating the curriculum, teaching critical thinking and problem solving, stimulating creative thinking, supporting collaborative decision making by the school staff. Dewey saw his school as a laboratory for studying how children learn and for identifying the possibilities and problems of the schools in view of the information gained. One hundred years later the problems still exist but so do the possibilities.

Dewey's school was important for him as well as ourselves. He continued to think about it for years after he left Chicago, and it influenced such major works as *How We Think* (1910) and *Democracy and Education* (1916). The influences of the school and the people who helped bring his ideas into fruition are clearly stated in the acknowledgments of these books. Two women in particular—his wife Alice and Ella Flagg Young—are acknowledged warmly.

The trouble is that the ideas are not developed fully enough in these major works to serve as guides to practice. But in the school records and reports and in articles written by Dewey for the *Elementary School Record* (1900a, 1900b, 1900c, 1900d), which he edited with Laura Runyon, a teacher at the school, these ideas come through very clearly.

A history entitled *The Dewey School*, chronicles the school's creation until Dewey's departure in 1904. The book, written by Katherine Camp Mayhew and Anna Camp Edwards, who taught at the school in its first years, was called, by the historian Lawrence Cremin (1961, p. 137), "a detailed and engrossing account." It is probably the most complete history of the school that we will get; certainly we will not have another by people who had firsthand knowledge of the school's underlying principles and everyday operation. Although Mayhew and Edwards put off their history until 1936, they had much material to work with and their continuing interest in the school for such a long period speaks to its importance in their own lives. Those who want an account of the school's history will need to go back to their book. My book is not intended to be a history; its concern is now: what we can learn from Dewey and his staff as we wrestle with the same problems that they worked out.

Unlike many writers on education today, Dewey saw the possibilities as well as the problems. Were homes not educating children the way they did when he was a boy? Schools could do this more systematically in connection with a civilizational theme that was developmentally appropriate and served to unify children's educational experience (in and out of school), thereby making it more meaningful. Was the world becoming smaller, providing ever more intercultural contacts? There were new opportunities to enrich the experiences of individuals and the society by bringing people together in order to solve the problems they held in common.

The civilizational theme in itself was a social unifier. All people had to go through the same processes of thinking and experimentation to solve the problems of living. People from other areas of the world are basically the same as we are, despite superficial differences. This valuable lesson from Dewey's laboratory school often is missed in today's multicultural education programs.

Educators in Dewey's time had an advantage that we lack. They could visit his school, attend his classes both on campus and by correspondence, and read about what the children and their teachers were doing. And they could, and did, contribute their own ideas to the solution of curriculum problems. It was in no sense a one-person operation.

I wish I could bring the school back, Brigadoon-like; what one might see, as I did, is that it was very modern. Perhaps a century is not as long as one might think; it was our century, yours and mine, after all. My own father, who was born in 1899, could have been in Dewey's kindergarten—how quickly we get back to the generation of Dewey and the teachers. Although I am unable to do magic and bring the school back, it is my hope that I have managed in these chapters to convey its substance and significance for today.

Chapter 1 deals principally with two lessons: the social nature of learning and developmentally appropriate practice. These ideas have continued to find support in the work of contemporary scholars and are unlearned lessons—at least the way that Dewey applied them. Chapter 2 examines the laboratory school idea as conceived by Dewey. The school was a desire achieved, but there was something almost providential about this event. The possibilities for laboratory schools today are discussed. We need a coherent curriculum and Chapter 3 examines Dewey's model, which has been oddly neglected. In Chapter 3, I discuss ways that the Dewey teachers capitalized on children's interests, activities, and natural talent for imagination. We have much to learn from these teachers regarding the use of imagination in early childhood education. Chapter 4 discusses the resources used by the teachers in developing a new curriculum and the two-dimensional curriculum that resulted. Often overlooked are the teachers' contributions to Dewey's pedagogical theory. They are discussed here. Ideas from Dewey's school for dealing with present problems of curriculum integration also are considered in Chapter 4. In Chapter 5, the teachers themselves describe their approaches to instruction and how well they did or did not work out. There are striking implications for today. (We seldom give teachers a chance to report on what worked and what needs rethinking in the way of instructional approaches.) The possible value of teachers' reports is considered in Chapter 5. Chapter 6 discusses how teacher cooperation functioned as a substitute for the kind of supervision based on levels of authority in an organization. A principal concern of the chapter is elementary teachers as subject specialists. A departmental form of organization, as it functioned in the Laboratory School, is a real lesson for today. Chapter 6 examines Dewey's idea of planning, which is very different from educational planning at the federal, state, and local levels today. Dewey's experience with multiage grouping, which resulted in a change of plans, is discussed. Chapter 7 is concerned with children's development as self-directing learners. Dewey's stages of development that emerged from the school's work are discussed and compared with the stage theories of Piaget and Kohlberg. Instruction-related approaches to discipline problems were worked out in the Laboratory School. They are discussed in Chapter 7. Stages of discipline with teacher and pupil responsibilities also are presented. Chapter 8 shows how all of the ideas in the previous seven chapters are interrelated and function seamlessly in a good school. Discussed in this final chapter is the issue of youth crime. Dewey's definition of character and his straight-from-the-shoulder ideas for preventing and dealing with youth crime are timely and could be helpful. The chapter concludes with a simple checklist concerning ideas from Dewey's school. The thought is that those who are interested might want to see how their school measures up. Some of the ideas are being applied, although not always well and not always with understanding; such understanding would enhance their effectiveness.

My only disappointment with this book is that it did not come out in time for the school's centennial in 1996. But I kept finding more and more information that might be helpful for today's schools and it was worth the extra time. Dewey continues to be a modern thinker and his school a modern school. I have a feeling that this will be so for a long time.

Acknowledgments

THIS BOOK WOULD NOT HAVE BEEN POSSIBLE had I not had access to the incredible resources on the Dewey school in the Regenstein Library at the University of Chicago. This access was conveniently available to me during my very profitable year as a Visiting Scholar at the Benton Center for Curriculum and Instruction in the Department of Education at the University of Chicago. I am deeply grateful to Philip W. Jackson, then Director of the Benton Center, for the invitation to be a Visiting Scholar.

My husband, Kenneth J. Rehage of the University of Chicago, deserves special thanks. Ken criticized the book in its conceptual stages and opened the door to invaluable resources. This is more than a figure of speech; when I first began my research the teachers' reports from the early years of the Laboratory School were being stored in a closet in Judd Hall. The cache has since been moved to the Regenstein Library. Ken's deep interest in the project has been lucky for me and for this book.

Ralph W. Tyler, who is no longer with us, generously shared his time and insights with me over a period of years. Ralph was impressed with how Dewey and the teachers tried to identify and build on children's assets and he saw this as something we need to do. I am impressed with how Ralph's life was an extension of Dewey's. This book has definitely benefited from his wisdom.

My former husband, Daniel Tanner of Rutgers University, shared with me his sharp insights into the implications of Dewey's school and made invaluable suggestions throughout the development of this book.

During the course of this project I have benefited from ideas and suggestions from Frances S. Bolin of Teachers College, Columbia University; Lynn M. Burlbaw of Texas A&M University; Lynne Cavazos of the University of California, Santa Barbara; Paula A. Cordeiro of the University of Connecticut; and Craig Kridel of the University of South Carolina. I owe special thanks to Richard L. Hooker and Allen R. Warner of the University of Houston and Trevor E. Sewell of Temple University for their continuous encouragement and support throughout the course of this project. No scholar ever had more supportive colleagues.

Appreciation is extended to Valarie Brocato, Suzy Taraba, and Krista Ovitz of the Department of Special Collections of the University of Chicago Library and to David Ment of the Teachers College Library, Columbia University for their assistance during the course of the research. William Harms of the News Office at the University of Chicago provided invaluable aid in locating and obtaining photographs.

Marion Ann Keller deserves special thanks for typing the manuscript with care and cheer.

❖ **1** ❖

Lessons Unlearned

It is not surprising that in a half-dozen years this school should not only increase in number, but that it should reach a position of commanding influence in this country.
—Wilbur S. Jackman, "A Brief History of the School of Education"

IT IS AMAZING WHAT TIME can do. Although influential in its time, the school that John Dewey established to test and demonstrate his ideas about children's learning has all but been forgotten. Dewey hoped that his school would provide direction to other schools, just as laboratories in scientific fields eventually lead to change. The purpose of his school was, in his own words, "to create new standards and ideals" and "lead to a gradual change in conditions" (Dewey, 1896c, p. 417). In what became known as the Dewey School, ideas that were original in his time were applied and modified as teachers worked with children. A century later, the ideas and practices still have been mainly disregarded. There are waiting for us in the records of this school, lessons yet unlearned about things that deeply concern us—educating children in the problems of living together as a community, nation, and world, and creating a new curriculum that is matched to child growth.

THE SOCIAL NATURE OF LEARNING

We like to think of our age and its problems as unique, and one can, of course, draw differences between our era and Dewey's. Violent crime among youth has continued to rise (Butterfield, 1996) and has grown more wanton. Some school districts with high rates of violence are attempting to prevent crime by training youth in "managing conflict" (Portner, 1994a, p. 21). Since the 1960s fear of crime has grown in the larger society, and protecting oneself from crime has become a way of American life. No one can ever get far enough away from crime and the worry about it.

Changing economic and family patterns have resulted in children receiving less parental guidance, and many children learn how to behave mainly from television (Brandt, 1993). No wonder, then, that some educators have come to feel that schools should do more to help children grow up to be socially responsible adults who behave in constructive and caring ways. Brandt's observation that "educators feel they must do something; the question is—what?" (p. 5) is no doubt correct. Dewey's school has much to say to us about the what. When he started his school, economic and family patterns were already in the process of changing. The entire conception for the school was calculated to respond constructively to these changes (Dewey, 1899). As we attempt to prepare children for their life responsibilities a century later, we can profit from the school's experience in awakening children to the needs of others and the desire and the power to give. This is so, even if Dewey's school happens to confirm the value of what we already are doing.

Fostering Social Sensitivity and Social Interest

Dewey was tough-minded. He saw the changing patterns and he told it like it was: Schools must compensate educationally for what was being lost in the home (1899). This was a particularly difficult challenge, and he met it experimentally and creatively. He attacked the problem on two levels—school organization and curriculum. He established his school as "a cooperative society on a small scale" (Mayhew & Edwards, 1936, p. 466) so that children "would be prepared to make their future social relations worthy and fruitful" (p. 467). He did this by making human occupations such as cooking, weaving, and carpentry the activities that led children toward understandings in the fields of organized knowledge such as chemistry, geology, and mathematics. Children learned by re-enacting the drama of human development.

A Curriculum Focused on Human Similarities. An important point not to be overlooked is that the curriculum developed by Dewey and his staff strove to teach human similarities. Not only Americans but all people share these similarities; they all cook, weave, sew, and build houses. They all have common economic and social problems stemming from changes in industrial organization. Getting separate ethnic groups to work together on these problems may be the one best hope of ending the bloody conflicts among them ("Peaceful Integration," 1991). One way that this can happen is through transfer from school experiences. But curriculum trends in the 1990s have promoted and perpetuated ethnic separatism "in the name of multiculturalism" (Honan, 1994, p. B3). Multicultural programs all too often focus on what Americans do not share as a people. A proposal for a multicultural curriculum in New York State, for example, tended strongly in this direction (Sobel, 1993). The philosophy of a society marked into indelible divisions can only pose a barrier to Dewey's ideal school as a cooperative community. More important, it hardly seems reasonable to expect that a curriculum that builds walls between people rather than focusing on what unites them could help them live peaceably.

Recognizing the Advantages of Changed Family Patterns. Since Dewey's day the trends that he saw have continued. There is less work done in the home to meet people's basic needs, such as food. The changes have come into existence and there are certain definite advantages. Who would want to reverse the changes that provide new professional opportunities for women outside the home? As Dewey (1899) pointed out in a lecture to parents and friends of the school, "we must recognize our compensations" (p. 12). Today the problem is just as he conceived it: to preserve the advantages opened by the changing patterns and to make the school "into a vital social institution to a very much greater extent than obtains at present" (Dewey, 1897a, p. 13) so that children learn to be socially responsible people.

Dewey's perspective on what he saw as a developing trend enlarges our own perspective—it certainly did my own—and it is worth our time to sit in his audience and listen. In his talk to parents, he observed that the home no longer was educating children the way it had in the old agrarian society in which each child shared in significant work and could see at first hand the whole industrial process. "We cannot overlook the factors of discipline and of character-building involved . . . " (1899, p. 10). "But," Dewey continued, "it is useless to bemoan the departure of the good old days of children's modesty, reverence, and implicit obedience, if we expect merely by bemoaning and exhortation to bring them back" (p. 11). It was the social conditions that had changed, and only an equally radical change in education would work in building character. The observation might have been made today.

Lessons in How to Imbue—and Not to Imbue— the Spirit of Service in Children

Dewey had been running his school for 3 years when he made the above observations. By then he felt able to make proposals for other schools based on his school's ideals and activities. Dewey (1899) contended that each of our schools must become

> an embryonic community life, active with the types of occupations that reflect the life of the larger society, and permeated throughout with the spirit of art, history and science. When the school introduces and trains each child of society into membership within such a little community, saturating him with the spirit of service, and providing him with the instruments of effective self-direction, we

shall have the deepest and best guaranty of a larger society which is worthy, lovely, and harmonious. (pp. 43–44)

Obviously Dewey's intent was that the spirit of service should permeate the entire curriculum and atmosphere of the school. Working together in close association with others on an activity meant that one's own work contributed to a common purpose and could build lifelong habits. In his later work at Columbia University Dewey (1916) went on to develop a means of problem solving that emphasized the social role of people. Always the spirit of service involved thinking, not just doing.

The point is an important one in light of recent requirements that students perform community service, a form of character education in some states (Hernandez, 1994). Such programs have been set up to develop a sense of civic responsibility in students. However, all too often they are merely add-ons to the curriculum rather than a true part of it and cannot be said to generate more than a sense of irritation among many students—as any seemingly disconnected requirements would do. In short, they put a penalty on students.

A perusal of literature on service programs will show that there are lessons unlearned about service. The programs often are not based on Dewey's idea that service is part of students' intellectual as well as social development. In fact, some programs convey the exact opposite—that doing has nothing whatsoever to do with thinking. Howard (1993), for example, sees service as "nurturing students' nonacademic strengths" (p. 43). According to a deputy assistant U.S. attorney general, requiring that students perform community service teaches them how to become good citizens and find out about available service opportunities (Portner, 1994b). For Dewey (1909), activity in helping others happens—or should happen—after reflection and the development of goals. Moreover, children and, of course, their teachers should look upon school subjects naturally rather than artificially. These subjects, after all, developed out of the need for human beings to find answers to their questions, and these questions were closely related with human needs. All school subjects should be taught to bring out their personal and social aspects, "stressing how human beings are affected by them" (Hook, 1975, p. xi). In geography, for example, the children in Dewey's school learned that the significance of a river or mountain is social, not physical.

The constitutionality of mandatory community service programs has been challenged on the basis that they ask students "to provide free labor to institutions or individuals" (Hernandez, 1994, p. B13). The problem with which we are concerned is summed up in one legal claim: "Coerced volunteering . . . destroys the spirit of helping others" (p. B13). No doubt Dewey would agree.

In addition to the diminishing influence of the home on children's character, Dewey identified other continuing trends of importance in reforming our own institutions. One in particular bears on the crime problem. Building on his early work in the Laboratory School, Dewey in 1916 identified social interaction as the key to the health of individuals and a society that grows ever more humane as individuals are united by common interests. At the end of the twentieth century, social interaction grows more possible and isolation has been established as a key to mental illness, social dislocation, and crime. Dewey's sociological and psychological ideas have been supported to a considerable extent by later scholars.

Social Isolation and Social Dislocation

Joblessness, teenage pregnancy, and crime are forms of social dislocation in our inner cities. In view of his own ideas, Dewey would have been interested in what William Julius Wilson, a sociology professor at the University of Chicago, had to say about social dislocation. According to Wilson (1987), recent increases in the rates of these problems "cannot be accounted for by the easy explanation of racism" (p. ix). The main cause is social isolation: "the lack of contact or of sustained interaction with individuals and institutions that represent mainstream society" (p. 60). The most disadvantaged African American youth rarely interact with persons who have had a stable employment history and "they seldom have sustained contacts with friends or relatives in the more stable areas of the city or in the suburbs" (p. 60). They are cut off. As Dewey (1916) pointed out "an alert and expanding mental life depends upon an enlarging range of contact with the physical environment," but, more important, with a widening "sphere of social contacts" (p. 100).

In Dewey's time, Asian Americans experienced exclusion from public schooling by the dominant white culture. In San Francisco, Japanese and Chinese children were kept out until the early 1900s (Peterson, 1985). What Peterson calls "cultural imperialism" (p. 6) has continued to fall away, and, as Tyler (1988) observed, more and more previously excluded groups have access to the curriculum. Improving access is an "unfinished task" (Tyler, 1978, p. 1), as is making the access worthwhile to learners.

Enriching Children's Lives Through Intercultural Contacts

Early in the twentieth century Dewey saw the breaking down of physical barriers between previously isolated nations, races, and ethnic groups as a continuing trend and he viewed it as an opportunity: The lives of individuals are enriched and their horizons expanded through a greater number of contacts with other cultures. Moreover, the society benefits from a "broader community of interest" (1916, p. 101) where one group does not shut out others.

Dewey's concept of democracy bears directly on present racial and ethnic issues in the curriculum. In bringing people together from previously isolated racial and ethnic groups to participate in an interest—Dewey does not say what it might be but presumably it could be a problem of mutual concern—teachers are not only creating community but enriching the experiences and releasing the talents of individuals. This is what education in a democracy is all about.

In the 1980s and 1990s a number of states passed laws saying that students need to appreciate other cultures and eliminate personal ethnocentrism. As indicated, the focus of multicultural programs is on teaching about other cultures—on cultural pluralism rather than developing the shared interests that Dewey believed are vital for a healthy and progressive society (and which he definitely tried to develop in his Laboratory School). It still remains for schools "to secure the intellectual and emotional significance of this physical annihilation of space" (Dewey, 1916, p. 100). At the close of the century this remains a lesson unlearned.

Dewey's idea that learning is ever social in nature continues to be something to take seriously in today's world. We need not worry about Dewey's ideas being out of date because they come from another time. He was clearly a man ahead of his time and we have yet to catch up. In the 1990s the physical barriers have continued to fall as American economic activities are directed toward emerging world markets in South Africa, Hungary, and the Middle East. But a unified society appears to be a forgotten—if not rejected—dream.

DEVELOPMENTALLY APPROPRIATE PRACTICE

The world is different, but the problems that Dewey and his school staff tried to learn more about and the ones that we are trying to solve are fundamentally the same. They always will be as long as there are children for whom we seek the best and a society that is rampant with problems and rich with possibilities. The teachers in Dewey's school were "seeking the best things for children" (Jackman, 1904, p. 6). Could that not also be ourselves?

In fact, although a century apart, we and they might all be colleagues where our concern for finding better ways of working with children is concerned. They might wonder, though, why we have not yet profited from the ideas generated by their school, and there is no better example than the recent emphasis on "developmentally appropriate practice" in early childhood classrooms (Elkind, 1991, p. 14; see also Slade & Wolf, 1994).

The Concept

The term "developmentally appropriate," which became popular in the late 1980s and 1990s has been well described by Bowman (1991):

The term evokes a vision of classroom experiences synchronized with each child's maturational/experiential status so that what is presented to be learned is consistent with the child's capacity to learn, thereby insuring school success. (p. 25)

As Bowman has observed, the "concept appeals both as an educational philosophy and as common sense" (p. 25). Moreover, it has long been in our legacy of ideas about educating young children. A century ago, Dewey insisted that we must find out "where the child really is," what he or she is capable of doing and "can do to the greatest advantage with the least waste of time and strength, mental and physical. We find here our indicators or pointers as to the range of facts and ideas legitimate to the child" (1897b, p. 365).

On the surface there is a striking similarity between the recent concern for developmental appropriateness and Dewey's; indeed they seem one and the same. But there are real and very important differences. In a word there is more to Dewey's idea. For Dewey, curriculum development was central. His main purpose in establishing his experimental school was, in his words, "the construction of a course of study which harmonizes with the growth of the child in capacity and experience" (1900c, p. 226). Obviously, the curriculum would be developmentally appropriate, but Dewey's eye was on the ball of curriculum development. He argued that the psychological or developmental view needed to be supplemented by the social in developing a curriculum. In his "Plan of Organization of the University Primary School" (1895a) Dewey wrote: "The ultimate problem of all education is to co-ordinate the psychological and the social factors" (p. 1).

The Cliché

There is a tendency for those concerned with developmentally appropriate practice to regard the curriculum as a given. Their concern is with placement of content, whatever that content happens to be. Philosophical questions about what is worth learning, and most important to learn, go unasked. Thus Elkind (1991) writes that "curricula need to be studied to determine their level of developmental difficulty" (p. 12). One can easily see how this could refer to any kind of curriculum, even one designed to teach racism. Schools need to be concerned about what is taught—its social value in a democratic society and worth to the child—as much as they are with whether children make too many errors because a problem or task is too difficult for them. This deep lesson comes from Dewey's Laboratory School. Unfortunately, it has never really been learned; our years of educational experience since Dewey are strewn with examples of curriculum adaptation, the idea that the school can best be improved by rearranging the existing curriculum in accord with child development findings (Tanner & Tanner, 1990, p. 166).

Dewey's objective in his Laboratory School was not to perpetuate the traditional curriculum by making it developmentally appropriate. It was to create a new curriculum in which developmental, intellectual, and social goals were viewed as inextricably intertwined. Developmentally appropriate practice can be an empty term. Without considering and questioning all curricular factors—what is taught, its worth to the child, and its importance to the society—the historically honorable concept of developmental appropriateness degenerates into mere cliché and education reform becomes less likely.

FOLLOWING DEWEY

There is a tendency in American classrooms to try one educational reform program after another, often in the name of Dewey. It is clear from the names given these ideas—developmentally appropriate early childhood programs, community service, cooperative learning, interdisciplinary curricula are examples—that we would like to have the kinds of schools that John Dewey fought for and for which he tried to develop a model in his Laboratory School 100 years ago. It is also clear that somehow we have lost our way.

The Disappearing Path

It is the fate of the famous to be best known in their day. Tragically, particularly for us in education, this includes the circumstances that surround their work and give it meaning. So it is to be expected that few students of education know that Dewey's most important ideas concerning early childhood and elementary education came mainly from the work that he and the teachers did in the school that he set up to study children's learning. His writing came out of his work with children, experience in running a school, development of curricula, talks to parents (who provided financial aid for the school), and contacts with other experts in education, most notably Ella Flagg Young. In a biographical essay written to commemorate Dewey's eightieth birthday, his three daughters said: "He regards Mrs. Young as the wisest person in school matters with whom he has come in contact in any way" (J. M. Dewey, 1939, p. 29). We will learn more about Young, who was supervisor of instruction in the school, and her work with teachers in Chapter 6.

The point here is that the further we get from Dewey's school—descriptions of what the children were doing and learning—the less likely we are to implement Dewey's ideas as he intended them to be. With each year the school recedes a bit more into the mists of time. As it is now, we get our Dewey in a highly distilled form. When we read about him, the ideas that he formulated while conducting his experimental school are mere skeletons, separated from their flesh and blood beginnings. Small wonder that those of us who would like to "follow Dewey" have such difficulty and often end up doing it in bits and pieces that may not match. This has been going on for the better part of a century. (The school ended in 1904.) Little wonder that so many of our attempts at reform are, to use one of Dewey's words, "scrappy" (1897c, p. 73). The model that gave us our most powerful and enduring ideas in American education is missing.

The Disadvantage of Being a Descendent

Educational reformers who lived in Dewey's time had an advantage that we lack; rather than being remote, the Laboratory School was of great importance to them in their own day. We are disconnected by time because we are not Dewey's contemporaries. Dewey got the word out about his school to his own generation; not only did he conduct the school, he wrote about it. He edited the *Elementary School Record*, a series of nine monographs describing the children's activities in detail and carrying such titles as "Kindergarten," "Curriculum," "Science," "Music," and "History." How deeply interested they were, those fellow American educators in the work that Dewey was doing for education in his school. Each issue of the *Record* contained, in addition to detailed reports of the children's work, articles by Dewey about his evolving educational principles. Dewey was saying things that had never been said in education and his readers had the sense that they were witnesses—if not active participants—in an educational revolution. They let him know about his influence on their professional lives. "For some years now," wrote a teacher educator from Pennsylvania to Dewey, "I have been accustomed to look to your school and the reports that come out in the Record as the freshest and best and most inspiring of the pioneer work in education" (Lukens, 1901).

During these years students and readers knew that Dewey's ideas and innovations were based on real experiences with real children and their teachers and parents. They knew it because they read his accounts, as well as those by the teachers, of how specific activities corresponded to the child's growth. And they came to the school to see for themselves. Visiting days were Monday, Wednesday, and Friday. (Visitors were asked "to conform to certain regulations, in order not to interfere with the relation of teachers and pupils to their work") (Dewey & Runyon, 1900, p. 1).

The students in Dewey's department at the University also had intimate knowledge of the school's development and some students were involved in studying pupils of the school to determine stages of child growth (Mayhew & Edwards, 1936). As might be expected, Dewey discussed the organization of the school curriculum in his course on the philosophy of education. Noted in the *University Record* was the following: "As far as is possible the work of the students is related to the problems of the University School" ("The Philoso-phy of Education," 1896, p. 422). Interestingly, the course also was offered by correspondence. Students taking it in this fashion were sent mimeographed copies of stenographic reports of the lectures, along with bibliographies and questions for discussion. Students of education in Dewey's generation were close to his practical experience in a way that we can never be.

Out of Dewey's experiences came the ideas that he wrote about in his books and that reformers try to follow in a manner that often is, through no fault of their own, like flying blind. It is indeed a paradox that Dewey, whose emphasis was ever on human progress through shared experience, left so little of his own experience in a form that would be truly useful to future genera-tions of school improvers.

Nevertheless, the school can be brought to life through its records, pri-marily through the experiences of the teachers in connecting the curriculum with the ideas behind the school. Teachers knew the general direction in which the school was to move and "worked in a cooperative way as participants in a common plan" (Mayhew & Edwards, 1936, p. 367). At a time when there is so much interest in collaborative curriculum development (Murphy, 1991), there are deep lessons to be learned from how Dewey worked with teachers. The only comment that will be made now—supervision in Dewey's school merits its own chapter—is that Dewey had faith in teachers' professional judg-ment to a degree equaled by only a few of his peers and rarely exceeded to this day.

The world is different, but most trends that Dewey identified at the end of the nineteenth century simply have continued, creating both problems and opportunities for our children. Certainly there is no better example than the constant changes in our lives brought about by technological and commercial development. In 1897 Dewey observed that new inventions and machines "are making over the whole scene of action year by year. It is an absolute impossi-bility to educate the child for any fixed station in life" (p. 12).

Dewey (1897a) wanted schools to prepare individuals to take charge of themselves and not only adapt themselves to the changes taking place but to "have the power to shape and direct those changes" (p. 12). This was the school's social responsibility, and this was what Dewey and the teachers in his Laboratory School tried to do pedagogically. Although we have similar goals—it is impossible not to have them in a democracy—they have never found expression in the curriculum the way they did in those 7 short years in Chi-cago. Today, it would be more accurate to say that technological changes drive the curriculum. There are lessons yet to be learned where the school's social responsibility for preparing individuals to direct change is concerned.

I began this introductory chapter with an observation about what time can do. I will end it on a somewhat contradictory note, about what time has not done. Although 100 years have passed since Dewey opened his school in 1896, the reforms that his school demonstrated for public education remain fresh and largely untried. What is needed is for these strategies to be extricated, dusted off, and looked at. Time also has given us an advantage over Dewey's contemporaries. As Dewey pointed out in 1936, "whatever there is of lasting value" in the school's work and the theory that inspired the work, "may suggest to others new and even more satisfactory undertakings in education" (Mayhew & Edwards, 1936, pp. 463, 436).

For now, we can look at our own problems and take what is of value from Dewey's school. What is the best way to introduce children to organized bodies of knowledge? How should higher-order thinking skills be taught? How can schools teach children social responsibility and habits of service to the community? How can supervisors work most effectively with teachers in curriculum planning? Should schools have multiage classrooms? What is the school's responsibility where cultural diversity is concerned? How can we save our at-risk children from lives of crime and drugs? These are some of the questions that we might ask Dewey, if the man himself were here. The next best thing—or perhaps an even better thing—is to see how the problems were dealt with in his school. It would be misleading, of course, to imply that answers to all of our educational problems can be found in the experiences of Dewey and his staff. But there are clear answers to some and implications for others. This introductory chapter has provided examples. The fact that they have been disregarded repeatedly by successive generations of reformers, including the present generation, is what makes them lessons yet unlearned.

❖ 2 ❖

A Laboratory School—The Forgotten Ideal

The laboratory school's main purpose is to make discoveries about educa-
tion—to set up experiments, and thus to modify theory by what is learned.
This is our right for existence.
—Francis S. Chase, "Purpose of a Laboratory School"

IF ONE DETECTS A TROUBLED SOUND in Francis S. Chase's statement, one is right.
Even in 1962 when the Chicago dean addressed the Laboratory School Administrators Association, it seemed clear that Dewey's laboratory concept was
not understood—or at least not followed—in schools with the label of "laboratory." The situation has continued up until the present. In this chapter I
will examine Dewey's conception of a laboratory school and permit him to
speak on exactly what he had in mind. I have chosen to begin with the story
behind the school because it seems to me that knowing what germinated the
idea in his thinking makes the lessons to be learned from the school more
meaningful and tangible.

Let me say at the outset that it is a very human story—complete with
childhood memories (Dewey's, in this case) about learning experiences in and
out of school and the hope that his children would have a more intellectually
satisfying school experience.

THE STORY BEHIND THE SCHOOL

The laboratory school was the outcome of the interplay of ideas and experience—Dewey's own personal experience and his study of the ideas that were
profoundly affecting the major fields of knowledge, in particular, philosophy,
psychology, and sociology. There is no question that Dewey was indebted to
the ideas of others, but these ideas underwent a metamorphosis in Dewey's
mind. They were tempered by his own experience, which was perhaps why he
had such respect for experience.

12

The Never-Ending Memory of Boredom

The influential experience begins with his boyhood. The school that he attended as a child in Vermont was certainly no worse and probably better than most schools in the mostly agrarian nation in the late 1860s. The classroom procedures were "traditional, mostly dull and uninspiring" (Dykhuizen, 1973, p. 4). He found the recitations especially boring. He rarely caused any disturbance but, according to those who knew him well, "his yawns and fidgetings mingled with those of his classmates in unconscious protest against the monotony he was forced to endure" (p. 4).

Education is seen by most people as something apart from assuming a share in household activities and responsibilities. While growing up, Dewey saw the school education of his friends being supplemented by such activities. The intellectual and civic discipline they (and he) were receiving left its impression on his thought. As Dewey's daughters wrote in their rich biography, "that his boyhood surroundings played a large part in forming John Dewey's educational theories is clear" (J. M. Dewey, 1939, p. 9).

By the time he had grown to adulthood and become a teacher, urbanization and industrialization had forever changed the educational landscape. As the Dewey daughters relate, the social changes "had interfered with the invaluable supplements to school education provided by active occupational responsibilities and intimate personal contacts with people in all walks of life which occurred spontaneously in his boyhood" (p. 9). According to these women, who were well steeped in educational theory themselves (see, for example, Dewey & Dewey, 1915):

> The realization that the most important parts of his own education until he entered college were obtained outside the school-room played a large role in his educational work, in which such importance is attached, both in theory and in practice, to occupational activities as the most effective approaches to learning and personal discipline. His comments on the stupidity of the ordinary school recitation are undoubtedly due in no small measure to the memory of the occasional pleasant class hours spent with the teachers who wandered a little from the prescribed curriculum. (J. M. Dewey, 1939, p. 9)

The Influence of New Psychological Theories

Dewey's ideas about education were influenced by the new outlooks in philosophy and psychology, particularly George H. Mead's (1934) conception of the social nature of self and William James's (1890) idea of the importance of inherent tendencies in normal human development. Examples of such tendencies are the child's impulse to communicate with others and to investigate. In an autobiographical essay, Dewey (1930) named James as the person who most influenced his thinking.

Like others of his generation, Dewey was profoundly influenced by Darwin's evolutionary theory, which overturned the notion that human destiny is predetermined by an Absolute. Dewey (1930) himself writes about the impact of evolutionary theory on his philosophy. Like others of his time, Dewey read into evolutionary theory that the possibilities for human development and destiny are endless, but, unlike others, he did not believe that the laws of nature guaranteed the ultimate perfection of humankind. Building on the ideas of Lester Ward, he put forward the view that human progress depends on the development and use of intelligence (L. Tanner & D. Tanner, 1987; White, 1943/1977). Dewey (1935) meant intelligence as a method: "the procedure of organized cooperative inquiry which has won the triumph of science in the field of physical nature" (p. 71). The children in Dewey's school would use the method of intelligence in common as they sought the answers to problems that had significance to the embryonic community. As Baker (1955) pointed out, "it was adherence to intelligent group deliberation and the experimental method which controlled the life of the school" (p. 152).

Dewey was indebted to James (White, 1943/1977) and quite probably to another great American thinker, Charles Peirce (Brent, 1993), for the philosophy that ideas must be tested by their consequences in action. James's and Peirce's pragmatism was individualistic. Dewey turned pragmatism into a social, rather than an individual, philosophy because he believed that philosophy should serve society. In truth, Dewey was a philosopher of modern times and his school, in what it sought to accomplish, was a school of modern times. Particularly important for us in the present day is Dewey's concept of community: Persons who share in steering the course of human destiny by solving problems. Applied in Dewey's school, this is a modern idea—too seldom applied but looking forward to the twenty-first century.

Obviously, certain events and trends in Dewey's life and time conspired with a very happy outcome: the organization and administration of a school for children. Or perhaps it was not the events that conspired but simply his tendency to observe what was happening around him and to develop his own ideas from the experiences. Before coming to Chicago, Dewey was head of the department of philosophy at the University of Michigan, an institution with close ties to the schools of the state. Called on frequently to give talks to teachers, he had many contacts with elementary and secondary schools in Ann Arbor. He became convinced from what he observed that "much current educational practice was at variance with what psychology taught about learning methods" (Dykhuizen, 1973, p. 78).

Dewey had three small children of his own. "His observation of them," wrote his daughters, "gave a practical emphasis to what he had learned from

James of the importance of inherent tendencies and caused him to attach great importance to proper development in the early years" (J. M. Dewey, 1939, p. 27). The conviction of the young professor and father that existing processes of schooling, particularly in elementary schools, were badly out of sync with the psychological principles for normal development and his dissatisfaction with "pure theorizing" (p. 27) without practical experience to check out the theories, led to the idea of an experimental school. The school that he envisioned "should combine psychological principles of learning with the principle of cooperative association which he learned from his moral studies. At the same time, it should release his children from the intellectual boredom of his own school days" (p. 27).

As Dewey himself wrote in 1900, when the school had been in existence for 5 years, the purpose was to adopt "working hypotheses" from psychology and discover the "educational counterparts" (1900d, p. 222). In other words, his goal was to show how education in school could be made consistent with "contemporary psychology" (p. 222), which it most assuredly was not. By contemporary psychology, Dewey meant developmental psychology, not behaviorism (1896b).

The Fertile Ground of Chicago

A honeymoon is when one gets what one wants. So it was between Dewey, a new faculty member at Chicago, and William R. Harper, the University president. Harper badly wanted Dewey on his faculty, and Dewey wanted an experimental school. Not that Harper was opposed to the idea; in fact, it fit perfectly with his plans for the new University.

An Instrument for Thoroughgoing Reform. The school that Dewey had in mind would create new ideals and standards for the curriculum and teaching conditions in public school systems. In a lecture, "The University School," he declared, "If it is advisable to have smaller classes, more teachers and a different working hypothesis than is at present the case in the public schools, there should be some institution to show this. This the school in question hopes to do" (1896c, p. 417). Its ultimate goal was reform of the most thoroughgoing sort.

Harper's University. Dewey's proposal for the school was enthusiastically approved by President Harper and the trustees. Harper was interested in a university of a kind almost unknown in American education; its purpose was not teaching but learning. It would exist not to spread old truths but to advance civilization by finding new truths and training the finders (Mayer, 1957, p. 22). Harper set out to build a faculty for his dream university. He wanted men and women who were leaders in their specializations so that his university would have top rank in different fields. He also admired breadth in certain scholars. Above all he wanted to create a true community of scholars: original minds in vastly different fields who had gotten to know one another and could talk with one another. By the 1890s the barriers between different fields were already almost unsurmountable. As Martin Mayer (1941), a Harper biographer, pointed out, "Harper was determined to break down the barriers" (p. 3).

Harper and Dewey. Harper not only knew what he wanted in a prospective faculty member, but could recognize it instantly. He saw it all in Dewey: a teacher, an eminent scholar in philosophy and psychology, a trainer of discoverers, and, above all, an original mind. There was something else, too—Dewey's interest in pedagogy. In direct opposition to taboos and tradition, Harper wanted graduate work in pedagogy to be offered at his university. He invited Dewey to join his faculty of scholars as head of the new philosophy department—including psychology and pedagogy. Dewey accepted, and, as time would tell, Harper made no mistake in the appointment.

In Dewey, Harper surely had found the breadth that he admired in a scholar. Dewey's mind was not compartmentalized; in fact, he tried to bring relevant fields together and link them with practical concerns. Education was a practical concern in which he had become increasingly interested before coming to Chicago.

The Grand Design. Dewey believed that a separate department of pedagogy should be founded and that it should be linked closely with psychology and philosophy. The department would have two major purposes: to prepare supervisors and professors of pedagogy and to engage in a program of research and experimentation. It would have its own school for trying out and demonstrating new educational theories and practices—the Laboratory School (Dykhuizen, 1973, p. 79).

Everything new seemed to be happening at the new University of Chicago in the 1890s. Never before had there been such a department in an American university. College professors in pedagogy, teachers in normal schools, city school supervisors, and superintendents either had to begin their work with inadequate preparation or study in Germany where, as Dewey pointed out to the Board of Trustees, "educational conditions are so different" (Dewey, personal communication, June 1896).

The heart of the plan was, of course, the Laboratory School to be conducted by the department. Dewey saw a school of demonstration, observation, and experimentation connected with the theoretical instruction as "the nerve of the whole scheme," for simply to "profess principles without their practical exhibition and testing will not engage the respect of the educational profession" (June 1896). Nor can it be expected to advance knowledge or improve practice. This, of course, continues to be true. Whatever the university field, "the service of knowledge entails not only the discovery of new knowledge but also the transmission of the best of established knowledge to students" (Shils, 1983, p. 44).

The Laboratory School was a part of Harper's vision for the University as well as Dewey's. Why Harper set so much store on this school is interesting. Harper had genuine pedagogical interests as well as talents. In fact, he was a veritable pedagogical pied piper. This giant among university builders was a remarkable teacher. In fact, so remarkable was he that he had raised the dead language of Hebrew to a subject of great popularity (Goodspeed, 1928; Mayer, 1957). Early in his career, Harper's all-consuming ambition had been to be a successful teacher of Hebrew. This was in a period when the teaching of ancient languages, particularly Semitic languages, "was rapidly becoming extinct in America" (Mayer, 1957, p. 12). The ambition was more than realized. At one point Harper was teaching Hebrew to more than 1,000 students by correspondence. He wrote Hebrew textbooks and initiated a journal, *The Hebrew Teacher*. He even founded a professional organization of Hebrew teachers, the American Institute of Hebrew. Dewey and Harper were joined by a common interest in teaching. Although this is Dewey's story, it, inevitably, is Harper's too.

Harper, almost single-handedly, fashioned a new kind of university. I am referring, in particular, to the encouragement given to professors to pursue original investigations. This atmosphere was crucial in the founding of Dewey's school. In fact, if it had not been for Harper's concept of a university teacher, it is doubtful whether the Laboratory School ever would have existed. In an early history of the University of Chicago, this point is made clear:

> The emphasis upon research had already been embodied in the development of Johns Hopkins University and to a slight degree at Harvard and Columbia. But nowhere in this country were research interests at all well represented, and the tremendous momentum given to the entire movement throughout the country by emphasis of this work at the University of Chicago can hardly be exaggerated. (Goodspeed, 1916, pp. 156–157)

Was it just a happy accident that Dewey found such a fertile field for his experimental school idea? Probably not, for the psychological ideas that influenced him were by then influencing others as well. But unlike others, he keenly felt the need to test them in practice. To find someone like Harper, whose image of an institution fit so well with his own ideal of inquiry, and who had a strong personality and the will to make things happen, was indeed remarkable.

RETRIEVING A RETRIEVABLE INNOVATION—LABORATORY SCHOOLS

If there was a single great idea behind the school, it was, without question, the experimental point of view. This viewpoint says that ideas must be tested in practice. Dewey viewed his school as a laboratory for testing and verifying new educational theories and principles. What has been the impact of this idea?

The idea of a school devoted entirely to testing educational theory has never really taken hold (Tyler, 1991). This is one of the great paradoxes in education, for it is just as true today as in Dewey's time that experimental schools connected with theoretical instruction in universities are needed. Not that we lack a model—in Dewey's school we have a model to guide us. Nor is the model itself obscure. Indeed, as noted in a history of the University of Chicago: "The world knows how strikingly influential the school was as a testing ground and a demonstration of what became known as progressive education" (Storr, 1966, p. 297). Moreover, how Dewey ran his school, particularly the ways in which he worked with the teachers, has continued to attract interest and admiration on the part of scholars (Cremin, 1961; Kliebard, 1988).

The Most Important Lesson

Arguably, the most important lesson from Dewey's Laboratory School is the idea of a laboratory school itself. One might expect a significant impact of this idea in light of the continuing concern for educational reform, discussed earlier. American practicality (and parsimony) would seem to lend itself to the idea that changes in instructional method ought to proceed only from careful testing so that their practical consequences are known. A school that by intention is experimental and established to test ideas that are used as working hypotheses, would seem to be in the practical tradition of Benjamin Franklin and the generations of practical people who followed him. In short, laboratory schools should be seen as a public necessity and the innovation should be well entrenched. Why hasn't this happened?

Ralph Tyler (1991) has given us some insights in his John Dewey Memorial Lecture:

> Apparently, this idea was not easily adopted. Most schools and colleges of education that have elementary/and or secondary schools have continued to employ their schools as the sites for practice teaching, or superior schools for faculty children and the children of other families nearby, but not as laboratories for the serious study of children's learning. There are a few noteworthy exceptions, but only a few. (pp. 1–2)

Our sense of what has happened to laboratory schools is enhanced by these words of Philip Jackson (1990):

Insofar as today's Laboratory Schools are concerned, the chief reason for continuing university support appears to be that the schools have proved useful over the years in attracting new faculty members to the university and in keeping a significant portion of the faculty and other middle-class families residing in the neighborhood, thereby enriching the local community and contributing to its stability. (p. xix)

Laboratory Schools: The Inventor Speaks

The Laboratory School was born of a need that still exists. Yet, as Tyler and Jackson indicated, what are called laboratory schools are often a far cry from what Dewey had in mind. Just because a university has an elementary or a secondary school, does not make it a laboratory school. Dewey's original idea has slipped into the murky past but it is still retrievable. Thanks to his own description of what laboratory schools are and are not, we can grasp the essentials of his innovation. Some readers may find laboratory schools applicable to their own situation.

Purpose. According to Dewey (1899) the most important work of a university education department "is the scientific—the contribution it makes to the progress of educational thinking" (p. 96). In order to make this contribution, it needs a laboratory. The laboratory school bears the same relation to the department that a laboratory has to physics or biology. It has but one purpose: to make discoveries about the education of the child by putting theory into practice in an experimental setting and modifying theory by what is learned. It does not exist to prepare prospective elementary or secondary teachers, or for the purpose of educating a group of children. "Only the scientific aim," Dewey said in 1899, "the conduct of a laboratory comparable to other scientific laboratories, can furnish a reason for the maintenance by a university of an elementary school" (p. 76). To be sure, he was aware of the political reality: It never hurts to have a good school. Three years earlier he was in the position of asking for the school and used this as an argument. "As a matter of policy," he wrote to the trustees, "it would be hard to suggest any way in which the University could so easily get such a strong hold upon the interests of a number of persons as by affording their children with as nearly as possible an ideal education" (Dewey, personal communication, June 1896).

In continuing his formulation of a laboratory school, Dewey (1899) tells us that it "is a laboratory of applied psychology. That is, it has a place for the study of mind as manifested and developed in the child, and for the search after materials and agencies that seem most likely to fulfill and further the condition of normal growth" (p. 96). In Dewey's school, the practical problem was to develop instructional approaches and materials to further child

growth, both intellectually and socially. The practical and theoretical problem in a present-day laboratory school would be fundamentally the same.

A laboratory school conducts its work under the assumption "that enough
is known of the conditions and modes of growth to make intelligent inquiry
possible" (p. 97). It is only by acting on present knowledge "that more can
be found out. The chief point is such experimentation as will add to our reasonable convictions" (p. 97).

Beginning with Convictions. There is absolutely no doubt that Dewey possessed such convictions when founding his experimental school. They are stated
clearly in his writings at the time. In "Interest in Relation to Training of the
Will" (1896/1903), he emphasized that true interest is an active quality that
children have when they become identified with a task or a project and the
goal is to them important. In "The Psychological Aspect of the School Curriculum" (1897b) he criticized the traditional view of a school subject as a set
of facts and principles mastered through effort rather than interest, and formulated the theory for a developmental curriculum. In "The Reflex Arc Concept in Psychology" (1896b) he criticized stimulus–response theory for reducing human behavior to "a patchwork of disjointed parts" (p. 358) and stated
his view of a developmental psychology. In "Ethical Principles Underlying
Education" (1897a), he insisted that the school must be "an embryonic yet
typical community life" (p. 14) if it is to prepare children for community life.
In "Pedagogy as a University Discipline" (1896b), he set forth the idea of a
laboratory school. These documents all were written in the period immediately preceding the founding of the school or in its first year. Immersing oneself in such classic works as "The Psychological Aspect of the School Curriculum" is to invite continually new insights both into the nature of knowledge
and how to lead children to the study of systematized knowledge. The old
articles are still useful; in fact, they have retained an incredible freshness. Perhaps it is because the problems they deal with have an enduring currency. We
and Dewey talk about the same things. As Cremin (1965), the late educational
historian, once quipped about a Deweyan idea: "To trace it to Dewey is, like
it or not, to trace it to ourselves" (p. 6).

The point here is that Dewey went in with a set of convictions and they
provided the basis for the teachers' enthusiastic investigations and curriculum
work. As will be shown later, it was the association of Dewey, the teachers,
and Ella Flagg Young that made possible the further development of these
ideas. *How We Think* (1910) and *Democracy and Education* (1916), two of
Dewey's most important works on education, came out of his work with the
teachers, supervisors, parents, and children at the school. The mere operation
of the school provides us with valuable insights about curriculum improve-

ment in an experimental school situation—or in any school. There are specific findings about curriculum unification as it relates to teacher supervision and school organization, and findings about the use of human resources in the university and community. There are findings about planning and findings about home and school relationships. These findings and others emerged from the school's work; those that seem to me revealing as lessons for today are discussed in this book.

Dewey's convictions about what a good school should be are evident in his statement of what motivated him: "a desire to discover in administration, selection of subject matter, methods of learning, teaching, and discipline, how a school could become a cooperative community while developing in individuals their own capacities and satisfying their own needs" (Mayhew & Edwards, 1936, p. xvi).

It is important to note here that some of the ideas that Dewey tried to infuse into his curriculum were being attempted by some public school systems well before he started his school. In the early 1890s in Detroit, for example, the elementary school curriculum was concerned with teaching children to think for themselves, find out for themselves "that all subjects are dependent and related, and to become self-reliant" (Moehlman, 1925, p. 150). But those schools did not enjoy the protection from carping critics that a university laboratory school has (or should have); in fact, they had trouble continuing their innovations (Tanner & Tanner, 1995). Nor were they engaged in research.

Dewey was quite aware that the business of discovery cannot be carried forward in an atmosphere shackled by tradition. "The demand," he tells us, "is to secure arrangements that will permit and encourage freedom of investigation; that will give some assurance that important facts will not be forced out of sight; conditions that will enable the educational practice indicated by the inquiry to be sincerely acted upon, without the distortion and suppression arising from undue dependence upon tradition and preconceived notions" (1899, p. 98). In a university setting these conditions are possible: Universities stand for freedom of inquiry.

Opportunities Multiplied. One's chances of attending a research university and learning to be an inquirer, or going on to become a college teacher who is engaged in discovery, have multiplied enormously since Dewey's time. This is because the number of research universities has increased vastly. Each represents an opportunity to study children's learning in an experimental setting. The laboratory problem that Dewey studied continues to be of critical importance: constructing a curriculum in light of the principles of child development and present social conditions. According to Dewey, "the problem by its nature is an infinite one. All that any school can do is make contributions here and there and to stand for the necessity of considering education both theoretically and practically in this light" (1899, p. 97). The need that Dewey identified to test out ideas with controlled populations, safe from the vicissitudes of changing educational fads and national policies, is, unfortunately, an unlearned lesson. It is not too late and the opportunities are certainly there.

❖ 3 ❖

The School as a Social Community

The much and commonly lamented separation in the schools between intellectual and moral training, between acquiring information and growth of
character, is simply one expression of the failure to conceive and construct
the school as a social institution, having social life and value within itself.
                    —John Dewey, "Ethical Principles Underlying Education"

THE LABORATORY SCHOOL OPENED IN JANUARY 1896. It was a small school—16
pupils from 6 to 9 years of age, one teacher, and an assistant—but it had a
large, and clearly conceived, ideal. By the time Dewey resigned in 1904, the
enrollment had grown to 140. There were 23 on the staff and 10 assistants
who were graduate students at the University. The ideal of a school as a simplified society in which children gained social experience and insight as well
as intellectual and manual skills and made a good start in each of the subjects
taught in ordinary schools was well on the way to being realized; indeed, some
said that it was (Cremin, 1961; Cronbach, 1981; Feffer, 1993; Ryan, 1995;
Tanner, 1991; Tyler, 1991; Young, 1916).

THE REMARKABLE COHERENCE OF DEWEY'S PLAN

"The attention of those interested in educational experiments is called to the
school conducted under the auspices of the Pedagogical Department of the
University of Chicago," said Dewey in the University newsletter (1896c,
p. 417). In his article, "The University School," he set forth its hypothesis
and the assumptions on which the developing curriculum was based. The
hypothesis "is that of the school as a social institution" (p. 418). Actually it
was more than a hypothesis; it was the organizing idea for a unified curriculum in which children's activities led "into the path of knowledge" (p. 419).
Not surprisingly, considering his own experience as a child and young person, Dewey stated that "education outside the school proceeds almost wholly

23

through participation in the social or community life of the groups of which one is a member" (p. 418), and he argued that education in the school should proceed the same way through language and personal contact, work, and play. He showed how in his curriculum theory each school subject developed from the child's activities. The activities were "the activities fundamental to life as a whole" (p. 418) and they were conducted in a simplified social environment—the school.

Today the idea that the school should function as a society in miniature has been reduced to such forms as cooperative learning and community service. It has become detached from the way Dewey meant, as "an organizing principle for the subject matter of the curriculum" (p. 419).

The Problem of Humpty Dumpty

Since the 1980s many American schools have recognized again the need to deal with the problems that concerned Dewey and his staff. One such problem is the need for a coherent curriculum. Whole language, writing across the curriculum, and interdisciplinary projects that involve study leading to action are examples of recognition of this problem (Tanner & Tanner, 1995). The recognition also has taken the form of a search for successful models that can be replicated. Large foundations and policy makers seek to "spread best practices" (Sommerfeld, 1994, p. 6). But the "best practices" are introduced piecemeal, often without regard for what comes before or after. They are not part of an entire plan but are targeted to one population or level of schooling, which makes curriculum articulation more difficult. Changes such as upgrading school subjects, interdisciplinary teaching, global education, building on children's experience, and community experience are fragments looking in vain for a unifier. (While they look, their effectiveness is being dissipated.) They call to mind nothing other than Humpty Dumpty. Can Humpty Dumpty be put together again? Not without a coherent plan, and that plan must begin in kindergarten.

Dewey was among the first to recognize the need for the educational system to respond to the enormous intellectual advance and accumulation of knowledge, and emphasized that the response must be coherent and continuous—beginning with kindergarten. In these comments (1896a) he directed attention to the problem and the solution, as he saw them.

It is as nearly certain as any educational expectation may be that if the increased demands as regards the number of languages, range of literary study, of history and of the physical and biological sciences are to be met, even half way, in the college and high school, the response must proceed from changing the methods in the lower grades, and by beginning work along these lines in the primary school—yes, and in the kindergarten. It is not a mere question of local expedience, whether it is advisable here and there to modify the traditional "three R's" curriculum. It is a question of the right organization and balance of our entire educational system, from kindergarten to university, both in itself as a system and in its adjustment to the existing social environment. (p. 354)

Dewey's Response—Still Timely. Dewey's developmental curriculum, which began with very young learners, was a response to that need. Since the 1980s many American schools have been engaged in reform efforts, some separately and others through reform networks such as Accelerated Schools (Levin, 1990) and Success for All (Slavin, 1989/90). These programs draw on elements in Dewey's theory of curriculum. Levin seeks to connect the school "Dewey-style" (Brandt, 1992, p. 20) with children's own experiences, and Slavin is concerned with cooperative learning, which was a central idea in the Laboratory School.

Today the search for models to use in school improvement goes on. One very promising model is there; however, it is all but unseen, perhaps because of its very obviousness. (After all, everybody knows that Dewey was America's most creative person in the theory and practice of education.) Dewey's model is coherent, has been tested, and contains the "Dewey-style" practices that are being introduced separately and, therefore, less effectively. There it is— if educators only would look. The curriculum worked out by Dewey and the staff bears strikingly on such concerns as character education, the nature of the kindergarten curriculum, horizontal and vertical curriculum integration, and how to teach children to inquire so that they can experience the thrill of invention, discovery, and creation. Intellectual development, social development, and curriculum integration were approached seamlessly and inseparably in Dewey's plan for the school, and the staff enthusiastically followed suit.

The Ever-Renewed Problem. Dewey probably would be the last to suggest that the Dewey school curriculum be taken carte blanche and superimposed on schools a century later. But the conceptual scheme is another matter because, plainly and simply, the problem of education remains the same. "In substance," Dewey wrote, "this problem is the harmonizing of individual traits with social ends and values" (Mayhew & Edwards, 1936, p. 465). He noted that "the problem is especially difficult at the present time because of the conflicts in the traditions, beliefs, customs, and institutions which influence social life today" (p. 465). This is fascinating as well as illuminating; it is so easy to think of our problems as new. Like many of the things that Dewey wrote, it could have been written today because it concerns a problem facing our generation: "The need to harmonize individual traits with social goals," he wrote in 1936, "is an ever renewed problem, one which each generation has to solve over again for itself; and, since the psychological make-up varies from individual to individual, to some extent it is one which every teacher has to take up afresh with every pupil" (p. 465). The problem was the same, but every pupil was and is different.

Putting Humpty Dumpty Together Again

Dewey's organizing idea of the school as a cooperative society is a monumental contribution and should be applied. It remains true that the "integration of the individual and society is impossible except when the individual lives in close association with others in the constant and free give and take of experiences and finds happiness and growth in the process of sharing with them" (Mayhew & Edwards, 1936, p. 466). Of course, this idea—which was and is so different from the notion that schools are merely places to learn lessons—influenced the selection of subject matter in Dewey's experimental school. "There was the need," Dewey wrote, "for working out material which was related to the vital experience of the young and which was also in touch with what is important and dependable in the best modern information and understanding" (p. 470). That is also our need. Dewey's model that begins with the "life activities with which young children are familiar" (p. 466) commends our attention. It is a lesson truly unlearned.

Today the idea that activities centering in the home can lead to knowledge in every subject is so far from the existing curriculum that it sometimes is dismissed as a kind of antique and not up to the demands of today's world (Dunleavey, 1995; Floden, Buchmann, & Schwille, 1987). In Dewey's school the child's activities led to abstract learning, social development, and curriculum integration (Cremin, 1961; Dewey, 1900d). These are continuous concerns of American educators (Tanner, 1991; Tanner & Tanner, 1995). We begin to wonder: Could we take this lesson and make it work for ourselves?

It is possible. But innovators take warning: Certain conditions had to be met for children's activities to lead to learning. Dewey's curriculum was a structured curriculum. Teachers began with the concepts that they wanted children to learn and planned the activities accordingly. In no sense was learning incidental—if by that is meant accidental. In too many efforts to follow Dewey, the difference has been misunderstood (Cremin, 1961; Ruenzel, 1995; Tanner, 1991). In the following section, I will discuss the learning opportunities presented by children's activities and interests and how they were utilized by Dewey and the teachers. I will indicate some missed opportunities; perhaps we can move beyond them.

CHILDREN'S INTERESTS AND ACTIVITIES:
INVESTING THE UNINVESTED CAPITAL

Our grandson, age 4, loves to cook. Of course, he doesn't really cook but he has a toy kitchen, including a stove and things to eat. The food is plain and simple. We place an order with Adam and after a respectable interval he returns bearing a toy light lunch for two. I can't help thinking that toy manufacturers know all about children's interests. Teachers know about them, too, because young learners do not leave their interest in cooking and other household activities at home. As Soundy and Genisio (1994) point out, "much of the dramatic play of 3-to-6-year-olds reflects straightforward imitations of home life" (p. 20).

In *The School and Society* (1899), Dewey made a similar observation in his lectures to parents. "If you observe little children," he said, "you will find they are interested in the world of things mainly in its connection with people, as a background and medium of human concerns" (p. 48). These interests are a kind of "uninvested capital" (p. 70) in the learning process. Children are interested in how people relate to the world in which they live through obtaining food, clothing, and shelter. Not only are these worthwhile and enduring interests, argued Dewey, but they provide clues as to the activities that help children learn important concepts. As a superb example, cooking was part of the Dewey school program through the elementary years. Year after year the children tested their foods for the presence of proteins, fats, carbohydrates, and other constituents. "Without knowing it, by successive, carefully interpreted, and guided steps, they had come to a realization that their kitchen was a laboratory, and that a certain phase of their cooking was a study of the chemistry of food" (Mayhew & Edwards, 1936, pp. 255–256).

Missed Opportunities

Schools rarely respond to children's interests in this way, at least in the sense of a total curriculum possessing scope and sequence. The Dewey school's approach of unified activities leading to curriculum differentiation is what Schwartz (1988) called "unapplied curriculum knowledge" (p. 35). The idea that young children's people interests can lead to learning when schools respond, rather than ignore or hop on a different train, has long been in our curriculum legacy (Cuffaro, 1995; Tanner & Tanner, 1995; Van Hoorn, Nourot, Scales, & Alward, 1993; Washburne, 1939) and is supported by knowledge in the field of child development (Bruner, 1985; Kagan, 1994; Mussen, 1989). But early childhood experts' viewpoints on the value of play differ (Katz, 1991). So do the viewpoints of supervisors and colleagues. Some principals may consider play in the kindergarten "too non-academic looking" (Goldhaber, 1994, p. 24) for their school.

Also as Katz (1991) pointed out, parental expectations "and their understandings and preferences" (p. 52) regarding their children's experiences influence how teachers respond to children's play activities. (Dewey took pains
to educate parents.) Last but not least, there is the teacher; that is, "what teachers are willing and able to do; teachers may be willing to implement some
practices, but for a variety of reasons may be unable to do so, and vice versa"
(p. 52). Schools are most likely to be both willing and able to build consecutive curricula with young children's interests and activities as a beginning point,
if emphasis is placed on the idea in education schools. This, unfortunately, is
not now the case. Continuity is a truly neglected problem. Words like continuity and sequence have taken a backseat to words like goals and evaluation,
and have nearly disappeared from use (Goodlad, 1984; Tanner & Tanner,
1995). "If there is anything that I would like to call loudly for it is consideration of the basic question of organizing a curriculum so that it might have
continuity, sequence, and scope" (Goodlad, 1984, p. 92).

It is safe to say that schools are not investing the uninvested capital. They
are missing the opportunities presented by young children's natural interests
in the basic activities of the home that involve food, clothing, and shelter. The
idea that these activities and interests are actually the roots from which organized knowledge can grow has simply become lost. To be sure, children's
dramatic play is seen by many teachers as a means of language development
or a way of teaching science concepts, but Dewey's conception concerned the
curriculum in its totality. "Just as two points define a straight line, so the present
standpoint of the child and the facts and truths of studies define instruction.
It is continuous reconstruction, moving from the child's present experience
out into that represented by the organized bodies of truth that we call studies" (Dewey, 1902, p. 11).

Investigative Play: The Need for an Organizing Center

There are differences, certainly, among those who view play as important in
learning. Some early childhood experts emphasize the function of "investigative play" (Goldhaber, 1994, p. 24). They have an integrated concept of learning and believe that children need "uninterrupted blocks of time in which to
construct understanding of their social and physical world" (p. 24). This is an
optimistic note and might be considered a lesson learned, for these ideas were
present in Dewey's school. It should be recognized immediately, however, that
the curriculum had an organizing center: "the idea of the school-house as a
home in which the activities of social or community life were carried on"
(Mayhew & Edwards, 1936, p. 43). What the teachers in Dewey's school hoped
to do was to use and guide the child's interest in the home into social activities and knowledge:

The reconstructed story of the building of the homes of the primitive peoples, as the youngest group imagined and reenacted it, took on a character as real in historical quality as the authentic accounts of the homes of the ancient Greeks— the history learned by older groups. (p. 43)

If a curriculum is to have continuity it must begin at the beginning—with young children. Unfortunately, this is a lesson yet to be learned.

Work and Play: Avoiding the Arbitrary Distinction

Since the 1960s there has been an ongoing play versus instruction debate in the early childhood field (Katz, 1991). Work and play in kindergarten often are conceived as diametric opposites. Dewey's ideas on the difference between work and play are of interest and importance and, of course, influenced the teaching in his school. "In their intrinsic meanings, play and industry are by no means so antithetical to one another as is often assumed," Dewey (1916, p. 237) wrote. He continued:

> Both involve ends consciously entertained and the selection and adaptation of materials and processes designed to effect the desired ends. . . . Persons who play are not just doing something (pure physical movement); they are *trying* to do or effect something; an attitude that involves anticipatory forecasts which stimu late their present responses. The anticipated result, however, is rather a subsequent action than the production of a specific change in things. Consequently play is free, plastic. Where some definite external outcome is wanted, the end has to be held to with some persistence, which increases as the contemplated result is complex and requires a fairly long series of intermediate adaptations. (pp. 237 238)

> When fairly remote results of a definite character are foreseen and enlist persistent effort for their accomplishment, play passes into work. . . . The demand for continuous attention is greater and more intelligence must be shown in selecting and shaping means. (p. 239)

> From a very early age, however, there is no distinction of exclusive periods of play activity and work activity, but only one of emphasis. There are definite results which even young children desire, and try to bring to pass. (p. 239)

A final comment is rich with significance for today's educators: "Work which remains permeated with the play attitude is art in quality if not in conventional designation" (p. 242). The teachers in Dewey's school did not make an arbitrary distinction between work and play. The youngest children were doing schoolwork but they also were engaged in dramatic play and using their imaginations.

Popular among contemporary viewpoints is the emphasis on play as a means of language and literacy development (Christie, 1991; Soundy & Genisio, 1994). Imagination is equated with the unreal and made up rather than the authentic. For example, according to Soundy and Genisio, "by the time children's dramatic play reaches its highest level of development it has evolved into a cooperative multidimensional activity that produces interrelated action sequences and highly imaginative themes" (p. 20). Children's play also can involve the real, and it is the real things that lead to conceptual learning.

What Dewey Took from Froebel

In the issue of the *Elementary School Record* devoted to kindergarten, Dewey (1900a) wrote that "in a certain sense the school endeavors throughout its whole course—now including children between four and thirteen—to carry into effect certain principles which Froebel was perhaps the first consciously to set forth" (p. 143). They were as follows: (1) the school's primary responsibility is to teach children to live in cooperative and mutually helpful ways, (2) the activities and games of children are capable of educational use and indeed "are the foundational stones of educational method" (p. 143), and (3) the school should reproduce on the children's level "the typical doings and occupations of the larger maturer society" (p. 143) of which they finally will become a part. Up to that point, said Dewey, the Laboratory School should be regarded as an "exponent" (p. 143) of Froebel's philosophy. The school was making the attempt to act on these ideas "with as much faith and sincerity in their application to children of twelve as to children of four" (p. 144).

Froebel's contribution was revolutionary. He made his generation aware of the fact that children's play is essential to their growth. Dewey told the readers of the *Record*, "We may suppose that he would have been the first to welcome a better and more extensive psychology . . . and would avail himself of the results to reinterpret the activities" (p. 145). Dewey took issue with Froebel's elaborate symbolism (children sweep a make-believe room with a make-believe broom, for example) but understood the reasons for it: Germany's political and social conditions in Froebel's time, which were such a contrast with the kindergarten's cooperative social life. American kindergartens did not have to resort to symbolism. "There certainly is change enough and progress enough in the social conditions of the United States of today, compared with those of the Germany of his day, to justify making kindergarten activities more natural, more direct and real representations of current life than Froebel's disciples have done" (p. 146), Dewey said, and he noted that there was still a disparity between Froebel's philosophy and German political ideals, which made German authorities suspicious of kindergartens.

Treatment of Imagination

If there was a single word to mark the difference between Dewey and then-current kindergarten practices, it would be the word "real." Dewey declared:

> There has been a curious, almost unaccountable, tendency in the kindergarten to assume that because the value of the activity lies in what it stands for to the child, therefore the materials used must be as artificial as possible, and that one must keep carefully away from real things and real acts on the part of the child. (p. 146)

> All this is mere superstition. The imaginative play of the child's mind comes through the cluster of suggestions, reminiscences, and anticipations that gather about the things he uses. The more natural and straightforward these are, the more definite basis there is . . . for making imaginative play really representative. (p. 147)

Dewey argued that the simple dusting, cooking, and dish washing that the child does in school are no more utilitarian to the youngster than a game. To the children these occupations are charged with the delightful mystery that is associated with whatever adults are concerned with. "The realities reproduced, therefore, by the child should be of as familiar, direct, and real a character as possible. It is largely for this reason that in the kindergarten of our School the work centers so largely about the reproduction of home and family life" (p. 147).

The idea that materials must be real fit in well with Dewey's conception of the school as a miniature society, for how could the society be realistic if children were kept away from real things and real acts? The question is an important one for today's educators, who, it must be observed, still lean toward the synthetic and artificial. One cannot overemphasize the importance of Dewey's idea for intellectual and social development: Imagination is most likely to lead to learning when it is connected with real things and real problems.

CHARACTER EDUCATION

Today there is much interest in including moral (character) education in the curriculum as a formal program. This is very different from the approach followed in Dewey's Laboratory School, where character education permeated every aspect of the curriculum and school life—without being given a name. The school followed the ideas on character education that Dewey advanced in "Ethical Principles Underlying Education" (1897a). Dewey pointed out that "the child is an organic whole, intellectually, socially, and morally, as well as physically" (p. 11), and argued that "the ethical aim which determines the work of the school must accordingly be interpreted in the most comprehensive and organic spirit" (p. 11). He then proceeded to do so: Children are future voters and family members, and probably will themselves be responsible for rearing and bringing up future children and, therefore, maintaining society's continuity. They will be workers, engaged in occupations that will both be useful to society and maintain their own self-respect and independence. They will be members of a certain neighborhood and community "and must contribute to the values of life, add to the decencies and graces of civilization" (p. 11) wherever they are.

For children to be able to fill these varied responsibilities, they must be trained in art, science, and history. They must gain command of the methods of inquiry and the basic tools of communication. They must have sound bodies, skillful eyes and hands, habits of perseverance and serviceableness. The idea "that there is any one particular study or mode of treatment which can make the child a good citizen . . . is a cramped superstition which it is hoped may soon disappear from educational discussion" (p. 11).

Dewey pointed out that since the society of which children are to be members is the United States, a democratic society, they "must be educated for leadership as well as obedience" and "must have the power of self-direction and power of directing others, powers of administration, ability to assume positions of responsibility" (p. 11). Obviously, character education programs that focus on resisting misbehavior do not meet that need. "Mere inhibition is valueless," said Dewey (1909, p. 54).

In somewhat stronger language, he added: "To say that inhibition is higher than power, is like saying that death is more than life, negation more than affirmation, sacrifice more than service" (p. 54). Dewey argued that it is unrealistic to "repress the child's powers, or gradually abort them (from failure of opportunity for exercise), and then expect a character with initiative and consecutive industry" (p. 55).

In Dewey's theory, the only restraint that is worthwhile from the standpoint of growth and development is that which comes through concentrating on a positive goal or end. Thus the Laboratory School followed a generative rather than a restrictive approach to character development. Children's attention—in fact, that of the entire school—was not on what not to do but on intelligent doing or investigation.

For Dewey, the social and the moral were one. This was not just an abstract philosophical point but it guided curriculum development and the choice of instructional approaches. The curriculum dealt with social life and was organized in a social way. According to Mayhew and Edwards (1936), "to those who taught and those who learned, what was social came to mean that which was ethical and moral" (p. 437).

Obviously, Dewey felt confident that his hypothesis concerning a unified approach to character was confirmed in the Laboratory School experiment, for he stated it again in great detail, in 1909. While schools continued to articulate character as their supreme goal, they still were not relating subject matter and teaching strategies to social life. Moral education was still viewed as teaching about certain virtues. The conception was narrow and pathological. In 1916, Dewey warned: "Moral education in school is practically hopeless when we set up the development of character as a supreme end, and at the same time treat the acquiring of knowledge and the development of understanding, which of necessity occupy the chief part of school time, as having nothing to do with character" (p. 411).

The Long Exercise in Futility

Since early in the twentieth century researchers have discovered (repeatedly) that adding moral education to the curriculum "didn't achieve anything" (Pritchard, cited in Bates, 1995, p. 16). The classic studies of Hartshorne and May (1929–1930) found that verbal moralizing about honesty, service, and self-control had no effect on children's moral character and behavior. According to Pritchard, "values clarification," a popular approach in the 1970s, where the teacher was a moderator rather than a moralizer and students made judgments about ways to act, had the same result (Bates, 1995, p. 16).

Actually, this is not so surprising. As everyone knows, people can talk one way and act another. "Actions speak louder than words" is what our mothers taught us. This simple truth is homely wisdom and common sense, but that does not make it less useful. Rephrasing what he doubtless heard first as a child, and confirmed later through observation and experience, Dewey (1909) warned: "There is nothing about the nature of ideas *about* morality, of information *about* honesty or purity or kindness which transmutes such ideas into good character or good conduct" (p. 11). Setting aside periods or time slots to teach about morals should not be expected to lead to students' moral development. There is nothing whatever to suggest that the ideas and conclusions that emerge from discussing moral dilemmas, as proposed by Kohlberg (1970) and Simon, Howe, and Kirchenbaum (1972)—or anyone else, for that matter—will be transformed into character or behavior. Yet the moral-dilemmas approach continues to be touted as a means of moral development (Geiger, 1994).

In the 1980s and 1990s some educators were "crusading for character education" (Bates, 1995, p. 16) in the form of special curricula in values. But this idea made some good teachers uncomfortable. (One can see why they are good teachers.) An interesting study of 20 state teachers of the year from across the United States found that they "are uneasy about formal values curriculums, saying that such programs compartmentalize values" (McLarin, 1995, p. B7). There is another alternative, but Dewey's approaches remain in shadow, not fully understood.

Generative Approaches in Dewey's School

Dewey's school was a venture in moral education. His philosophy as it was worked out in the school was as follows:

> The business of the educator—whether parent or teacher—is to see to it that the greatest possible number of ideas acquired by children and youth are acquired in such a vital way that they become *moving* ideas, motive-forces in the guidance of conduct. This demand and this opportunity make the moral purpose universal and dominant in all instruction—whatsoever the topic. (1909, p. 2)

Dewey saw clearly what every teacher knows: Teachers' and learners' attention must be "for the greater part of the time, upon intellectual matters," and "it is out of the question to keep moral considerations constantly uppermost" (p. 2). But he emphasized that "it is not out of the question to aim at making the methods of learning, of acquiring intellectual power, and of assimilating subject-matter, such that they will render behavior more enlightened, more consistent, more vigorous than it otherwise would be" (p. 2).

Thus, when children learned to think critically and to *act* on their judgments, they were behaving morally and developing habits of resolving dilemmas in this way. Dewey and the Laboratory School teachers sought "to bring intellectual results into vital union with character so that they become working forces in behavior" (p. 4).

Of course, schools need more to go on if they are to follow Dewey's unitary approach to character development. Teachers should begin by believing in a unitary approach. Teachers already follow this approach, often unintentionally, when they teach such values as perseverance, responsibility, and concern for others, without giving much thought to the crucial issue of a values curriculum. "Curriculum or not, teachers teach values" (McLarin, 1995, p. 1). Teachers intentionally should make the setting and intellectual program such that children are helped to develop independence, perseverance, and thoroughness, and that children gain the self-confidence that comes from knowing that they have a way to go about solving problems. Children should feel that they are actors, not just onlookers in the saga of human development. In the Laboratory School, cultivation of this highly moral attitude and behavior began with the youngest children. The key was the civilizational theme. By re-enacting the drama of human invention, they learned that all humankind was engaged in a continuing moral venture of which they were a part and that they could continue. They learned that the results of inventions are not always sweetness and light. Mayhew and Edwards (1936) pointed out that children saw

> that while successive inventions of machines have led to the eventual betterment of social life, the immediate results have often been at the bitter cost of the discarded hand-worker whose plight illustrates an ever-present social problem caused by technical advance. Industrial history thus taught on a background of actual experience with materials and processes will always have more than a materialistic or merely utilitarian meaning. For the children of this school it carried many social and moral implications of unsolved problems of human relationships. (pp. 313–314)

The moral value of history will be discussed in more detail in Chapter 4. For now, the point of importance is that this field of knowledge—like all others—was taught to bring out its moral aspects. Although the school was a miniature community, it was not isolated but was connected with the world and its problems.

The Laboratory School sought growth of character in the following ways. First, the school was organized as an informal community in which each child felt that she had a share and her own work to do. Second, the spirit of the school was one in which teachers were there to help if a child had a problem, and so they modeled concern of one person for another. The atmosphere was stress-free. As will be discussed in Chapter 7, the approach to discipline was generative rather than restrictive. Children with difficulties were directed into activities that they found exciting and satisfying, thus channeling energies toward growth.

Third, emphasis was placed on how to work out problems. In later years, alumni would speak of how well they learned to deal with problems as one of "the character building results of the Dewey School" (Mayhew & Edwards, 1936, p. 406). One alumna reported:

> As the years have passed and as I have watched the lives of many Dewey School children, I have always been astonished at the ease which fits them into all sorts and conditions of emergencies. They do not vacillate and flounder under unstable emotions; they go ahead and work out the problem in hand, guided by their positively formed working habits. Discouragement to them is non-existent, almost *ad absurdum*.

Many alumni think that their school was best simply because it was their school. Allowing for these cautions, we may derive useful insights from this alumna's observation. Just as Dewey insisted, problem-solving skills and attitudes learned in school can have direct personal as well as social results throughout one's lifetime. Thus, if children are provided with a way to tackle problems, they gain both courage and self-confidence and are more likely to lead satisfying lives (as opposed to lives of perpetual frustration).

Fourth, the school sought to develop the kind of habits that lead children to act in certain ways. For Dewey, "a habit is something deeper than a series of similar acts" (Kilbridge, 1949, p. 20). Acts are connected not to constitute conduct but because they are related to "an enduring and single condition—the self or character as the abiding unity in which different acts leave their lasting traces" (Dewey & Tufts, 1908/1936, p. 198). Practice in working out problems, accepting responsibility, meeting new situations, cooperating with others, and engaging in real and practical work left their traces.

Fifth, there was an emphasis on creative activity. Dewey insisted that "every method that appeals" to the child's "capacities in construction, production, and creation, marks an opportunity to shift the center of ethical gravity from an absorption which is selfish to a service which is social" (1909, p. 26). He pointed out that "ever since the philosophy of Kant, it has been a commonplace of aesthetic theory, that art is universal; that it is not the product of purely personal desire or appetite, or capable of merely individual appropriation, but has a value participated in by all who perceive it" (pp. 26–27). In the Dewey school, girls as well as boys developed manual skills, and even the youngest children carried on constructive work with tools.

In addition to making Christmas presents, children made bookshelves for rooms at home and were "encouraged to undertake tasks for their own convenience and comfort" (Ball, 1900, p. 183). In later years, some alumni particularly expressed the feeling of good fortune that constructive work was a part of their educational process (Mayhew & Edwards, 1936, p. 406).

Obviously, developing manual skills was not an attempt to teach the child to be a carpenter. According to Nicholas Murray Butler, it was "mental training through the hand and eye, just as history is mental training through the mental and other powers" (cited in Ball, 1900, p. 177). According to another educator, it was "the cultivation of the hand so that it may be able to express the ideas of the mind" (cited in Ball, 1900, p. 177). Or, as one alumnus put it: "We learned to use our eyes and hands" (Mayhew & Edwards, 1936, p. 406). These ideas and practices need to be strengthened in our own curricula; the trend is in the opposite direction. In the 1980s and 1990s most states increased graduation requirements in academic subjects as a way of improving education. The industrial and studio arts courses were taken away from youngsters' programs of study. Some school districts reduced or dropped their offerings in the studio and industrial arts. Such schools experienced an increased dropout rate (Rannels, 1991; Tanner & Tanner, 1995). The loss to individual children who were unable to develop in the one area they were good at and so opted to leave school was enormous, as was the loss to society in the form of tangible objects that never will be produced or enjoyed by others (not to mention the opportunities forever lost to shape character in personally and socially valuable ways). The value for character development of providing experiences where children develop manual skills is a lesson unlearned.

Finally, in Dewey's miniature community adults and children really talked with one another. The point is crucial for today's schools because it has become increasingly clear that mechanical instruction—even by humans—does not feed the human spirit. The result may be that children also lack humanity. (Something that chills the hearts of us all.) In the Laboratory School, teachers did not treat the children with condescension or confine their exchanges to direct instruction. As Nel Noddings (1994) has pointed out, conversation can be valuable for moral education: "Even if the purpose of conversation is rarely explicit moral education, matters of moral interest will arise. Adults and children will express themselves, and opportunities for exploration, debate and correction will arise" (p. 114). This was certainly the case in the Laboratory School where such opportunities led children to new paths of investigation. As Noddings reminds us, "Many children and adolescents lack opportunities to engage in real conversation with adults" (p. 114). All children need to have such opportunities, for they are an essential part of character education, indeed of normal human development.

"The demand," wrote Dewey "is for social intelligence, social power, and social interests. Our resources are (1) the life of the school as a social institution in itself; (2) methods of learning and doing work; and (3) the school studies or curriculum" (1909, p. 43). The school must represent a real community life; the instructional approaches must appeal to children's constructive interests, "permitting the child to give out and thus to serve" (p. 44); and the curriculum must be organized to enable children to be conscious of the world in which they have a part to play and the demands they must meet. "The rest," Dewey said, "remains between the individual teacher and the individual child" (p. 44).

Dewey's Developmental Curriculum— An Idea for the Twenty-First Century

All studies arise from aspects of the one earth and the one life lived upon it. We do not have a series of stratified earths, one of which is mathematical, another physical, another historical, and so on. . . . Relate the school to life, and all studies are of necessity correlated.

—John Dewey, *The School and Society*

THE YOUNG CHILD IS AN INTEGRATED BEING who by nature sees the world in an integrated way and whose mind seeks connections. But the school teaches him early to see the world in fragments named science, art, social studies, reading. Later this is bound to cause problems because whatever one's calling, one must connect it with other areas in order to function. No field exists in isolation and the curriculum (whether in elementary school or college) must be designed to show students how to make the connections. In the 1990s, leaders in the engineering industry listed the deficiencies they found in engineering graduates, such as the inability to communicate effectively. What they found most troubling however, "is that many graduates are unable to connect seemingly unrelated areas such as politics, social issues, and engineering" (Cage, 1995, p. A16). In response to these criticisms, engineering schools began designing their curricula in an attempt to show engineering majors "that engineering does not exist in isolation" (p. A16). The idea is not new but it shows what could be done in education at any level. We know from his work in the Laboratory School that Dewey would be concerned with extending the curriculum principle downward to elementary and secondary education, which has yet to happen in any significant way.

Dewey tried to tie the curriculum to reality so that it did not go spinning off by itself as an isolated world existing only in the school's rarefied atmosphere. Dewey did not invent the idea of an interdisciplinary curriculum. At the time he started his school, educators were trying fervently to figure out how to unify the curriculum. Some of their most interesting (but not necessarily promising) ideas may be found in the chapters of the National Herbart Society Yearbooks (1895–1900). In 1895 the meeting of the Herbart Society rang with discussions on the merits of various subjects to serve as a concentration center or core for the curriculum (Tanner & Tanner, 1990). Never since has a group of educational theorists given this topic so much attention, or has there been such interest in totally unifying the curriculum based on the nature of knowledge. In Dewey's Laboratory School, the problem of curriculum integration was approached from the vantage points of both the nature of knowledge and child experience. The needs of a democratic society were always there to figure in the equation.

In the late 1890s, the change in theoretical outlook was clear, and some teachers tried hard to correlate the curriculum following the Herbartian idea that some subject—literature, for example—should serve as the organizing center. Often they found that when they tried to put subjects together, one subject took over. Attention was paid to this very problem in Dewey's school, and insights on how to correlate subjects come from Dewey's and the teachers' experience. "All studies grow out of relations in the one great common world," wrote Dewey in 1899 (p. 92). When children live "in varied but concrete and active relationship to this common world," their studies are unified naturally, and "it will no longer be a problem to correlate studies. The teacher will not have to resort to all sorts of devices to weave a little arithmetic into the history lesson, and the like" (p. 91).

What Dewey was saying was that if the subjects are related to real life—which is their origin and purpose to begin with—curriculum correlation unavoidably results. Replete with common sense, the idea looks equally promising today. Like many of the world's great ideas, it appears too simple to be true, but is. Good teachers continue to find this out for themselves (Tanner & Tanner, 1995).

In this chapter I discuss the sources that the Dewey teachers drew upon in developing a curriculum that was integrated without sacrificing intellectual values. Putting ourselves in the historical setting of a century ago, we see that this was a time when knowledge and specialization were increasing rapidly, with attendant social problems. It was a time and a curricular challenge much like our own. Putting ourselves in the teachers' situation, we find just a simple plan—meant to be a working document rather than anything final (Dewey, 1895a). The plan changed as new problems and possibilities presented themselves. Dewey's idea of planning is so important that it deserves a section by itself, which I have given it in Chapter 6.

DEVELOPING A NEW CURRICULUM:
WHAT THE TEACHERS HAD TO HELP THEM

It is one thing to place confidence in one's staff to develop an experimental curriculum and, clearly, Dewey had confidence in the teachers' ability to put the theory of the school into practice. Mayhew and Edwards (1936) were very clear on this from their own experiences, as was Young (1916) from hers.

It is quite another thing, however, for the confidence to be realized in a successful outcome. Obviously, the teachers used resources that would be good for us to know about. Needless to say, one resource was Dewey himself. He was a presence to the faculty and, "as leader, sought to get the faculty group to problemize their difficulties in relation to the theory" (Baker, 1955, p. 141). This kind of leadership is enormously important and just as possible today. Besides Dewey, there were people in leadership positions—a general supervisor, principal, and department heads—but they did not dictate what and how to teach. Moreover, there were no materials on the market geared to Dewey's view of education. The mystery deepens. What did the teachers in this famous school have to go on or use? The material on the school provides us with leads that hit home where our own efforts to improve a curriculum (or even develop a new one in a new school) are concerned.

Theoretical Knowledge

If teachers are to improve the curriculum, they should work with concern for theoretical principles (Grossman, 1992; Tanner & Tanner, 1995; Zumwalt, 1989). This must happen at the beginning—actually at the preservice level—because ways of working without such concern soon become hardened into habit (Dewey, 1904b; Grossman, 1992).

The Dewey teachers did not have a complete theory to work with. In fact, if they could have looked ahead a century, they would have known of their contribution to the ideas that Dewey would later develop and that have inspired so many teachers. Dewey's Chicago decade (1894–1904) has been of increasing interest because, as one scholar put it, "that Chicago phase had to have been fateful to have provided the foundation for so long and productive a career" (Krupnick, 1995, p. 6).

The Dewey teachers might have been greatly surprised (and perhaps saddened) to read that Dewey's theory of education was virtually complete before he started the school. According to Cremin (1961), the late historian, "there were few dramatic changes in Dewey's pedagogical theory as a result of the Laboratory School" (p. 140). Cremin cited as evidence an article written by Dewey in 1901 dealing with social occupations. Cremin probably assumed that the social occupational theme was present in Dewey's school plan in 1895. We will never know why he made this assumption; perhaps it was based on something that Dewey himself wrote. Dewey devoted considerable attention to the social occupational theme in his summary of the plan, published in 1936 (Mayhew & Edwards, p. 5). However, Dewey's 1895 plan and his 1936 summary are different. What one finds in the actual plan itself is a civilizational theme; there is no mention of an occupational theme. The truth is that the idea for a social occupational theme was the solution to a curriculum problem and came later. In 1934, in a draft of the school's history on which she was working, Katherine Mayhew wrote, "During the school's second year the scheme of social occupations was outlined" (p. 5). This is consistent with reports in the University of Chicago's *University Record*. On May 21, 1897, for example, the *Record* announced that "after this year the beginning will be made with a study of social occupations."

The portrayal of Dewey's pedagogical theory as virtually complete and unchanged not only is inaccurate but ignores the significant contributions made by teachers, supervisors, and graduate students to its development. Dewey owed them a debt that he would continue to acknowledge (1910; Mayhew & Edwards, 1936). Theory development in education is—or should be—a collaborative affair.

Working with an Incomplete Theory. The teachers in the Dewey school were in the unique position of working with an incomplete theory. This was difficult, but it was not all bad; it was, after all, what they were there for and they learned along with Dewey. Theirs was a situation rich with opportunity; testing educational ideas made them investigators as well as teachers. Adding to the challenge and feeling of adventure was that they had been teaching in conventional schools. As Soltis (1994) points out, this feeling of hope, joy, and adventure is essential for an "educational reformation . . . if it is to happen" (p. 245).

As in any investigation or voyage of exploration, the situation was fraught with uncertainty. The Laboratory School was a virtual fishbowl and it is certain that the teachers were subjected to criticism. For example, Dewey hypothesized that intellectual initiative and independence of judgment—qualities that are essential in a democratic society—are incompatible with closely constrained movement. (He apparently felt that the hypothesis was confirmed in the school, for it was stated with clarity and firmness in *Democracy and Education*, 1916.) The teachers put into practice the idea that mental activity cannot be separated from opportunity for physical movement. The visitors who streamed into the school found what they saw foreign to their own experience and, therefore, displeasing. Twenty years later, in a review of *Democracy and Education*, Ella Flagg Young (1916) wrote:

Teachers and superintendents visited that school carrying with them the ideals of order and discipline by which their efforts were daily directed. Instead of straight rows of children's heads they found children moving physically as if outside of school; instead of raising their hands, or making other physical signs to indicate a desire to answer a question, children spoke out and expressed themselves as if in good society outside of school. . . . Visitors as a rule had not intended to devote time to seeing children in school acting as they would in society. Their ideals of order by which the school was to be estimated contained no elements corresponding to this. (p. 7)

In developing curriculum, teachers drew on their own knowledge specialization. They based their work on Dewey's (1896c) idea that concept development begins with the child's activities. As Katherine Camp (1903), director of elementary science teaching, stated the matter: "From the point of view of this psychological principle the problem of elementary science, then is: What *activities* furnish opportunities to be used in the growth of scientific method and concepts?" (p. 1). This question could be applied to each and every field of study.

Written Works as Sources. According to Young (1916), who knew what was going on in the Laboratory School and the Department of Pedagogy, "as his university courses were given it was frequently urged that Professor Dewey should publish his theory of education" (p. 7). The point of importance is that the teachers did not begin their work in 1896 armed with Dewey books on childhood and learning.

Until 1895 Dewey's published works on education were few and mainly concerned the high school, understandably since that was his teaching level before he received his doctorate. In 1895 he published a book on the teaching of arithmetic, which he co-authored with James McLellan (McLellan & Dewey, 1895), and an article on the application of child development to education (1895b). It was in the autumn of that year that he presented his plan for the experimental school, but it was "privately printed, not published, and is to be so treated" (1895a, p. 1).

It was not until the year the school opened that Dewey published two particularly significant articles for teachers' curriculum design efforts. In "The Reflex Arc Concept in Psychology" (1896b) Dewey attacked stimulus–response theory for giving us a concept of learning "in disjointed fragments" (p. 370), and therefore an inadequate view of individual development. The reflex arc notion was based on the assumption that each response is a completely new experience. Dewey argued that the so-called arc is "virtually a circuit, a continual reconstruction" (p. 360). This idea of the continual reconstruction of experience lay at the heart of Dewey's educational theory and he would develop it further in subsequent writings.

The second article, "Interest in Relation to Training of the Will" (published in 1896 and reprinted in 1903), was an excellent counterpart to the first. Writing in the National Herbart Society Yearbook, Dewey pointed out that while interest and effort were being viewed as opposing ideas, both concepts often were misconstrued—interest being thought of as sweetening some bitter pill of learning, and effort as external occupation of the child with a task. "Genuine interest in education is the accompaniment of the identification, through action, of the self with some object or idea, because of the necessity of that object or idea for the maintenance of self expression" (p. 12). When effort is thought of by teachers as opposed to interest, there is by implication "a separation between the self and the fact to be mastered or task to be performed" (p. 12). The child leaves school a divided self. "Externally we have mechanical habits with no psychical end or value. Internally, we have random energy or mind-wandering, a sequence of ideas with no end at all because not brought to a focus in action" (p. 12).

Today the problem is not so much that interest and effort are viewed as opposites but that the student's identification with a task or idea because of its importance to him, often is considered extraneous. What is to the point is passing high-stakes tests, and teachers often teach to the test (Madaus, 1988; Tanner & Tanner, 1995). The political use of test scores has caused student motivation and interest to be put on the back burner in many classrooms because the urgency for high scores makes everything else seem either secondary in importance or of no importance whatsoever. Meanwhile, we have many divided selves leaving the school, graduates as well as dropouts. This need not be. Dewey counsels us:

> When we recognize that there are certain powers within the child urgent for development, needing to be acted upon, in order to secure their own due efficiency and discipline, we have a firm basis upon which to build. Effort arises normally in the attempt to give full operation, and thus growth and completion, to these powers. Adequately to act upon these impulses involves seriousness, absorption, definiteness of purpose, and results in formation of steadiness and persistent habit in the service of worthy ends. But this effort never degenerates into drudgery, or mere strain of dead lift, because interest abides—the self is concerned throughout. (1903, p. 12)

Certainly, absorption, seriousness, and steadiness are what we value in all persons. A lesson from the Dewey school is that there may be better ways of achieving these qualities than what we are doing now. We need not be creating divided selves.

The two articles were a marvelous resource for teachers in the experimental school, who were, of course, freer to apply them than the teachers in most other schools. With these articles, teachers had a learning theory: Learning does not take place in fits and starts but when a purpose arises from the learner's own experience. An operant conditioning curriculum, which philosophically differs little if at all from rote and recitation (Dewey, 1896b), is not concerned with the learner's interest or purposes. On the other hand, when children are engaged in an activity of interest to them that presents difficulties, they look for a method of coping with the difficulties and thus acquire new skills. The activities supply occasions for creating difficulties and motives for dealing with them, and there is no sudden transition as children acquire new skills. Additional opportunities are provided for the child to use her newly acquired skills and complete the learning circuit. In this circuit, what is learned must be present to the child as a desirable end or objective and therefore as a motive to exert effort.

Certainly, one publication can change the world—witness Darwin's *Origin of Species* (1859/1860)—and the Dewey teachers had at least two as they began their work in October 1896. These articles were concerned with learning, however, not about content—the time-honored fields of knowledge that grew and must continue to grow from human experience. In April 1897 Dewey published "The Psychological Aspect of the School Curriculum" (1897b), which dealt with precisely this issue. The title of the article, with its emphasis on how subject matter knowledge is experienced and grows, was a new (and controversial) idea that was already in operation in his school. Dewey believed that a child must actually experience a subject, that is, must feel the part that it plays in human life, in order to build a strong foundation in that subject. His statement on this was a kind of plea:

> We must take into account the distinction between a study as a logical whole and the same study considered as a psychological whole. From the logical standpoint, the study is the body or system of facts which are regarded as valid, and which are held together by certain internal principles of relation and explanation. The logical standpoint assumes the facts to be already discovered, already sorted out, classified, and systematized. It deals with the subject-matter upon the objective standpoint. Its only concern is whether the facts are really facts, and whether the theories of explanation and interpretation used will hold water. From the psychological standpoint, we are concerned with the study as a mode or form of living individual experience. Geography is not only a set of facts and principles, which may be classified and discussed by themselves; it is also a way in which some actual individual feels and thinks the world. It must be the latter before it can become the former. (pp. 360–361)

Dewey's article deals with how a subject becomes a subject, not only ideally in the mind of a child but truly, as it relates to some aspect of human life. Many of us (myself included) have taught a subject without thinking of how it originally developed to meet some typical need of social life. If we teach a subject in this way, we are bound to do it mechanically, and so the mechanics are all that we can give our students. But if we can see the subject as the result of a needed function, the way that the Dewey teachers did, it is a marvelous gift for ourselves and our students. Dewey's words splendidly evoke this idea for us:

> There is no fixed body of facts which, in itself, is externally set off and labeled geography, natural history, or physics. Exactly the same objective reality will be one or the other, or none of these three, according to the interest and intellectual attitude from which it is surveyed. Take a square mile of territory, for example; if we view it from one interest, we may have trigonometry; from another standpoint we should label the facts regarding it botany; from still another, geology; from another mineralogy; from another, geography; from still another standpoint it would become historical material. There is absolutely nothing in the fact, as an objective fact, which places it under any one head. Only as we ask what kind of experience is going on, what attitude some individual is actually assuming, what purpose or end some individual has in view, do we find a basis for selecting and arranging the facts under the label of any particular study. (pp. 361–362)

In essence, this was Dewey's philosophy of knowledge, which is as relevant to elementary school pupils as it is to graduate students. It was the task of the Dewey teachers to provide children with experiences (cultivating a garden, for example, or a visit to a farm) that would lead to the gradual differentiation of the school subjects. The teachers' problem was "to clarify, build up, and put in order the content of experience, so that in time it will grow to include the systematic body of facts which the adult's consciousness already possesses" (p. 363).

Articles written by the Dewey teachers show a clear understanding of his idea that the school should build on the child's experience and the relation of this conception to the teacher's own area of expertise. In the lead article of the first number of the *Elementary School Record*, Lillian Cushman (1900) applied Dewey's developing theories to her field of art. It is only by giving an artistic expression to their own life experiences that children can get any real aesthetic training, she told readers:

> [W]hen this correlation is obtained subject matter will arise out of [the child's] life and interests. While a part of these are common to all, others are modified by the local environment and by the activities of the school. Our six-year-old children whose studies are grouped about the activities of the farm, model in clay the vegetables and fruits, the domestic animals, the farmer himself plowing, sowing or engaged in any other occupation which may interest them. (p. 6)

She pointed out that there is no cut-and-dried list of subjects for expression; children in a different school would seek a "vital realization of other things that already have a hold on them. . . . In a public school located in a suburb, I obtained the freest expression when the fifth grade represented a skating scene" (p. 6). She then moved on to a discussion of how art technique can be presented most effectively using Dewey's idea that knowledge is a kind of link between a difficulty in action and a further successful activity. "It is first necessary to create a consciousness of need," she advised (p. 7). "To illustrate: nothing is more uninteresting, meaningless to the child, than exercises in perspective," but when she has an illustration in mind over which she is "brimful of enthusiasm" and a difficulty in perspective prevents this, "the tables are turned. Instead of forcing instruction upon unwilling minds, the teacher now gives assistance which the children ask. Needless to say that the results are vastly different" (pp. 7–8).

Dewey's influence on Cushman is evident. Art, like other disciplines, grows out of the experiences of individuals, and like other disciplines its technical aspects are best learned when the individual has a real need. It is also likely that Cushman's work had an influence on Dewey's psychological theory. She presents stages of child development as they relate to art instruction. Dewey's developmental stages were an outcome of the school's work (Dewey, 1900d).

It should be noted here that in Dewey's experimental school aesthetic experience was not a special kind of activity confined to art. As Dykhuizen (1973) pointed out in his Dewey biography, Dewey held "that the consummatory fulfillment in aesthetic experience is potential in all experience" (p. 260). Solving a problem, writing a story, playing a game to completion are examples. In our day as in Dewey's, this kind of pleasure is universal and, as Foshay (1995) has observed, is a key to enriching children's school experiences (p. 205). The point is enormously important. The potential for enjoyment exists "in every organized school experience . . . as well as the more informal, environmental aspects of the school experience" (p. 205). The potential is there but realizing it is another matter. The press of time and the need to cover the material often cause us to neglect the pleasure element in a completed piece of work and what it can mean for children's lives, particularly if a struggle was involved in completion. As Foshay reminds us, we are responsible as teachers "to take into account the aesthetic quality of the school experiences we bring about and to make students aware of the aesthetic element in their own responses" (p. 205).

Curriculum Differentiation and Integration: Having One's Cake and Eating It, Too. Dewey sought both conceptual knowledge in the subject fields and an integrated curriculum. This was his powerful idea, and my own judgment is that it was implemented successfully. But the question is, How? What kept the curriculum from disintegrating as the teachers tried to build up under-standings in the subject fields? It was an organizing theme that ran vertically through the school—in the case of Dewey's school, social occupations. From the teachers' reports, we learn that only 2 hours a week were devoted to work on the theme itself. However, it was a potent force for keeping the curriculum together as teachers made a conscious effort to relate work in the subject fields to the theme. The teachers' reports were by subject field.

Like Dewey, we want students to develop subject matter knowledge and we want for them an integrated curriculum. But we tend to begin with a differentiated curriculum, which is a violation of Deweyan learning theory. In this theory, the problem of curriculum integration is seen in reverse. The Dewey teachers began with an undifferentiated, unified curriculum and sought to build up conceptual knowledge in the subject fields, thereby differentiating them. The existence of an organizing theme that ran vertically and horizontally throughout the curriculum afforded coherence. However, there was no guarantee that this would always happen, and it was suggested that teachers state the relationship between their subject matter and other schoolwork in their reports (Laboratory Schools Work Reports, Addenda, 1898–1899). As in the case of human liberty, eternal vigilance was required.

Dewey's article on the psychological aspect of the curriculum focused on the relation between curriculum and instruction. But teachers had to take it from there. In the beginning they followed a simple and sensible format for curriculum planning.

A Two-Dimensional Curriculum. The curriculum that Dewey and his teachers developed had two dimensions: the children's side (activities) and the teacher's side (logically organized bodies of subject matter: chemistry, physics, biology, mathematics, language, literature, history, music, and physical culture). As noted elsewhere, "Ultimately, development of the curriculum depended on teachers keeping the two dimensions clearly in mind" (Tanner, 1991, p. 107). At first, in order to do so they organized their plans using headings, "From the Child's Standpoint" and "From the Teacher's Standpoint" ("School Record," 1896a, p. 419). Readers of the *University Record*, which published a report of the school's activities every Friday, were informed that the child's standpoint "refers to the series of activities through which the child passes in becoming conscious of the basis of social life," and the teacher's standpoint, "to the opportunities afforded for the enrichment and extension of the child's experience in connection with these activities" (p. 419).

The Cardinal Rule. On reading the plans, one notes that the teacher's standpoint is first. The "opportunities"—ideas and concepts—are classified by subject, followed by the child's standpoint. For example, in the report, "From the Teacher's Standpoint" (pp. 419–420), the plan in mathematics was to teach measurement (liner, surface, volumetric, and gravimetric measurements). These concepts were taught not via teacher lecturing but by involving the children in cooking and sewing, both of which constantly demand measurement. In this way children got an idea of what mathematics really is, instead of the abstract relationships. "Drill based on weights and measures used" (p. 420) was included in the report from the teacher's standpoint. Clearly, teachers were not above using drill when needed.

Drill aside, the point of importance is that the teachers began with the subject field and planned children's activities that called for progressively more complex understandings. They did *not* begin with the activities and try to extrapolate ideas from the subject field.

The fact that teachers used the headings in their reports carries a suggestion of doubt on Dewey's part that they could keep the two dimensions of the curriculum in mind otherwise. If there was doubt, it was of short duration. By December 1896, the subheads had disappeared from the weekly reports. The reports now assumed a narrative form. For instance, the report of December 4 stated:

> Groups IV and V (ages 7–11) have taken Chicago as the center of work in Geography and are working in two directions; one, the location of points within Chicago itself, starting from their own home and the school house as centers, and the other in placing Chicago with reference to important localities of the United States. . . . The drawing of a map to scale introduces linear measurement, and practice in multiplication is given in connection with inches, feet, yards and rods. ("School Record," 1896b, p. 460)

The form of the report may have changed, but the two dimensions of the curriculum were still clearly in evidence.

As the curriculum developed, the form of the reports evolved accordingly. As noted, it was suggested that teachers state the connection between the subject matter for the week and the other work of the school (Laboratory Schools Work Reports, October 1898).

The fact that teachers received guidance from Dewey in the weekly meetings is well known. What often is overlooked is that the communication went both ways. As the Laboratory Schools Work Reports clearly show, teachers shared their insights as well as experiences with him. While they were doing so, Dewey's theoretical ideas were being refined and further developed.

The School Plan

The idea of starting an experimental school is all very well. But the desire— which Dewey had had since Ann Arbor—was a pretty thin basis for such a venture. To be sure, his colleagues and their friends had children of school age, but did this group know about his thinking on education? Would they want their children to have the kind of schooling that was based on Dewey's ideas?

Happily, the answer to both questions was yes. Dewey and his colleagues were formulating new outlooks on psychology, with educational implications. As Mayhew and Edwards (1936) pointed out, this group and "others in related departments of the University made up a united and enthusiastic group of investigators and teachers" (p. 1). Dewey was an active member of the Illinois Society for Child Study and the work of this group was "being watched and commented on by leaders in psychological thinking" (p. 4). Some of his earliest statements were published by this Society and the National Herbart Society. According to Mayhew and Edwards, the idea for a school that would test Dewey's developing theories became a reality because of his colleagues' desire "that their own children should experience this kind of school" (p. 5).

The Plan as Resource. Whether teachers had access to the *Plan* in the form in which it was submitted to the trustees is difficult to determine. In a sense it is also unimportant. The ideas in the *Plan* were published for all interested persons (Dewey, 1896c) and were referred to constantly in the weekly meetings held by Dewey and the teachers.

The entire conception of the school in terms of social objectives and the nature of childhood and learning is put forward in Dewey's *Plan* (1895a). The framework for a two-dimensional curriculum is present, minus the power and certainty of Dewey's theoretical statement in "The Psychological Aspect of the School Curriculum," which was published 2 years later. The subjects listed from the teacher's standpoint look ordinary enough: arithmetic, botany, chemistry, physics, zoology, geography, history, geology, mineralogy, physiology, and geometry. They become more interesting when we stop to realize that very young children were embarking on the study of these fields. How these bodies of systematized knowledge were to be learned—via children's constructive activities such as cooking, carpentry, and sewing—made Dewey's school different from other schools. In fact, the difference was nothing short of revolutionary. There were other differences as well. Children of different ages, abilities, and temperaments would work in groups together; Dewey believed that a school, as an intermediate institution between the home and society, should give the child an opportunity to be a participating member of a community.

An important idea behind the activities, which was discussed in Chapter 3, was Dewey's conception of the psychological nature of the child. Dewey argued that children are inherently active with strong impulses to investigate, to share with others what they have found out, to construct things, and to create. Dewey stated this concept as a curriculum principle: The child's impulses are an enormously important educational resource, and opportunities should be provided for children to develop them through engagement in activities. Dewey emphasized this principle in his *Plan*.

Purposes of Activities. In addition to providing the experiences that Dewey felt would lead to the study of systematized knowledge, activities were the means of achieving curriculum synthesis. Activities had social as well as intellectual purposes. Communication is the basis of community and the process of education is unremittingly social. The impulse to communicate with others was a resource not only for individual development but for helping children to participate in socially valuable relationships with others. In Dewey's *Plan*, the activities called for communication through drawing, speech, and written records. Dewey pointed out that literature is simply a form of communication and artistic expression. While this hardly seems like a revolutionary idea now, it should be remembered that in Dewey's time, fields of knowledge were treated as if they existed for their own sake, not as a means of facilitating communication and action in the real world (Tanner & Tanner, 1995; Vaihinger, 1935). Dewey (1895a) insisted that in his school (or any school), speech, writing, and reading be primarily viewed not as expression of thought but as social communication. He warned: "Save as it realizes this function, it is only partial (and more or less artificial) and fails, therefore, of its educative effect, intellectually, as well as morally; its complete, or organic, stimulus being absent" (p. 4).

The School's Values. A long time before Dewey conducted his school, competition (a value of economic individualism) had become the predominant value of schools. Competition was the keynote of the marking system and was met at every turn in schoolbooks ranging from readers to arithmetic or economics texts. In addition, children were divided by groups according to their age. Neither the spirit of competition nor the division of children into grades or classes was in keeping with Dewey's concept of a school. In his *Plan*, he made this conception clear. The school, Dewey (1895a) wrote, "must have a *community* of spirit and end realized through *diversity* of powers and acts" (p. 2). The idea was to substitute "the cooperative spirit involved in division of labor for the competitive spirit inevitably developed when a number of persons of the same presumed attainments are working to secure exactly the same results" (p. 3). Dewey insisted that a good school will develop interest in others; that is, the child will be responsive to others' needs (such as for consideration). The school should lead children to an understanding of social relationships—ranging from those in their experience to the ideas and beliefs of their wider community (society and the world). It should help the child to take control of and direct his own power to accomplish ethical and desirable social goals.

This emphasis on the social as well as the intellectual runs through Dewey's *Plan*.

To return to the present, periodically the dominance of the competitive spirit has been challenged. In 1995, a leading newspaper reported that "more and more of the nation's most demanding high schools no longer rank seniors" (MacFarquhar, 1995, p. B6). It was believed by many teachers as well as students at one school, for instance, that eliminating the ranking "would encourage students to take a broad array of courses and cut down on the cheating and plagiarism that they attributed largely to rivalry over rank" (p. B6). One of the results of ranking is that students "shy away from arts and other classes that carry less weight when grade point averages are computed" (p. B6). Doing away with ranking nudges college admissions offices to look at a student's individual high school program.

This is only one small crack in the encrusted tradition of competition. In fact, it has become the fashion to put whole schools in competition with one another for high test scores, particularly (but not exclusively) in school districts serving large numbers of disadvantaged children. As Oakes (1995) observes, such changes as substituting a cooperative spirit for competition require an "unsettling rethinking of the most common and fundamental educational beliefs and values. They also require a fundamental realignment of political interests" (p. 9). As she points out, "That is an incredibly tall order for school reform" (p. 9). The fact that the ideas still generate controversy is a sign of hope, for it means that they are alive. Indeed, *The School and Society* (1899), in which Dewey enunciated these same ideas, has been in print since it was first published by the University of Chicago Press the summer after the lectures to parents were given (Harms, 1990). It is as if he were still alive and among us.

A century after Dewey's school, it is more important than ever to create a sense of community. Indeed, a culture that is increasingly diverse—and increasingly values diversity—makes this an imperative. Some schools seem to have learned the lesson well. The following paragraph is from the mission statement (in a sense, a mission fulfilled) of the Manchester GATE School (1995), a public elementary school for gifted children in Fresno, California:

> Since our students come from all parts of the district, there is a need to create a sense of community. We do this by offering a full co-curricular program of music, sports, activities and events. Almost 350 students participate in the instrumental music program while another 100 attend rehearsals before school for our vocal groups. Over 400 students participate in extra-mural sports, while Manchester's interscholastic athletic teams have distinguished themselves in all sports. Drama opportunities are available in many classrooms and in schoolwide functions as well. Our Parent–Teacher Association and teaching staff . . . [are] instrumental in these efforts. There is also a need to have these students develop leadership

skills and to develop a sense of community service. Components of our program, such as partnership with Sierra Hospital, and the GATER Block "M" Award [for any fourth, fifth and sixth grader] lend themselves to this development of community service.

The foregoing calls nothing to mind so much as Dewey's famous words in *The School and Society* (1899): "What the best and wisest parent wants for his own child, that must the community want for all of its children" (p. 7). All children should have the opportunity to participate in activities that build a sense of community and, not incidentally, enrich each individual life. Sadly, for children and our society, they do not.

In clear fashion, Dewey indicates that the children in his school will be treated as individuals. Each child will be studied so that her activities will "properly express" her "capacities, tastes and needs" (1895a, p. 12). This is truly a lesson unlearned. Today the individual child has receded dangerously from the literature. As Tyler (1991) pointed out, "Most of the current publications on problems of teaching and learning focus on groups rather than on individuals" (p. 7). We have done fairly well at studying and recognizing group differences; this is, of course, a focus of multicultural education. But no child should get her identity from the school simply as a group member.

Interestingly, there is no limit on how large a group can be; it can be a television audience, for example. The idea of the group is more economically appealing than that of the individual. But it is not more economically sound in the long view. To ensure children's continuing intellectual and social growth, class groups should be small enough to permit individual analysis. This is a lesson from the Dewey school about which he was adamant (1904a).

Turning to the idea of a plan itself, Dewey believed that if a school plan was to lead to a better kind of schooling, it should be direction pointing, not a set program. A good plan continues its development as it is applied. Dewey proposed this kind of plan for his school:

> The principles of the school's plan were not intended as definite rules for what was to be done in school. They pointed out the general direction in which it was to move. . . . As the outcome of such conditions and others as changes in the teaching staff, equipment, or building, the "principles" formed a kind of working hypothesis rather than a fixed program and schedule. Their application was in the hands of the teachers, and this application was in fact equivalent to their development and modification by teachers. (quoted in Mayhew & Edwards, 1936, p. 366)

Academic, social, and individual development are treated interactively in Dewey's school plan. It was truly a magnificent resource for teachers—not just a plan but a statement of philosophy as well.

The University

We come now to one of the most important and interesting resources used by the teachers in developing curriculum: the University of Chicago. When the teachers asked for help, it was given quickly and enthusiastically by University departments, especially in all fields of science. Mayhew and Edwards (1936) experienced this assistance. They state that department heads as well as faculty members "were generous with their time and facilities," and "in addition to this whole-hearted aid in material ways, intellectual resources were freely put at the disposal of the teachers" (p. 10). What resources they were; some of the scientists and sociologists would go on to worldwide acclaim. More important for the children, these distinguished individuals loved their work and communicated the excitement of their discoveries:

> At that time Thomas C. Chamberlain was elaborating his planetesimal theory of the origin of the solar system and came to talk about it to the children. John M. Coulter planned and guided the experiments on plant relations. Others who cooperated were Charles O. Whitman in zoology, Jacques Loeb in physiology, W. I. Thomas and George Vincent in sociology, Frederick Starr in anthropology, Rollin D. Salisbury in geography, Albert A. Michelson in physics, Alexander Smith in chemistry, and Henry C. Cowles in ecology. (p. 10)

The University was very close to and interested in its school, which was one reason why teachers had "easy accessibility" (p. 10) to scientists who were or became leaders in their fields. As Mayhew and Edwards point out, many of these individuals "had, in addition to special attainments, unusual pedagogical interests which led to their giving constant intellectual and material help to the teachers of the school" (p. 10).

There was yet another reason why the teachers drew so freely on the University's resources: Dewey's view that education is education. Put somewhat differently, there is no reason why children in school and adults in a university should not be studying and working on the same problems, which they sometimes were at Chicago when Dewey was running his school. Dewey said to the parents, in 1899:

> I wish to add one more word about the relationship of our particular school to the University. The problem is to unify, to organize, education, to bring all its various factors together, through putting it as a whole into organic union with everyday life. . . . Already we have much help from the University in scientific work planned, sometimes even in detail, by heads of the departments. The graduate student comes to us with his researches and methods, suggesting ideas and problems. The library and museum are at hand. We want to bring all things educational together; to break down the barriers that divide the education of a

little child from the instruction of the maturing youth; to identify the lower and the higher education, so that it shall be demonstrated to the eye that there is no lower or higher, but simply education. (p. 92)

Education Is Education: The Idea in Action. The teachers took advantage of the relationship with the University to train students' inquiring minds and to convey the reality of what they were studying (Camp, 1900). Group X, for example, comprising 13-year-olds, the age of today's eighth graders, were deeply interested in photography. The year before they had made pin-hole cameras in the shop and wanted to perfect them and move on to actually taking, developing, and printing pictures. Their teacher, Georgia Bacon, felt that they were ready "so far as interest went, to grapple with the study of light, already planned for their autumn program" (Mayhew & Edwards, 1936, p. 225).

The previous year this group had studied various theories of the earth's formation and the major physical forces that have formed and are continually forming the continent of North America. The work was further differentiated into the fields of physics and biology. As Group IX, they had studied various forms of energy, gravity, electricity, and heat in relation to their geological study. In the field of biology, they had studied function, with particular emphasis on the respiratory system and digestive tract relative to kinds of food and ways of preparation. Thus, the transition had been made naturally by means of practical science to the study of more abstract concepts in biology and physics.

What is particularly interesting about the Deweyan approach to learning an academic discipline is that it recently has been rediscovered (without necessarily giving credit to Dewey). For example, according to a renowned theoretical physicist, "physics is indeed human; it can and should be made to appear so in our teaching and writing. This is the first and foremost task of the physics teacher" (Weisskopf, 1989, p. 23). Weisskopf suggests that teachers emphasize the "human angle of our science" (p. 23) by following the historical approach. Emphasis can be put on such understandings as: "Daily experience with heat, boiling water, and steam had to be abstracted, or generalized, in order to achieve a comprehensive view of heat that can be applied to all concrete examples" (p. 24). The historical approach might help to make clear why it is necessary to study phenomena under contrived conditions. "It would show that such a seemingly 'unnatural' approach to nature has indeed revealed the essential traits of nature and established a deeper relation between man and his environment" (p. 24).

According to Weisskopf, a second way to convey the idea that success has evolved and is continuing to evolve from human activity is the early involvement of students in experimental research:

He or she will see how important all these wires, amplifiers, and gadgets are for penetrating the essential processes of nature and—if the student has not made a very bad choice of a team—will witness the deeply human enthusiasm with which most physicists try to get at these processes. The student will participate in the immense joy of finding something new, even if it is only a tiny bit of personal insight. (p. 24)

If Weisskopf could be transported to Dewey's school in the fall quarter of 1900, he might view with pleasure Group X's work in science. The course was taught by Arthur Jones, a student of Professor Albert Michelson. Mayhew and Edwards (1936) describe the situation vividly:

Mr. Jones came each day fresh from his own laboratory study and was unusually successful in his experiment of recalling the course of the college laboratory so that children were able to carry on simplified experiments demonstrating the same principles. (p. 225)

The group's work was related to the camera's use and its parts and dealt with the laws of focusing and perspective. Also encompassed in the course were other instruments, such as the telescope and microscope. Weisskopf would see that

[m]any excursions were made to the University laboratory to see perfected instruments, such as the interferometer and spectroscope, for demonstrating what they (the children) could only roughly approximate or estimate. This connection with the University and adults who were studying and working on the same problems steadied and heightened the children's appreciation of the importance and reality of their work. The actual work was a series of experiments on light, bringing out the principles involved in the construction of an image in a convex lens. (pp. 225–226)

Although the children were ready for photography and got as far as taking pictures, developing the pictures was impossible as there was no darkroom and not even space for constructing one. Inadequate facilities continually plagued Dewey and the teachers. Nevertheless, the children continued the study of light and various theories about its nature in the spring quarter.

There are two ideas of great importance for today's teachers in the work of Group X. Bringing children into contact with adults who are working on similar problems helps children to understand how their own work is related to the real world. This contact can be in the form of visits to laboratories, or college faculty can come to talk to the children. Granted that such arrangements were easier in Dewey's school, for in those days the University was more intimate than it is now, it is still true today that the fields of knowledge become alive as experts convey their excitement to children.

Second, it is better for learning to view education as an organic whole than to view it as segregated by level. Problems are imbued with interest when children know that the adult world is working on the same things. The same can be said about teaching: Connection with mature scholars who are working in the same field of knowledge makes teaching more interesting. One senses that following Dewey's idea was a pleasure, and still could be.

ACHIEVING CURRICULUM INTEGRATION IN THE DEWEY SCHOOL: SOME IDEAS FOR THE PRESENT

"In order for educational experiences to produce a cumulative effect, they must be so organized as to reinforce each other," wrote Tyler (1949, p. 83). In improving our curricula it is important to consider the vertical and horizontal relations of learning experiences. If we look at the relation between the activities in fourth-grade geography and fifth-grade geography, we are concerned with vertical curriculum relations (and, hopefully, continuity and sequence), and when we examine the relation between fourth-grade geography and fourth-grade science, we are concerned with horizontal curriculum organization. As Tyler pointed out, continuity and sequence are not the same. Consideration of sequence means attention to "having each successive experience build upon the preceding one but to go more broadly and deeply into the matters involved" (p. 85). Actually, this is a restatement of Dewey's idea of learning as a circuit rather than a closed circle.

As most teachers know, integration concerns the horizontal relationships of learning activities. The purpose of integration is to provide students with a unified view and, in so doing, offer a more effective curriculum. As Tyler warned, if the experiences are conflicting or lack connection, students develop "compartmentalized learnings which are not related to each other in any effective way" (p. 84) in the students' own everyday lives. Thus, when children develop skill in handling mathematics problems, the school faculty should plan ways in which the skills can be used in science, social studies, shop, and other areas so that they are part of the child's growing capacity for use in daily life situations. Dewey created a new school so that this might happen. Integration is, admittedly, more difficult if one starts with an old school and an ongoing curriculum, but it can still happen. Moreover it is the educator's responsibility to make it happen.

Problems with Integration

Today's educators face certain issues when helping students to develop a unified view. Dewey and the teachers addressed many, if not most, of these same issues in attempting to break down the "traditional barriers" (Mayhew & Edwards, 1936, p. 24) that separated the school from children's lives—a purpose of his school. Subject matter was introduced very early through the activity program, yet children were generally unaware that they were learning content in history, geography, economics, manual arts, and ecology. They could not give it a name, nor did this seem to be a problem for the teachers or children. As teacher Althea Harmer (1900) noted about children studying the effect of industries on the social life of a community:

> All these aspects meet in and radiate from the continuous and direct activity or occupation of the children themselves. From the standpoint of the child there is but one thing going on: he is occupied with making things, with weaving, etc.; he is busy in doing something which appeals alike to feeling, perception, imagination, judgment, and manual skill, utilizing them in an activity which interests him. (p. 80)

The curriculum was doing what it was supposed to do.

A Rose Without a Name. Today in some early childhood programs, children learn subject matter through activities. Sometimes, however, the fact that the children cannot name the knowledge fields from which the material is drawn is troublesome to teachers. For instance, a second-grade teacher was "badly shaken" when the children in her class were unable to respond to a visitor who asked what they were learning in social studies. The children just looked at the visitor blankly. "They didn't know what 'social studies' meant" ("Teaching Across Disciplines," 1994, p. 3). The teacher concluded that she ought to have given her students a conception of the subject fields and their meanings, which she feels "students should know and understand" (p. 3). Certainly Dewey and the teachers in his school would not agree, nor would their experiences support this conclusion. The sources of geography, history, and perhaps other fields as well are well-planned activities. If these second graders were grasping (although naively) the connection between their activities and generalizations in the social studies, their teacher was on the right track. A teacher ought not to allow herself to be intimidated by visitors if she is being true to her philosophy. (The Dewey teachers could tell her a thing or two about that.)

The "Smother" (Dominant Field) Problem. The tendency of one subject to dominate is a problem, too. Put somewhat quaintly, one subject becomes "a 'handmaiden' to another" ("Teaching Across Disciplines," 1994, p. 3). Literature, for example, might be simply a tool of history. But is that all bad? It depends on what the teacher has in mind. If the idea is to develop chunks or

blocks of integrated curriculum simply because it is the thing to do, one subject might well overwhelm the other. In that case, one starts with a mechanical approach, which invites the interdisciplinary effort to fail. On the other
hand, there might be a philosophical reason for wanting one subject to dominate or be the core. This was the case with history and literature in Dewey's
school. "As regards the study of literature," wrote Dewey (Mayhew & Edwards,
1936, p. 31), "perhaps the most striking departure from methods pursued in
other progressive schools is that literature is regarded as social expression. It
is approached, therefore, through the medium of history, instead of studying
history through the medium of literature. This puts the latter subject in its
proper perspective" (p. 31).

Dewey gave as an example the study of Greek history. In developing the
curriculum, the teachers discovered that nearly all books for children were
written from the literary side. "Many of them in addition make the myth fundamental, instead of an incident to the intellectual and social development of
the Greek people" (p. 31).

There is a point here about how one starts to integrate curriculum. Dewey
began with a total conception in mind rather than trying to blend two, or three,
or more subjects. Certainly he would suggest that we do the same. Before discussing his organizing theme and its possible applicability, a word of comfort:
Curriculum flops are nothing out of the ordinary when trying something new,
and Dewey certainly had his in the first year or two of his school. One would
not know it from the literature because it was never made much of, but Dewey's
first attempt to use an organizing theme did not work well. That it is so little
known and only a foggy part of his school's history, is due to the fact that he
came up with another idea that worked famously: the occupational theme.

The Organizing Theme

Like humans and other vertebrates, a curriculum must have a backbone to hold
it together. Dewey would agree—he used the same word in describing the
purposes of his occupational theme. Noting that much of children's play is
haphazard efforts in miniature to reproduce social occupations, he wrote:

> The occupations articulate a vast variety of impulses, otherwise separate and
> spasmodic, into a consistent skeleton with a firm backbone. It may well be
> doubted whether, wholly apart from such regular and progressive modes of ac-
> tion, extending as cores throughout the entire school, it would be permanently
> safe to give the principle of "interest" any large place in school work. (1900b,
> p. 85)

Theme-based approaches used by today's teachers tend to be concerned
with the horizontal relation of learning experiences; that is, they are usually,

at best, year-long units. Dewey's approach to curriculum integration was continuous and developmental. (He used the words *regular* and *progressive*.) Not surprisingly, horizontal integration was facilitated by the vertical core.

Interestingly, the teachers' typewritten weekly reports are by subject field. This is because the teachers in the Dewey school were specialists and the activities were planned from the teacher's standpoint. But the curriculum was not compartmentalized; the subjects were related to each other through the steady presence of the organizing theme and, most important of all, through teachers talking over their work, finding where their activities "reinforced one another or failed to converge" (quoted in Mayhew & Edwards, 1936, p. 370), and revising plans accordingly.

Choosing a Theme That Works: Dewey's Problem and Ours. No matter how eager our experimentation, we are confronted by vexatious problems in putting our ideas into classroom use. For Dewey the first 2 years were hard. Subject matter and staff had to be selected and plans had to be revised. On December 6, 1897, he wrote to Harper: "The school had a great many problems of its own to work out—this because it incurs so many departures from existing methods and so much experience to get hold of the right instructors that it could not take shape at once. . . . That period however is now ended, or will be at the end of this year. The main problems of selection and adjustment of work have been solved" (J. Dewey, personal communication).

The light at the end of the tunnel was in sight. Dewey and the teachers could refine and build on what had been learned. According to Mayhew and Edwards (1936), the practices of the school's "second period (1898 to 1903) grew out of or were revised on the basis of the courses and methods that had proved successful in the first" (p. 39).

It is what happened during the first period concerning the selection of a theme that is important for dealing with present problems of curriculum integration. Dewey chose a civilizational theme for the school. His plan was to have children engage in the basic activities that make up civilization and on which they depend. Dewey realized that present social life was simply too complex for children to understand, while past life, if treated as past, is inert and remote. However, through children's interest in their own activities, they "can be led to analyze the existing complex social structure by following up the growth of homes, foods, etc. . . . from the pre-historic cave-dweller through the stone and metal ages up to civilization, etc." (1895a, p. 11). This was Dewey's plan.

The Need for Focus. Dewey's idea for a civilizational theme was remarkable because it was doubly developmental. It concerned the development of humankind "in skill, understanding, and associated life" (Mayhew & Edwards,

1936, p. 6), and the development of the child in skill, understanding, and the ability to use his capacities for the good of the community. The trouble was that the theme—and, therefore, the activities—lacked focus. There were too many activities unrelated to anything explicit: "Cooking had been done in an elementary fashion, some constructive work in connection with a study of American Indians, some effort to reconstruct society from the Robinson Crusoe base" (Mayhew, 1934, p. 6). The fact that in 3 short years the school would have perhaps the most important experimental elementary curriculum the United States has ever produced inspires in us a curiosity about what happened to effect the transformation. Clearly the curriculum was a long way from being anyone's ideal, in discouraging shape, indeed. In the answer there is a lesson in leadership.

Doing What Good Leaders Do. Dewey did what good leaders are supposed to do: tap the ideas of other bright and creative persons so that teachers might have a more consistent line to follow in their work. Thus the social occupational theme, for which the school is so famous, was born. The theme emerged from the collaborative efforts of Chicago faculty, graduate students, Dewey, and the teachers to continually improve the curriculum organization. It seems likely that the idea of an occupational theme was the suggestion of two students, Frederick W. Smedley and Daniel P. MacMillan, who were in Dewey's seminar in the 1896–97 academic year. According to Mayhew and Edwards (1936), "It was in the seminar where the fundamental concepts basic to the school were worked out" (p. 389).

That the occupational theme was a new development is clear from Dewey's (1897c) own report in the spring of 1897 in the *University Record*: "After this year the beginning will be made with a study of social occupation at the present time" (p. 73). History, manual training, and science would be unified as children learned "how society has grown to be what it is" (p. 73). The new theme's purpose was to stimulate inventiveness while "giving an insight into actual history and to carry this out in a somewhat playful series of occupations" (Mayhew, 1934, p. 6). This would require much experimentation on the teachers' part. Not all occupations were practical in an elementary school setting and not all met the objective of giving insight into how discoveries and new inventions ushered in periods of social progress as well as conditions that blocked progress. Also not all were continuous—lasting through years.

The Teachers' Choice. An occupation that clearly met human needs, that developed in an ordered progression, and that could provide a powerful stimulus to children's inventiveness and lead them to historical insights was the textile industry. It was selected by teachers as the type of industry that could be studied in the school. Children learned the progression of the industry. In primitive conditions, skins and furs were used for clothing. Later, each home became its own producer: From raw material to finished garment, clothing was made by some member of the family. From the household grew the domestic system: A workman with a small amount of capital purchased wool from a dealer and distributed it among families to be spun and woven; he collected the cloth and sold it at a profit. The idea of importance here was that the merchant was separated from the manufacturer.

With the introduction of machines and further specialization, the domestic system evolved into the factory. The weavers, as a result of this system, were obligated to leave the country and live around the village spinning mills. Eventually, factory life was concentrated in big cities near trade centers. As large amounts of capital were invested and machines were invented and improved, the factory system was introduced.

Children in Dewey's school studied the three stages of industrial development and carried out the whole process. They saw the value of implements and invented mechanical devices for converting raw materials into cloth. They grew in understanding and respect for what other people had done in the social past. They wanted to experience the process as it developed. Not surprisingly, one child, at least, became a connoisseur of woven objects. Perhaps there were others. The point is that the children grew in the moral qualities of respect for the contributions of others and an understanding of the intellectual continuity of the human past as well as a sense of future possibility. They also used what they were learning in their daily lives.

Fresh from her work with the children, Althea Harmer (1900)—the teacher in the textile room—wrote:

> The way in which the children enjoy carrying out the process historically is shown in the scorn they express for the child, of perhaps less imagination, who jumps at every short-cut possible; while at the same time they adopt the short-cuts which legitimately follow in the course of historical development. They rejected the carder and carded patiently with their hands, at the same time appreciating the advance made in using the whirling spindle instead of the weighted stick in spinning. One boy of ten acquired much appreciation for rugs and hangings at home, which showed its intelligence in his judgment of the adaptation of design to the kind of weaving and material used, as well as in the color effects produced. (pp. 78–79)

Harmer goes on to point out that the children were learning to exercise judgment and, since the acts of judgment followed one another in logical steps, they were gaining an insight into the logic of history itself. Their work correlated with shop work—the spindle and loom were made in the shop—and it connected with the work of the art department regarding colors, designs, and so on. The children developed concepts that would transfer later to the study of economics and make it more concrete. They were able to understand chemical processes as they prepared raw material, dyed, and steamed. They also came to understand the effects of industry on the social life of a community and how the social life affected its history.

Suggestions from the Crucible of Dewey's Experience

By 1900 the curriculum bore little or no relation to its fragmentary and meager beginnings. What lessons for today are embedded in the stunning development? There are at least three, not necessarily in order of importance. First, it is all too easy to give up on an idea, saying that it does not work. If it is a good idea, it simply may need to be reworked, and suggestions should be sought from others. Whether one should turn to experts for assistance is moot. (This would not have worked for Dewey because they all had fairly traditional ideas.) Anyone with a creative solution that works is probably, by definition, an expert—at least in my book. This could be a graduate student (as in Dewey's case). Reading also may help, and the books should not necessarily be new. Books may hook us on to something that is promising but simply has been forgotten.

Second, plans should be tentative. This was Dewey's concept of planning and it keeps things from being labeled failures prematurely. The point cannot be overemphasized that if Dewey had viewed his first plan as written in stone, he would have had to pronounce his school a failure after 6 months. His purpose and philosophical view never wavered: Children's concept of the social meaning of what they are studying should develop continually. Thus plans and instructional approaches were revised continually with that purpose in mind. Having a purpose—a philosophical view—is what keeps us trying. Without an underlying philosophical purpose concerning the curriculum as a whole, we are likely to attempt a mechanical blending of the subjects and, with its failure, are only too glad to drop the idea rather than make revisions.

Third, we are deceiving ourselves if we think that horizontal curriculum integration will do the whole job single-handedly. The curriculum should have a backbone—a vertical theme to hold it together. This is surely one of the most important lessons from Dewey's school. Such a theme can be related to both the school's social purposes—which are academic as well as concerned with human relationships—and the child's psychological development. In Dewey's school, subject matter and instruction were related to his idea of the school as a community in microcosm. The theme activities themselves took only 2 hours a week. It was the fact that they radiated to other subjects that unified the curriculum.

"We do not expect to have other schools literally imitate what we do," said Dewey in 1899. "A working model is not something to be copied; it is to afford a demonstration of the feasibility of the principle, and of the methods which make it feasible" (p. 94).

The Laboratory School at the University of Chicago demonstrated the feasibility of a vertical theme—contributing valuable insights on curriculum integration from which we can profit. Today there is much interest in bringing in more history to enrich the social studies—in the need "to help children connect past events to the present" (Dunleavy, 1995, p. B7). The experience of Dewey's school with a historical theme provides valuable groundwork. Dewey's civilizational theme emphasized the development of the knowledge of humankind—all peoples on earth. As the world shrinks, people's experiences and problems become more alike. Dewey's idea seems to grow in merit.

❖ **5** ❖

The Teachers Speak

Our "higher" education will not really be higher until elementary teachers
have the same right and power to select and organize proper subject-matter,
and invent and use their own methods as is now accorded in some degree
to teachers of older students. In recollection of many things in our school
practice and results that I wish had been otherwise, there is compensation
in the proof our experience affords that the union of intellectual freedom
and cooperation will develop the spirit that is prized by university teachers,
and that is sometimes mistakenly supposed to be a monopoly of theirs.
—John Dewey, quoted in Katherine Camp Mayhew and
Anna Camp Edwards, *The Dewey School*

THE TEACHERS IN DEWEY'S SCHOOL had much freedom in developing curriculum—a power that tends to be accorded only to university faculty. The teachers and the curriculum both blossomed. In Dewey's words, "vitality and constant growth were gained" (Mayhew & Edwards, 1936, p. 366). Why, then, are elementary teachers given so little intellectual freedom in comparison with university faculty? Perhaps because people who want teachers to have this freedom are rarer than we like to believe. Indeed we may believe that teachers aren't as smart as professors and, like most of our favorite prejudices, it may be hidden from us.

Another reason is surely that we are without professional memory about where this freedom has existed and in what circumstances it is most effective. Dewey's school, in particular, the teachers' typewritten weekly reports, provides a memory. The reports, which are in the possession of the University of Chicago, are also invaluable for clearing up certain misconceptions about the curriculum. For example, it is widely believed that the curriculum in Dewey's school consisted of a series of projects. It didn't. The reports show very clearly that the teachers used a number of approaches—including discussion, field trips, writing, laboratory experiments, and experiences in the practical and fine arts.

64

The teachers' reports, however, were not intended to enlighten posterity but had a purpose in their own time—to provide data for the problems studied and discussed at the weekly informal teachers' conference and in University classes and seminars. According to Mayhew and Edwards (1936), "All the teachers in actual daily contact with children of all ages furnished, in these reports, the data for further inquiries and conclusions," and "the value of such material to the Department of Pedagogy of the University, engaged as it was with the problems of educational science, became almost like the systematic and cumulative clinical records of medical science" (p. 374). The reports also provided an opportunity for the teachers to organize their thoughts on what they had been doing.

Today, administrators miss a great opportunity. Teachers turn in plans (often used as a bureaucratic device), but seldom is information sought from teachers as to whether "such and such a thing worked and another did not," which "would lead to needed modification or even to the decision that some line of work must be begun over again on a different basis" (Dewey, quoted in Mayhew & Edwards, 1936, p. 371). Many supervisors do not grasp how essential such information is for school renewal and improvement. My own view is that such reports—if not formalized beyond usefulness—can only strengthen teachers' professional autonomy.

The teachers' reports are a treat because they show what a top-notch staff did to involve children actively in learning, always with the development of their creative intelligence and character in mind. The guidelines under which the reports were written are also a kind of buried treasure. They were intended to help teachers think clearly about the reasons for what they were doing, as well as to look ahead to the work that was to grow from what they were trying to accomplish. The reports provide convincing proof that under certain conditions teachers can develop curriculum.

Perhaps most important of all, through the reports, the teachers can speak to us of their work, as if by magic, a century after their school. There is a lesson here, of course: Records should be kept of innovative work. Most of the innovative work done by schools goes unrecorded—and dies forever. This chapter concerns what the Dewey teachers and the children did—with gratitude for both the teachers' work and the preservation of their records.

THE TEACHERS' REPORTS

In the fall quarter of 1898, the Laboratory School adopted its final departmentalized form of organization, "thus harmonizing with the University" (Mayhew & Edwards, 1936, p. 8). The teachers' weekly reports are by subject field. The traditional subject designations literally jump out at one and seem rather surprising. This is Dewey's school? we ask. Somehow we expected something different. History, geography, literature, French, Latin (foreign languages were introduced early), science, mathematics, music, art, wood shop, cooking, and physical education seem to reflect a subject-centered view of the curriculum. We strain to know what is different and as we read it becomes clear: The reforms are in terms of instruction and the underlying philosophy. Changes in instructional approach lead to changes in content (although the reverse may not be true).

Old Labels and New Meanings

Subject labels do not tell us that the school was concerned with developing social insight and sympathy or how the teachers capitalized on opportunities for doing so. For instance, in fall 1898, a group the age of today's first graders were learning in history how occupations are adapted to the physical features of environment. As they studied the homes and commercial activities of Holland, they engaged in imaginative play using chairs and blackboard to represent the dikes. In her entry for the week of October 21, their teacher wrote: "An effort was made to bring out the kinds of occupations followed by the poorer classes, the women harnessed up to canal boats and the heavy work done by them" (Laboratory Schools Work Reports, 1898–1899, p. 17).

Developing social insight and sympathy required that teachers take advantage of such opportunities. To take a second example, a group the age of today's third graders spent part of the spring of 1899 learning about China in connection with their theme, "progress through exploration and discovery" (Mayhew & Edwards, 1936, p. 125). In her entry for June 2, their teacher, Laura Runyon, reported the following:

> The children asked again about the sedan chairs, and were shown a picture of one. Someone wanted to know how much money the carriers got, and were told "only a few cents a day." They were surprised at this, and were questioned again on "population" and "means of subsistence," and seemed to realize how closely one crowds on the other. One of the boys said, "Well, why don't people give them a few cents extra; that isn't being kind!" No attempt had been made to elicit sympathy—simply the facts had been stated. (Laboratory Schools Work Reports, 1898–1899, pp. 148–149)

In her report at the close of the school year, she wrote:

> From the point of view of getting a rational idea of the explorers and their aims, the work of this year has been very satisfactory. The children seem to have a fairly correct idea of what made Columbus and the other explorers great, and on the other hand to recognize that some of their deeds were not commendable. They

also seem able to contrast their own times with those of the men they study, and also to compare different countries. (Mayhew & Edwards, 1936, p. 138)

Her report is particularly interesting in view of our own concern that the discoverers and explorers be treated honestly. We did not invent this idea. The point here is that intellectual honesty, social insight, and moral development are all inseparable. Dewey (1897a, 1909) insisted that they be treated as part of the same process, and what is so striking is that the teachers were able to recognize the opportunities for doing so and capitalize on them.

Thus, the curriculum was being changed. The old subject matter designations referred to a new and better education. As Cremin (1961) pointed out: "History became a vivid picture of why and how men have come to their successes and failures" (p. 139). The teachers' reports reflect a curriculum that by fall 1898 was well planned and sequential and "always with the social in mind" (p. 139).

Finding Meaning in the Reports for Ourselves

In seeking meaning from the reports, it is important to understand Dewey's view of intellectual freedom and how it differs from more recent notions of professional autonomy that date back to the teacher empowerment movement of the early 1990s. The differences are striking.

From Dewey came one of the first pronouncements that elementary teachers should have intellectual freedom. Today, however, we speak of professional autonomy rather than intellectual freedom. According to Shepard (1995), for example, university researchers who want to help teachers find new ways to assess student learning should take care not to "undermine professional autonomy" (p. 38). Her concern is understandable. A wave of legislation on accountability in the 1970s and 1980s reflected the view that teachers are technicians, not professionals. Policy makers embraced what Darling-Hammond and Snyder (1992) call "the bureaucratic model" (p. 17): Curriculum decisions are made at higher levels in the system. "Teachers are held accountable for implementing curricular and testing policies, most often prescribed at the district and state levels, whether or not the prescriptions are appropriate in particular instances for particular students" (p. 17). However, this model proved to be unrealistic for at least two reasons: Teachers inevitably are involved in curriculum development, and treating children in standardized ways does not help many children to learn. Discussions in the 1990s began to focus on teacher empowerment and autonomy. In fact, it was almost impossible to read an article on teaching without coming across some mention of professional autonomy. After decades of neglect, it would seem that the professional model, as Dewey conceived it, is making a comeback. Or is it?

The Insufficiency of Autonomy: Dewey's Dilemma and Ours. Professional autonomy is an insufficient peg on which to hang our hopes for school improvement. This has become equally evident to teachers, supervisors, and university researchers. A teacher with professional autonomy may follow ways of teaching that have become habits and through her emotion have become untouchable. Or a teacher's autonomy may be limited to finding ways of helping students to do well on standardized tests. Policy makers have not detached themselves effectively from the factory-production model of schooling, and curriculum is still test-driven. Autonomy in this case is only a rather disheartening label.

Perhaps most tragic is when teachers actually have the prerogative to make selections of content and instructional approaches and are indeed expected to do so, but have neither the time in the school day nor the assistance. Along with granting teachers autonomy, some school systems have eliminated departments of curriculum and instruction, thereby depriving teachers of their support infrastructure (Tanner & Tanner, 1995). For these teachers and the children with whom they work, the era of professional autonomy is an age of lost opportunities.

The point is that no matter how able the teacher, autonomy is not enough. In fact, if carried to its logical conclusion, autonomy could eventuate in a fragmented curriculum as each teacher does his or her own thing. This possibility was what Dewey wanted to avoid, while, on the other hand, he did not want to put a cap on teachers' artistry and resourcefulness. As the administrator of an experimental school, Dewey had to answer the question: How much freedom and responsibility should teachers have in selecting subject matter and the way that it is presented to children? The same question is before educators and policy makers today, so we are interested in his opinion, particularly since it is based on his experience. Reviewing that experience, he warned:

> In an experimental school it is more difficult than elsewhere to avoid extremes. One of them results in a continual improvisation that is destructive of continuity and in the end of steady development of power. The other relies upon definite presentation of ends and methods for reaching them to which teachers are expected to conform. (Mayhew & Edwards, 1936, p. 366)

In the end he opted for more freedom, not less, "avoiding hard and fast plans to be executed and dictation of methods to be followed" (p. 366). Dewey understood brilliantly how a school's ethos can "control" (p. 367) the work of individual teachers and bring about unity. Chapter 6 discusses this and the manner in which the directors assisted teachers. To return to the question of how much freedom, Dewey later wrote that if the school were to be "tried over again" (p. 366), he would still prefer to err in the direction of too much rather than too little. Nevertheless he felt that there could have been more assistance for teachers.

There is clearly a lesson to be drawn here, and Dewey as much as said it: Avoid extremes. We have not paid attention. He would have been troubled by the general lack of intellectual freedom for elementary teachers, on the one hand, and the failure to give teachers assistance where needed, on the other.

Intellectual Freedom. If one has to err, one errs in the direction of too much freedom, this lesson also can be drawn from the school's experience. The freedom that Dewey referred to was not just any kind of freedom—to teach what one wants, for instance—it was a very special kind, intellectual freedom. Using one's mind creatively when engaging in curriculum development and the act of testing one's ideas, which is what intellectual freedom was about in Dewey's school, are probably far more useful as guides for school improvement than the more general concept—professional autonomy. While it might justifiably be argued that intellectual freedom is a part of professional autonomy, it was significant enough in Dewey's school to be considered in its own right.

What the Dewey teachers had to go on was a set of theoretical ideas (some in rudimentary form). They had the freedom to work out a curriculum that was based on these ideas but had to locate their own resources, some of which were intended for well-read adults and adult scholars. Teachers used up-to-date scholarly resources to guide children toward understandings that often spanned several disciplines. For example, Laura Runyon used an article from an anthropological journal to obtain facts about a small nomadic people in equatorial Africa—their houses, weapons, food, dress, and economic and social systems. The class was a group of 10-year-olds and the subject was history (world exploration). In her entry for February 3, 1899, she reported:

> The feeling that the pygmies have against stealing was illustrated by the custom of selecting from a plantation a bunch of bananas, yet always leaving in its place a package of meat—regarded as payment. The children were asked whether they thought this justifiable. All at first thought that the practice was perfectly right. They were asked, What if the owner of the bananas had plenty of meat, and wanted the bananas, and by other illustrations led to see that value attached to anything must be an agreement. The papers written were in most cases satisfactory so far as memory of the facts was concerned, but several were lacking in sentence structure and spelling, and in order to give these children personal help, I excused the three who had the fewest mistakes and let them read aloud the article in the journal. They found some hard words, but enjoyed the attempt to read the facts for themselves. (Laboratory Schools Work Reports, 1898–1899, p. 66)

In connection with the theme activities, the Laboratory School curriculum ranged widely across world cultures. Thus global studies were begun early.

Today in many schools this would be viewed as an innovation. Even at the secondary school level, it is still necessary to argue that students should be "given the opportunity to move out of their own culture and into other people's histories, cultures and traditions" (Zevin, 1993, p. 82).

The form of this opportunity is always important, if it is to be an opportunity and not a penalty on students and teachers. In Dewey's experimental school, the study of societies was simply an integral part of the curriculum; that is, it was appropriately connected with history, geography, art, science, and so on. It was not tacked on to an already existing curriculum. (Again, this is the advantage of a new school, but curriculum reconstruction is always possible in an old school.)

Use of Primary Source Materials. There were textbooks for teaching American history but they would never do; the teachers found them to be generally without sustenance, a series of dates and battles. Those textbooks were designed for a different kind of teaching and learning: by rote (Finklestein, 1989). The Dewey teachers found primary source materials that made history come alive. It is my own sense that teaching this way must have been fun.

For example, for 9-year-olds studying colonial history,

> [t]he isolation of the colonies was made clearer by studying means of transportation at this time. Parts of the journal of Hezekiah Prince, who traveled from Maine to Virginia on horseback, were read to the children, describing the corduroy roads, bridle paths, and Indian tracks which had to be followed. We found a description of the first postal system established by Governor Spotswood, located each town where mail was received, and found the time taken for news to be received in Williamsburg from Philadelphia and other towns. Selections from *The Colonial Cavalier*, by Maud Wilder Goodwin, were read from time to time to show the dress and customs of the time. ("University Elementary School," 1899a, p. 63)

An Idea Whose Time Has Come. The children also engaged in historical conjecture, attempting to guess how a city's problem, for example, might have been met. In their study of Chicago's early development, a group the age of today's sixth graders tried to work out the problems of city government as they would arise. One was the water supply. The time was the 1830s.

> The Chicago River water had been used during the early years, when it was a clear stream. But the building of towns on its banks and the beginning of navigation rendered the water unfit for use. The children were told of the custom, for a time of carrying pure water about in barrels and selling it from house to house. Then wells were sunk, but in the rapid growth of the city these were unsafe.

So a private company undertook to supply pure water, and made a crib in Lake Michigan and laid pipes. Owing to bad management, however, these were not laid deep enough and during a severe winter the water froze, burst the pipes, and a water famine resulted. When these facts had been related the problem of how the matter could be remedied was laid before the children. Some suggested that the company lay the pipes deeper; some that the city buy out the company and manage the supply. This brought up the general discussion of municipal ownership versus private companies, and the children brought out the ideas that the city would have more money to construct better, and as it would not expect a profit, could supply consumers more cheaply than a private concern. The children were told that the city assumed the management of the water supply, and the various changes that have been made up to the present time. ("University Elementary School," 1899b, pp. 122–123)

Thus teachers did not merely use a lifelike instructional approach; it was real. This is an idea whose time has finally come, at least in the area of assessment. Assessments increasingly are viewed as opportunities to extend learning rather than simply to determine what has been learned. The foregoing illustration from the final year of the nineteenth century is very consistent, for example, with what the writers say in the National Society for the Study of Education's yearbook on performance assessment (Baron & Wolf, 1996). However, in the Laboratory School, the idea was part of instruction, not confined to assessment. Also it was utilized throughout the curriculum.

In science, for example, a group the age of today's sixth graders selected and staked out plots of ground in the spring of 1899 for the purpose of studying the behavior of the plants growing on them. In her entry under botany for April 14, their teacher, Anne Moore (who was actually a teaching assistant), wrote:

They have begun to make a list of all the different kinds of plants they can discover. Most of the plants are as yet small seedlings and require careful observation to be distinguished from one another. The names of only a few are known, and at the outset the difficulty of some mode of designating them presented itself. One of the children suggested the drawing of the seeds until they are sufficiently well developed to be identified. This plan was adopted and the children are now engaged in completing their lists by the use of this method. (Laboratory Schools Work Reports, 1898–1899, p. 36)

Intellectual Responsibility. At the heart of the concept of intellectual freedom lies intellectual responsibility. If teachers are to be independent and thoughtful about their work, their professional preparation must cultivate this habit. In 1904, Dewey observed that in preparing prospective teachers, the "far-reaching matter of intellectual responsibility is too frequently ignored" (1904b, p. 13). The effort must be to make teachers "thoughtful and alert student[s] of education" whose knowledge of the subject field, and "psychological and ethical philosophy of education" (p. 15) have become incorporated into their working power. Dewey warned that "only when such things have become incorporated in mental habit, have become part of the working tendencies of observation, insight, and reflection, will these principles work automatically, unconsciously and hence promptly and effectively" (p. 15).

What is so interesting is that these insights about teacher education came right from experience, his own, in the Laboratory School. Dewey found that while some teachers understood the underlying principles in adjusting subject matter to the needs of individual children and in teaching cooperation in daily living, others did not. He wrote:

> [T]he younger and less experienced teachers, who served as assistants, often failed to see this connection and were inclined to be impatient with the personal phase of the discussion [in the weekly meetings] when it concerned children they did not have to deal with. Experience showed that "principles" were too much taken for granted as being understood by all teachers; in the later years an increasing number of meetings were allotted to the specific discussion of underlying principles and aims. (quoted in Mayhew & Edwards, p. 370)

Embedded in Dewey's experience is a lesson for today. It is still true that we ought not to take for granted that teachers have the theoretical foundations for putting instructional approaches to really effective use. Although the direction in teacher education is to put greater attention on the teacher's intellectual responsibility, rather than simply focusing on immediate (and, sad to say, mechanical) proficiency, teachers in general still lack what Dewey (1904b) called "control of the intellectual methods" (p. 11) needed for personally developing skilled practice. Some teachers were prepared during the competency-based movement of the 1970s, but whatever the reason, unless teachers understand educational principles and have the attitude of developing content and instructional approaches based on these principles and unless they have the habit of observing and thinking, school improvement is impossible. Idea-oriented meetings of the sort that Dewey held with the teachers can fill some of the need, but unfortunately such meetings are rare.

Intellectual Sustenance. Supervisors have, on the whole, shown little concern for teachers' intellectual interests, and many teachers feel intellectually starved (Poplin, 1992). Dealing with ideas concerning the curriculum can be a source of intellectual pleasure and growth, for schools are related to our deepest beliefs about what individuals can and should be. The pleasure literally flows from the teachers' reports of a century ago. It is just as possible today.

Guidelines for the Reports

In October 1898, the teachers were given guidelines on what to include in their weekly reports. We can't be sure that it was Dewey who wrote them but the internal evidence suggests that it was. Certainly he would have approved them since they were absolutely vital to the work of the school. There were three simple guidelines. The first concerned subject matter; teachers were to indicate what was studied. That would seem unremarkable, but Dewey said:

> The report should in all cases indicate not merely the actual subject matter, but the reason for taking it up, its antecedents, and the points which are being led up to. (It will not, of course, be necessary to repeat this in every week's reports provided a full statement is made in some one. In all cases, however, the further work that is to grow out of what has been undertaken should be indicated.) (Laboratory Schools Work Reports, Addenda, October 1898)

Some experimental schools had curricula that lacked continuity and coherence. Dewey would have none of that. What he and the teachers were after was a sequential curriculum in which each year's instruction led up naturally to the problems and subject matter presented in the following year and that provided for the gradual differentiation of the content into the special fields of knowledge. Clearly the teachers were professionals, not mechanical toys or technicians. They need not repeat what was said in a previous report.

The second guideline, dealing with the fine and industrial arts, was that the reasons behind such work must be stated clearly:

> In all hand work, whether carpentry, sewing, etc., or art work, the reason or motive for the work should be definitely stated, its connection or lack of connection with the other work of the school, and the uses if any, to which the objects made are to be put. (Laboratory Schools Work Reports, Addenda, October 1898)

The concept of activity in some progressive schools was activity for its own sake, rather than with a definite outcome in view. Not so in the Laboratory School. The handwork was a way of learning facts and concepts—of working out processes and developing appreciations. These ideas formed the basis for handwork in the school. For example, learning technique in art leads in a natural way to "aesthetic taste or capacity to appreciate artistic excellence in at least some of its classic forms" (Dewey, 1916, pp. 285–286). Weaving could help children not only learn but feel and experience the history of invention. Dewey was, of course, particularly concerned with the relation of handwork to the other things that children were learning about. Thus teachers had to articulate the connections, and this was not just to show Dewey that they were clear in the teachers' minds. First and foremost, he needed to know if children could learn effectively in this way, if they would develop "ingenuity in planning and power in execution" (Dewey, 1897c, p. 72), and if they would develop the ability to work cooperatively with others. The answer to each was yes (Dewey, 1900a).

The third guideline dealt with instructional approaches. It concerned Dewey's conception of an active situation. Instructional approaches were all-important—the manifestation of all that the school stood for. Therefore, if any guideline could be identified as the most important, it would be this one. What Dewey wanted was concrete and practical: creative new ways of communicating subject matter that would replace rote and recitation in a school organized as a community (Childs, 1939).

Creative new ideas there were in those reports. Although some seem uncontroversial and unremarkable now, such as discussion and field trips, these were once innovations (and still would be in some classrooms). The curriculum of the Dewey school also influenced such innovations as projects in agricultural education, the inquiry-discovery method, science laboratories, home economics, vocational education in a comprehensive setting, and, of course, curriculum synthesis.

Not surprisingly, the third guideline was quite detailed. Mild-mannered though he might appear, Dewey did not hesitate to describe what he wanted:

> So far as possible the mode of getting at the topic should be indicated. This involves in History a statement of the uses of conversation, discussion, dramatization, class readings and references to literature; also the study of pictures, visits to museums, historical places, etc. In the case of Science it involves a statement of experimental work performed, materials and apparatus used (also as to whether these were supplied ready made to the children or worked out by them). The problem or point to be found out should be clearly stated instead of saying that simply they were studying about such and such a thing. Observational and field work should also be definitely reported on, also reading matter, whether in or out of class. In hand work both the personal and social relations and objects (if any) be given and also a statement on the technical side. In science, history and geography all instruction and expression work growing out of the subject matter should be stated, and whether in the same class, or through other teachers. The amount of writing in each subject should be stated, and whether done on blackboard or on paper; in class or study hour; whether record of work done, summary of discussions or more original composition. (Laboratory Schools Work Reports, Addenda, October 1898)

Dewey's third guideline reflects the view that learning occurs through a wide variety of experiences. Today this idea has been formulated into an approved educational practice: "Because learning occurs through a wide variety of experiences teachers should provide a wide variety of ways to learn" (Tanner & Tanner, 1995, p. 633). Nevertheless, in many classrooms, the teacher's repertoire of instructional approaches is primarily that of having students read the textbook and recite or write answers to questions about the textbook. Expanding this limiting repertoire to include participation, observation, analysis, experimentation, dramatization, and construction would be adopting an approved practice in education that can be traced directly to the Dewey school.

Teachers' Reports Today. Are teachers' reports suitable for today's schools? This depends on their purpose and the ethos of the school. In the Dewey school, the reports furnished the material for the weekly meetings. As Kilpatrick (1939) pointed out in an essay on Dewey's influence, "the teachers were pioneering, and pioneering in the true sense always requires creative thinking" (p. 461). More to the point, perhaps,

> [t]eachers then, as now, must always be learning ever better how to run a school. There is no end to the experimenting, and so no end to the learning. Never can insight quite catch up with life's emerging problems. Life is like that. Study must go on forever. (p. 461)

The Dewey school was alive with study. In such schools, and there are many, reports might be useful in effecting improvements in the school program, but only if teachers have professional autonomy (intellectual freedom) to exercise initiative and responsible self-direction in the context of collaboration with fellow teachers and other members of the professional staff. One shudders at the thought that the reports could become a bureaucratic device. Teachers' reports require an entirely new mindset. They are based on the idea that plans should grow out of what has been learned by teachers as well as students. The work for the following week (or month or quarter) should be based on knowledge about the effectiveness of instructional approaches with given groups and individual children. A great problem in education today is that plans are written in stone, so to speak. This is an invitation to disaster when things do not work the way they are supposed to, which happens all the time. Worse, teachers are prevented from using their knowledge, combined with experience, to improve the chances of more effective instruction in the future.

HOW TEACHERS ACHIEVED SYNTHESIS

Teachers in Dewey's school did not engage in team teaching as the concept is used today. Each teacher reported on what she did that week; there were no joint reports. Again, it was the theme that united. For example, a group of 7-year-olds whose instruction emphasized "progress through invention and discovery" learned about metals in both history and science. In her entry under history for the week of January 6, their teacher Katherine Camp wrote:

> The consideration of the beginning and use of metal occupied all the time in both history and science. Time was divided about as follows: A little time was spent in discussion of this period [the early metal ages, when metals were first heated], the rest of the time in experiments with and examination of copper, tin, and a little time spent on lead and zinc to bring out the general characteristics of metals as related to their uses, as observed by the children. For example the use of iron for strength and hardness and withstanding the fire. They knew very little about copper, tin or bronze. In experimental work they melted copper wire and pounded it while hot. They melted tin, cooling the drops in water to see that the spherical form was assumed and the form was preserved by being cooled in water—or if dropped from a sufficient distance in the air. This was done because they asked about lead bullets, which they had all used. They were shown copper ore containing metallic copper, and were told it was found in this shape with most metals in what they called stones. They then differentiated those stones containing metals which men could get out from other stones, and were given the word "ore." (Laboratory Schools Work Reports, 1898–1899, p. 3)

Mary Hill followed with her entry under science:

> Worked with metals in connection with their history. They examined a piece of copper ore and found out how the people in the early metal ages probably smelted their ores. They also heated wires of various metals and hammered the hot ends. (Laboratory Schools Work Reports, 1898–1899, p. 3)

Teachers correlated the curriculum in creative ways. Cooking and French seemed naturally to go together then as now, and Lorelei Ashleman, who taught French, did not miss the chance to make a connection. The group comprised youngsters the age of today's fifth graders. In her entry for the week of April 14, she wrote:

> After a review of their vocabulary on the parts of the human body, they were given the subject of the kitchen. The purpose of this was to associate French with their cooking lessons, which I learned could be conducted in French.
>
> The vocabulary was presented to them in as many different ways as was practicable and calculated to make a vivid impression. They visited the kitchen to see the various appurtenances and utensils, heard the words pronounced and read them aloud from the board. The usual tasks of the cook, such as lighting the fire, putting on the water, opening the oven, etc., were illustrated and expressed in French.
>
> The next day they were questioned about what they had done the day before and taught how to answer. This conversation was written on the board, and

they were asked to read it aloud and copy it to take home. Much stress was placed on ear-memory, and the ability to pronounce.

Before leaving the subject they were asked to write a composition on the kitchen of at least five sentences. This seemed particularly distasteful to them, and several who failed to bring papers had to spend the recitation time making up this work. They seemed to enjoy the spell-down and word game, which we had at the end, very much. (Laboratory Schools Work Reports, 1898–1899, pp. 36–37)

Experienced teachers and supervisors generally will recognize that guidelines are not enough to achieve curriculum correlation. No matter how admirable and sincere the efforts of individuals, like Mlle Ashleman, the basic structure of the curriculum remains the same. What really knit the Laboratory School curriculum together was the nature of the activities (re-enacting inventions, for instance), which required that teachers with various specializations help one another. An entry by teacher Georgia Bacon concerning the numerical work of her group (youngsters the age of today's seventh graders) gives a fairly good idea of how this worked in the school.

In connection with Miss Harmer's work they needed to know the ratio of revolution of the small to the large wheel in spinning. They got the diameter of the large wheel and worked out the circumference and divided it by that of the small wheel, using the rule that the circumference is approximately 3 and 1–7 times the diameter, which they had used in finding the contents of a globe last fall. The numerical work involved a division of fractions, and as they were rusty in this, an hour was spent in practice. (Laboratory Schools Work Reports, 1898–1899, p. 39)

It is worth noting here that as it became apparent that "many of the children had not had sufficient practice to make it possible to take up concrete problems" ("University Elementary School," 1898, p. 221), separate periods of numerical work were included in the curriculum. Clearly, the teachers' reports were taken seriously.

What was called "rather formal work" (p. 220), however, did not mean that skills were divorced from their use, or that the children did not discover the methods used to solve problems themselves.

Their work in fractions began with the rules used in measuring in the shop. They were given ½, ¾ and ⅔ of a foot to add. They themselves discovered the method of reducing each to twelfths and then adding. (p. 221)

Thus, what the teachers called practice involved understanding rather than rote learning. A kind of integration was taking place as well. For Dewey, the connection of skills and subject matter to the everyday world of occupations and action was the simplest and best way to achieve correlation. The teachers seem to have learned the lesson well. Have we? The answer is a resounding no.

Contrasts with Present-Day Approaches. Dewey began with ideas for a curriculum that would meet the developmental needs of individuals and society. These ideas underwent changes and development in the course of the experiment. As noted earlier, he moved to a departmental form of organization, but there were safeguards against fragmentation. Teacher collaboration and integration of subject matter were built into the curriculum. One had to collaborate with colleagues to make the kind of instruction in Dewey's *Plan* work.

All too often, schools start the other way around. They begin with a new organizational tactic on the basis that it is the first step toward supplying needed coherence for the curriculum. The trouble is that the first step may be all that happens; they never get around to the subject of the curriculum. We are witnessing this today in middle-grade schools. The recommended arrangement is interdisciplinary teams of teachers (Epstein, 1990). The teachers on the team represent such individual subjects as science, social studies, English, and mathematics. The teams may be interdisciplinary but the curriculum is likely to be the conventional subject curriculum. Although at first glance the arrangement may seem analogous to Dewey's departmentalized form of organization, a closer look shows that they are different.

In contrast to Dewey's specialized departments that ran vertically throughout the school, and thereby fostered continuity of learning, the teams are organized by grade level. As educators generally recognize, true curriculum coherence must occur vertically as well as horizontally. Although there are indeed opportunities for horizontal curriculum articulation, this may not be the team's focus. Some teams emphasize the guidance function. In any event, an interdisciplinary team is not a curriculum design, nor will it necessarily give birth to one.

Curriculum correlation was fostered in Dewey's school by regular planning meetings. Unfortunately, such meetings are not one of what Sarason (1971) once referred to as "the existing regularities" (p. 63). The lack of planning time is a "troubling issue" (Malen & Ogawa, 1992, p. 187) in curriculum improvement. Indeed, a national study of middle-grade practices found that only about a third of the schools that use interdisciplinary teams give the teams at least 2 hours of scheduled common planning time each week (MacIver, 1990). The study's conclusion was that "the majority of teams do not have the common planning time they need to become truly effective" (p. 460). Common planning time is a lesson unlearned. If teachers are on a treadmill, nothing good will happen.

What must be kept in mind is this: An organizational tactic will not produce a more coherent curriculum. Organizational arrangements are—or should be—derived from a plan for the curriculum. Fundamental to Dewey's plan were two conceptions: the relation between the psychological and logical aspects of the curriculum, and the school as the means by which a society grows. Organizational arrangements in the school were based on these ideas.

Correlation and the Individual Teacher. Correlation can be defined as: "an effort to develop certain common relationships between or among two or more subjects and still retain the usual subject divisions" (Tanner & Tanner, 1995, p. 350). That is one kind of correlation and it was pioneered by teachers in the Dewey school. We tend to think of correlation only in the sense of collaboration. However, correlation also occurs when an individual teacher organizes a subject so that it relates to the world of human experience, both past and present (Childs, 1939; Dewey, 1899). Clearly, teacher Georgia Bacon had this kind of correlation in mind in her report for the week of February 3. The subject was history:

> We did not go into all the battles of the French and Indian wars, because the boys had an idea that history was just a series of battles, so I wanted to skip over that and give them an idea that history was a development; and to arouse their interest in the social and economic side of things. We took up Braddock's expedition and defeat so that they would get an idea of the difference between the English and American soldiers and how Americans came to feel their power and the possibility of their doing things. (Laboratory Schools Work Reports, 1898–1899, p. 84)

An individual teacher can indeed achieve correlation by having children personate the lives and solve the problems confronted by real people. This approach is found frequently in the teachers' reports. Granted that there was a unifying theme, the actual work was still planned and carried out by a teacher and her group.

We need not guess how the idea worked in practice; the teachers explain very clearly. Mary Hill does so in her report on the work of a group of 11-year-olds in the fall of 1899:

> The method pursued in history has been to select, so far as possible, the great men of the period to be considered, and, through a study of their lives, to gain an idea of the industrial, social, and political status of their country, and the problems confronting them. With these conditions in mind, the children attempted to find solutions to the problems. . . .
>
> Prince Henry the Navigator was selected for study. Through him, as founder of the observatory at Sagres, where were gathered the noted geographers, as-

tronomers, and explorers of all nations, the children gained an idea of the knowledge on these subjects at that time, and what facts the discoverers had on which
to base their plans. The children then had before them the problem which occupied navigators for the succeeding two centuries—a short route to the East.

It was interesting to note how nearly the solutions of the children corresponded to those attempted by the discoverers. The difficulties which caused
failure in these attempts were partly suggested by the pupils and partly by the
teacher; for instance, one child, stepping to the globe said, "I would just sail
right up north around Europe and Asia and come down that way;" but the children immediately exclaimed that the ice fields stood in the way. They finally
concluded that the sailors would creep farther and farther down the coast of Africa
until they proved false the popular theory that the ocean boiled at the equator,
and then would strike boldly south until they rounded the southern point of
Africa. The teacher told of the voyage of Dias in which he passed the equator
and found the climate growing cooler as he continued south, and of his success
in rounding the Cape of Good Hope; then of Vasco da Gama's trip to India by
the same route. (Dewey & Runyon, 1900, p. 91)

By organizing a single subject in this way it is impossible not to develop
common threads between subjects. More important, perhaps, the subject
matter comes from real problems: how they might have been and were solved.
The instructional approach follows approved educational practices and would
be considered excellent today.

Unexpected Outcomes: One Teacher's Story. In the teachers' reports we find
symptoms of some of our own difficulties: children who are uncooperative and
somewhat vindictive (although undeniably advantaged, not disadvantaged) and
children who are sexist—and flaunt it. These problems appear in the report of
a lesson that did not go as planned. The teacher was probably Laura Runyon.
In addition to telling what happened, she explained the actual or probable
causes. We can tell that it helped her to write about it—another advantage of
reports—and also that she would do things differently the next time, at least
with this group. Although absorbed in her work, she did not lack a sense of
humor. She must have been a wonderful colleague.

"Primitive life was not studied by this group last year," she wrote. "Accordingly, it was decided to go rapidly over this subject" ("University Elementary School," 1898, p. 220). (It was probably the case that the children, who
were about 10 years of age, had not been long in the school.) Among the
instructional approaches used with this group was the enactment of tribal life
in England:

> It was difficult to get city-bred children to imagine the conditions of forest life,
> and there was a constant tendency to regard the whole thing as a "camping out"
> expedition. It was attempted at first to have each member of the class personate

the leader of the tribe, and work out for himself the conditions most favorable for supporting life. But this seemed only to recall stories they had heard of summer parties where pleasure and not existence was the thought uppermost. The boys showed a tendency to have only men in their tribes, or at best, only two or three women, whom they said, "would be enough to do the cooking." So this plan was given up and the story substituted, in which the girls could have an equal chance.

In deciding on the number in the whole tribe an unexpected dislike to having many children came out. An average of two to a family was deemed entirely too large, and it was only by citing known cases in the class, where there were five and eight in a family, that this small average was finally accepted. But that the antipathy was not wholly overcome appeared when the children wrote up the crossing of the English Channel to go to France. Here two members of the class had the raft overturned and *all the children drowned*! ("University Elementary School," 1898)

The report says something about the homes that the children who went to the Dewey school came from. One might argue justifiably that their advantaged background made them snobbish and difficult. But the clue to what went wrong lies in the material itself. The experience of prehistoric tribes was too remote. In relating subject matter to the real world of human problems—which is the child's world just as it is anyone else's—it is probably better to begin with present-day societal problems. In that sense the curriculum of the Lincoln School at Teachers College, Columbia University a few years later was a definite advance (Buttenwieser, 1969; Tanner & Tanner, 1995). But this in no way diminishes the importance of Runyon's contribution. We learn from her insight that the problem of material that is too remote from the world of the child can exist in any school—even one serving children who are growing up in an economically and socially advantaged environment. It is good to be reminded of this. Our age tends to associate a too-remote curriculum with schools serving disadvantaged children.

On the other hand, many urban children from tough neighborhoods actually experience our most critical societal problems today. A curriculum problem relates to the use of their experiences in learning facts and concepts. A popular notion is that the frightening and unsavory features of the child's environment can be used for learning facts and concepts. According to an observer in a school where children have witnessed shootings in the neighborhood, the experience could be the beginning of a "conceptual journey" to understanding about bills wending their way through the U.S. Congress—in this case gun control (Schachter, 1994). She concludes, "Dewey would have liked that" (p. 37). Perhaps. Where the doubt comes in is that this is only one instructional approach and there is an entire curriculum to be considered as well as its purposes. In other words, there are larger issues here at stake and one is escape, in a way that only schools can help people escape. According to Dewey (1916), the school has the responsibility "to see to it that each individual gets an opportunity to escape from the limitations of the social group from which he was born, and to come into a living contact with a broader environment" (p. 24). In that sense, the problem is not so very different from Laura Runyon's.

Dewey (1916) counseled that the school is a "special environment," selecting the best features of the existing environment and striving to "reinforce the power of the best" (p. 24). Relating the curriculum to the everyday world is a way of achieving synthesis, but the "world" should not be interpreted too narrowly and, above all, not in terms of the pathological. Art, culture, and science are also part of the child's world. When they are taught accordingly, the school is transmitting those environmental features that "make for a better world" (p. 24).

Contemporary Positions on Curriculum Synthesis: Missing Dewey's Point. All too often, contemporary discussions about the need for curriculum integration sound like a stuck needle, endlessly replaying old arguments about "the separate subject curriculum" (Beane, 1995, p. 622) versus curriculum integration. Dewey hated dualisms, and arguments are still couched in either–or dualistic terms. According to one writer, for example, the focus of curriculum integration is on "life as it is lived now rather than on preparation for some later life or later level of schooling. It serves the young people for whom the curriculum is intended rather than the specialized interests of adults" (Beane, 1995, p. 622). What is missed here is Dewey's idea of the developmental curriculum. In Dewey's theory of knowledge the direction is from unity (the way children naturally see things) toward greater abstraction (the way adult scholars see things). Never is one pitted against the other.

Moreover, correlation is achieved when the content and material of the subject—history, science, geography, and so on—concern the activities of real people, living or dead. The subject becomes active rather than inert when the students themselves solve real, as opposed to contrived, problems (Dewey, 1916; L. N. Tanner, 1988). We see examples of all of these things in the teachers' reports.

When a single subject is related to the everyday world, a marvelous thing happens—other subject fields are brought into the picture. In science, for example, when students test for the purity of water systems in their own and other communities, they learn facts and concepts in mathematics, political science, communications, and geography as well as science. Not least in importance, they learn social responsibility (Wood, 1990).

Contemporary arguments about curriculum integration versus separate subjects are not just boring, they are tragic. Clearly, there have been wasted years.

For a century, protagonists have missed the point of the developmental curriculum. Teachers, children, and, yes, the fields of knowledge have been the losers.

PROJECT-BASED INSTRUCTION IN DEWEY'S SCHOOL AND OURS

It is remarkable how influential the Laboratory School was on Dewey's later work. After leaving Chicago, he continued to build on one idea in particular that stemmed directly from the school: teaching children how to think. Young children are natural inquirers, and a purpose of science instruction in his school was to build on this endowment from nature and "instill a practical sense of the methods of inquiry" (Dewey, 1897c, p. 72). Six-year-olds worked in the laboratory and benefited equally with 10-year-olds regarding the development of intelligence and the awakening of their "spirit of curiosity and investigation" (p. 73). More important, perhaps, the idea that a child should use language "as a means of discovering something otherwise unknown, and of sharing with others" (p. 74) what the child has found out, encompassed all curriculum areas, not just science.

Thinking as Problem Solving: A Lesson from the Laboratory School

It is rather exciting to have the teachers' reports because they show how the inquiry approach can work in all curriculum areas. It was this idea in particular—that the experimental method can be applied to all sorts of problems—that Dewey built into a revolutionary approach for education: the idea of thinking as problem solving. For Dewey, inquiry, thinking, and problem solving were all the same.

In his experimental school, he had learned that not only do carefully planned consecutive activities in weaving, cooking, and the manual arts "inevitably result in students amassing information of practical and scientific importance in botany, zoology, chemistry, physics, and other sciences, but (what is more significant) in their becoming versed in methods of experimental inquiry and proof" (1910, p. 169).

The Amazing Story of *How We Think*. If we are to believe what Dewey wrote in the preface to his book, *How We Think* (1910)—and there is no reason why we shouldn't—his revolutionary concept of thinking as problem solving grew out of ideas that were tested with teachers and children in the Laboratory School. In that preface he acknowledged indebtedness to the teachers and supervisors and particularly to Ella Flagg Young, who was "then a colleague in the University and now Superintendent of the Schools of Chicago" (p. iv). He also expressed his "fundamental indebtedness" to his wife, Alice,

by whom the ideas of this book were inspired, and through whose work with
the Laboratory School, existing in Chicago between 1896 and 1903, the ideas
attained such concreteness as comes from embodiment and testing in practice.
(p. iv)

The acknowledgment to Alice seemed tinged with sadness. A dispute with
Harper over Alice's becoming principal (she had held various supervisory
positions in the school, including director of instruction) was the final straw
in a series of tiffs with Harper that finally led to the Deweys' departure. The
Deweys had been true professional partners, a relationship that was not possible in the same way in New York, where Dewey was not running a school.
      Dewey concluded from the Laboratory School that helping children learn
the practical methods of inquiry and teaching them to think should begin early.
Realizing that the key to whether this happens is the teacher, and inspired by
Alice, Dewey wrote *How We Think*—a kind of handbook for elementary teachers. *How We Think* analyzes the thinking process into its component steps and
describes the school conditions necessary for forming good thinking habits.
A particularly interesting chapter, "Activity and the Training of Thought,"
gives suggestions for organizing activities so that they present problems to be
solved by experimentation and lead to specialized scientific knowledge. Not
surprisingly, Dewey suggests occupations as an organizing theme and the
source of problems for the elementary curriculum.

Preventing Thinking. In *How We Think*, Dewey criticized some of the things
school do that threaten thinking. One is the value placed on a quick response.
Schools fail to recognize that "sometimes slowness and depth of response are
intimately connected" (p. 37). Dewey pointed out that "many a child is re-
buked for 'slowness,' for not 'answering promptly' when his forces are taking
time to gather themselves together to deal effectively with the problem at hand"
(p. 38), and that "the depth to which a sense of the problem, of the difficulty,
sinks, determines the quality of the thinking that follows" (p. 38). The press
of time for a quick answer can lead only to a superficial response—what Dewey
calls gliding "over the thin ice of genuine problems" which "reverses the true
method of mind training" (p. 38). Unfortunately, for teaching children to
think, schools today seem more than ever to be nervous places.
      In *How We Think* Dewey says fresh things about thinking that we redis-
cover periodically. For example, he argues that the term "thinking" refers to
various ways in which things gain significance: "Thinking is specific, in that
different things suggest their own appropriate meanings, tell their own unique
stories, and in that they do this in very different ways with different persons"
(p. 39). He clarifies misconceptions about thinking. (For instance, in most
people's minds thinking is associated only with books.) "Thinking," he says,

is not like a sausage machine which reduces all materials indifferently to one marketable commodity, but is a power of following up and linking together the specific suggestions that specific things arouse. Accordingly, any subject, from Greek to cooking, and from drawing to mathematics, is intellectual, if intellectual at all, not in its fixed inner structure, but in its function—in its power to start and direct significant inquiry and reflection. What geometry does for one, the manipulation of laboratory apparatus, the mastery of a musical composition, or the conduct of a business affair, may do for another. (p. 39)

Activities as "Projects"

In *How We Think*, Dewey lays out the criteria for selecting and organizing activities. There are three simple criteria: (1) the activities should be adapted to the children's stage of development; (2) they should have "the most ulterior promise as preparation for the social responsibilities of adult life" (p. 44); and (3) they should be maximally influential in "forming habits of acute observation and consecutive inference" (p. 44). Truly educational activities will develop children's habits of thinking and the ability to build on what they have learned. The tendency of many schools in Dewey's time was to view activities either as a relief from intellectual work or as magical means for developing mental power, as Dewey wrote, obviously with tongue in cheek, in the belief "that any exercise of the muscles trains power of thought" (p. 44). (What became known as the activity movement in education was a reaction to the formal school in which the learner was to remain motionless. Understandably, activity was defined in terms of gross, overt movement. Overlooked was that learning is itself an active process.)

The three criteria came from the Laboratory School and, after all these years, are dependable guides for selecting and organizing activities and projects.

Interestingly, Dewey does not use the word "project" when describing activities for teaching children how to think, in his book by that name. However, by the time Dewey published a revised edition of *How We Think* (1933a), things had changed: Activities known as "projects" increasingly had found their way into the school. Projects where students are involved in activities that require thinking as well as doing, can be effective as an instructional approach. (Home projects, where a student tests new seed or a new method of farming, have long been used in agricultural education.) As everyone knows—but many forget from time to time in education—doing is not thinking. Real thinking and real education should have the elements of the complete act of thought.

Dewey believed that children would learn to think if they worked on projects of interest to them. "*But interest is not enough*," warned Dewey (1933a, p. 219), with uncharacteristic sharpness, in the revision. The reason for his warning was as follows. His view of thinking as a developing process, either short or long, that involves seeing a real problem through, from setting it up to testing plans of action to see which idea solves the problem, was absent in most of the projects that were finding their way into thousands of classrooms. For most teachers in the 1920s and 1930s, a project meant making something.

Why were projects so rarely based on Dewey's conception of thinking as problem solving? Someone ran away with the idea and turned it into something else. William Kilpatrick (1918)—one of Dewey's former students—interpreted and popularized Dewey's idea, and what emerged was the "project method," which put "the purposeful act" (p. 320) at the center of the educational process. In Kilpatrick's version, there was just one condition necessary for an activity to be labeled a project: "purposing" (p. 320) by the child. This was merely child interest under another name. For Dewey, on the other hand, interest was just one of the conditions to be met to make a project worthwhile as an instructional approach.

Conditions for Projects (or Activities). Today there is much interest in projects. Most of us generally recognize that projects are of great potential value. They can be a way of acquiring scientific knowledge, unifying school subjects, and teaching problem solving. Yet today, as in Dewey's time, we can learn to use this instructional approach more effectively. I have yet to find in the literature better help for a project than Dewey's four simple rules in the revised edition of *How We Think* (1933a): (1) the project must be of interest; (2) the project must involve thought; (3) the project must awaken new curiosity and lead the students' minds into new fields; and (4) the project must involve a considerable span of time for its execution. Again, as with activities in the first edition, the plan and objective must have the potential of development. It is the teacher's responsibility "to look ahead and see whether one stage of achievement will suggest something else to be looked into and done" (p. 219). A curriculum is not a parade of unrelated projects or activities but a consecutive development.

Problems with Projects Today. A problem confronting educators in the 1980s and 1990s is somewhat different: Should a curriculum consist of projects, even assuming that they are related? Some think so. There can be no better example than the situation in which one middle-grade teacher found herself, called "project-based science" (Scott, 1994). She had decided to participate in a project with 10 other experienced middle-grade teachers and a group of researchers from the University of Michigan to improve science teaching. In the project-based approach, students collaboratively studied a "driving question" (p. 76). Project-based science was described by the researchers "as a comprehensive approach to science learning by which students study a relevant problem over a period of time" (p. 76). This might be a few weeks or several months, depending on the question and the approach taken in answering it. An example of a semester-long unit is "What's in Our Water?" (p. 78).

The researchers underlined the advantages of the project-based approach. In finding the solution to the problem, students learn to think critically; carry out experiments; collect and analyze data; and use computers and telecommunication technology. The researchers presented project-based science this way: "an integrated approach that blends the skills and background information gleaned from math, language arts, geography, and science"; since the investigations are collaborative in nature, all of these experiences are even more valuable and students' "appreciation for social responsibility" (p. 76) is enhanced.

It is the sense that a problem is real that attracts students. According to teacher Carolyn Scott, as the "What's in Our Water?" investigation proceeded, "students became increasingly convinced that they were studying a problem that was authentic and substantial" (p. 85). New skills, sensitivities, and concepts were learned. Students "who were at first reluctant to think critically" (p. 86) developed critical-thinking skills. They now understood such concepts as the source and treatment of local water; nitrogen cycle; causes, consequences, and possible control measures for acid rain; and the political aspects of environmental pollution. Their knowledge was demonstrated by their responses (and questions) in discussions, written results of their investigations, and tests.

That projects are a means of enabling students to gain knowledge and develop skills relevant to problems of the real world was evident to this middle-grade teacher. Yet she found the idea of a curriculum comprising a series of projects to be lacking in appeal and, indeed, unacceptable. Some of her reasons have to do with the drain on her energy, time (there never seemed to be enough time in a structured day), state and district curriculum requirements, and so on. Another reason is simply that a single instructional approach, whatever it is, can be terribly limiting. She writes:

> Even if the constraints of time and energy presented no obstacles, I believe my science students would receive more benefits from the project-based science approach if it were integrated into a school year punctuated by units of varying length and intensity and involving a variety of learning styles. At the risk of sounding too simplistic, I want to say "Don't overdo a good thing." My gut feeling is that the pursuit of two or three 6–9-week intense driving questions is not only strenuous for the teacher but also for the students, who need some short-term, less rigorous experiences as well. (Scott, 1994, p. 92)

Dewey never proposed that the curriculum take the form of a series of projects. His disciple, Kilpatrick (1925), did. The activities and projects in the Laboratory School were means of recognizing that children are inherently active with impulses to investigate and create. These impulses were, as noted, capital to be invested in learning as well as moral and social development. The movement of development was "away from direct personal and social interest to its indirect and remote forms" (p. 257). This is not to say that older children in the Laboratory School no longer engaged in projects. They did. By the age of 13 they devoted themselves to their own specialized projects in one or another of the subject fields. In the words of Mayhew and Edwards (1936), "The heretofore intensely satisfying story of what man had done paled before the exciting and fascinating thing that each boy or girl felt he might do," and "the study of history became far less important than the making of his own history" (p. 223).

As we compare the place of projects in Dewey's school with their place— or possible place—in our own, three points seems to be particularly important. First, the activities and projects were part of a conception of education that pervaded the entire Laboratory School. Trying to remove projects from Dewey's school would be like trying to remove the threads from closely woven cloth. As Feffer (1993) points out, "As in all things Deweyan, each part of the curriculum was integrated with other parts in an organic conceptual unity" (p. 119).

This is not the case in most schools today. If projects are to be of optimum value, what is needed is curriculum reconstruction. This might begin with a commitment by the total school faculty to use problem solving as a unifying approach to instruction. The commitment is important but it is what happens in individual classrooms that matters. In a formal project, based on Dewey's complete act of thought, teachers and students use a variety of ways to obtain knowledge to solve a problem: resource persons, field trips, laboratory work, and libraries. The project approach, which is based on inquiry and problem solving, has many manifestations. Teachers apply Dewey's problem method when they bring in resources from outside the classroom to straighten out some intellectual difficulty, for example. Scott learned a lesson in this regard from her experience with project-based science. She concluded:

> I would supplement our endeavors with resource people and places beyond the classroom. . . . Although the water and acid rain topics, as presented in the NGS [National Geographic Society] Kids Network units, do not correlate with my life science course objectives, the project-based science *approach* seems effective for students in today's classrooms. . . . In particular, I would extend our focus in life science to broader applications, to relevant issues of today. (Scott, 1994, p. 91)

The second point is really a cautionary note. In Dewey's conception of a project, children (or adults) are involved in a situation in which they are truly interested. Some difficulty generates a real problem for them to solve. They are interested enough to define the problem, make the needed observations, and so on. An example in the Laboratory School was the kind of activity "which reproduces, or runs parallel to, some form of work carried on in social life" (Dewey, 1900c, p. 82). A problem such as the development of the textile industry requires continual observation, planning, and testing out ideas in order to successfully carry on the practical side. We find this in the Laboratory School in every curriculum area, for example, history, where the children tried to determine the best routes for discoverers to take, based on fifteenth-century knowledge.

Typically, however, in the middle-school, project-based science, the problems were not formulated by the students as the result of some perplexity. They were questions raised by someone else for inquiry. They were driving questions. It was probably the driving aspect, a sense of being interrogated, that drained the teacher's and students' energy instead of generating further problems to be solved. As I have noted, the Dewey school was not a pressure cooker; the atmosphere fostered reflection. The difference is certainly significant for teaching thinking.

Third, although abstract thinking is one sought-after outcome of activities and projects, it "represents *an* end not *the* end" (Dewey, 1910, p. 142). Good schools do not involve children in activities or projects with the idea that activity will be replaced with the ability to abstract. In Dewey's words,

> The power of sustained thinking on matters remote from direct use is an outgrowth of practical and immediate modes of thought, but not a substitute for them. The educational end is not the destruction of the power to think . . . it is not its replacement by abstract reflection nor is theoretical thinking a higher type of thinking than practical. . . .
>
> Methods that in developing abstract intellectual abilities weaken habits of practical or concrete thinking, fall as much short of the educational ideal as do the methods that in cultivating ability to plan, to invent, to arrange, to forecast, fail to secure some delight in thinking irrespective of practical consequences. (pp. 142–143)

The learning style of some children leans toward the practical and "every opportunity that occurs within their practical activities for developing curiosity and susceptibility to intellectual problems should be seized," says Dewey (p. 144). In that way we broaden their education. As for those whose style or inclination is toward intellectual matters and abstraction, "pains should be taken to multiply opportunities and demands for the application of ideas" (p. 144). According to Dewey, "Every human being has both capabilities, and every individual will be more effective and happier if both powers are developed in easy and close interaction with each other" (p. 144).

The implication for projects, activities, and units in the curriculum of today is clear. Opportunities to solve problems should be present throughout the curriculum. Students should be engaged in problem solving in the real sense, as opposed to mechanically using a model problem with model procedures (L. N. Tanner, 1988). Of course, teachers should get to know their students in order to develop both kinds of thinking.

As Katherine Camp pointed out in 1903, each new activity should grow "more and more definite and controlled" (p. 8) as children progress in their development. Meanwhile projects are, or should be, fun. "To be playful and serious at the same time is possible, and it defines the ideal mental condition," wrote Dewey (1910, p. 218). "What is termed the interest in truth for its own sake is certainly a serious matter, yet this pure interest in truth coincides with love of the free play of thought" (p. 219). Solving a problem is akin to doing a puzzle, but in a good school the puzzle is so interesting that the solution is transformed into power and energy—and the desire to solve new puzzles. This was Dewey's school and can be our own.

Children work in their garden in the school yard. All photos courtesy University of Chicago Laboratory Schools.

Children apply principles learned in their classes as they cooperate in building and furnishing a clubhouse.

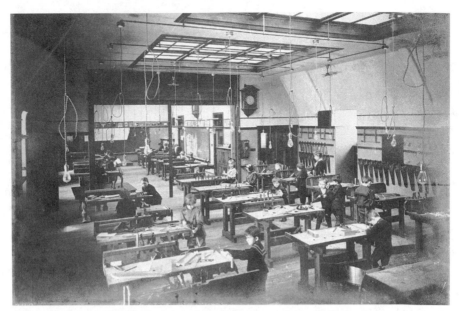

Children make articles in the shop for use in connection with their other work.

Children eat a gourmet lunch they planned and prepared in their French class.

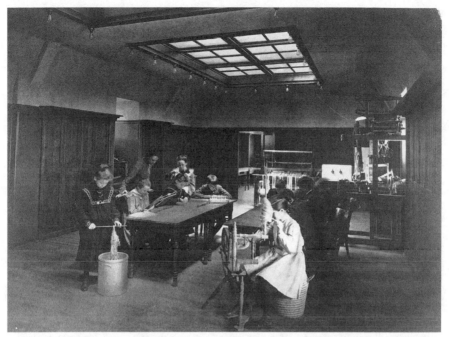

Children study industrial history by working out the entire process of making cloth.

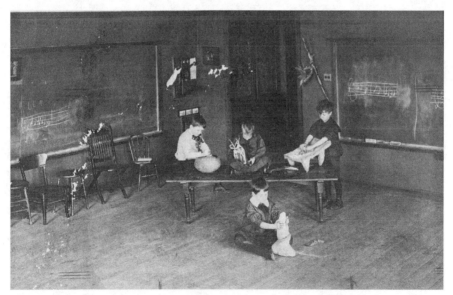

Children use the technologies of early peoples to turn grain into food.

Children study the nature of community life with the help of model houses.

Children study elementary botany.

❖ 6 ❖

Administration and Supervision

The school cannot take up the question of the development of training for citizenship in a democracy while the teachers are still segregated in two classes, as are the citizens in an aristocracy.

—Ella Flagg Young, *Isolation in the School*

BY "TWO CLASSES," Ella Flagg Young, who was general supervisor in the Laboratory School, meant (1) administrators and supervisors, and (2) classroom teachers. Young was Dewey's doctoral student and in her dissertation, completed in 1900 and published by the University of Chicago Press in 1906 as the first in the Contributions to Education series, she described her dislike for this division, especially in regard to supervision of teachers. The "benumbing" effect of "the voice of authority of position," the robbing of teachers' professional responsibility as "initiators in the individual work of instruction," and their relegation to "a class of assistants whose duty consists in carrying out instructions of a higher class which originates method for all" (pp. 106–107) were findings in Young's study. She had experience as a member of both classes—teacher and assistant superintendent in the Chicago schools. Later she would become superintendent.

In this chapter, we are concerned with how Dewey conducted his school, that is, his approach to school organization and administration. In efforts to apply his ideas about children's learning, the administrative aspects often are ignored. It is almost as though Dewey never had anything to say or contribute in this area, but he did. In fact, Dewey's ideas on school organization and approaches to teaching are part of a whole conception. The meaning for school improvement is clear: The lessons we have discussed on selection of content and instruction cannot be applied with any reasonable expectation of success without the matching organizational milieu. This is a Deweyan policy. As he explained its workings: "Cooperative social organization applied to the teaching body of the school as well as to the pupils. Indeed, it could not apply to the latter unless it had first taken effect with the former" (Dewey, in Mayhew

95

& Edwards, 1936, p. 371). Large differences between administration and the way teachers work with children are apt to lead nowhere (except, maybe, to an increased level of frustration).

One of Dewey's many original contributions is his idea of teacher cooperation as a substitute for the kind of supervision that is based on levels of authority in the organization. "Association and exchange among teachers was our substitute for what is called supervision, critic teaching, and technical training," he wrote (p. 371). The idea undoubtedly turned out well. He concluded:

> Experience and reflection have convinced me that this principle is fundamental in school organization and administration. There is no substitute for it, and the tendency to magnify the authority of the superintendent, principal, or director is both the cause and the effect of the failure of our schools to direct their work on the basis of cooperative social organization of teachers. (p. 371)

Dewey and Young were pioneers in organization theory. Three-quarters of a century later, the kind of organization they created in the Laboratory School would be labeled an *organic*—as contrasted with a *mechanistic*—form of organization (Burns & Stalker, 1972). How the organic system functioned and the lessons that can be drawn are described in this chapter. The main concern of the chapter is with leadership. As we look for ways to improve our own leadership, the Laboratory School provides some illustrations that merit our attention. There was, in particular, a distinctive way of thinking and acting that characterized the general supervisor. (Young's leadership is, in my view, a model in itself.) Besides leadership, the chapter is concerned with planning, the form of school organization, and relations with parents. I will begin with Dewey's remarkable concept of planning, from which the other approaches emerged.

DEWEY'S CONCEPTION OF PLANNING

According to Mayhew and Edwards (1936), who were teachers in the school, "The first six months was a 'trial-and-error' period and was chiefly indicative of what not to do" (pp. 7–8). The need for flexibility and adjustability was evident. For one thing, "there were no precedents for this type of schooling to follow" (p. 7), and, for another, there was the need to study the individual child "and to experiment with subject matter and method to find out what ministered best to [the child's] growth" (p. 7). Dewey himself stated in his *Plan of Organization of the University Primary School* (1895a) that "it will be understood to define the general spirit in which the work is undertaken, not to give a rigid scheme" (p. 1).

Planning Today: The Troubling Difference

Today, educational plans are detailed outlines and are not expected to change as teachers find new potentials and previously unrecognized problems. As a result, educational planning is not as effective as it might be (Elmore & Fuhrman, 1994; Murphy, 1991; Tanner & Tanner, 1995). It is worth looking at Dewey's conception of planning closely as it has deep implications for our own school improvement efforts. Tyler (1991) described it well:

> In his school, he developed plans and initiated activities based on the informa-
> tion he was gaining in studying the students' learning; but as he sought to imple-
> ment these plans, he found unexpected difficulties and potentials not previously
> recognized. He realized that information being gained in implementing a plan
> usually suggested modification of the plan for it to be effective, modifications
> even in the aims as the potentials and problems were identified. He reported
> that planning should be a continuing process and not to develop a firm outline
> of aims and operations.
>
> As I have observed educational planning at the local, state and national level,
> I find little evidence of the impact of Dewey's conception of planning. Most
> educational plans embody standards that are not expected to change as the plans
> are implemented. Most schools have not learned to develop and utilize a con-
> tinuous planning procedure. (p. 5)

Today we want to revitalize schools, but rigidity and revitalizing do not go together; in fact, they are antithetical concepts. There is a fact about change that needs to be faced: Rare is the approach to change that can be adopted without any modification by those involved; in fact, it is probably nonexistent. New instructional approaches and other school changes should be refined and modified based on "rich feedback information . . . gathered through a number of ways including continuous discussion and reflection by those involved" (Cordeiro, 1994, p. 172). This was the way Dewey's school operated.

A Lesson Unlearned. The idea that plans should be expected to change as they are implemented and the need to use a continuous planning process are lessons yet unlearned. Indeed, we seem to be moving in the opposite direc-
tion. The national standards developed for the academic subjects listed in the Goals 2000: Educate America Act are highly detailed outlines on a subject basis (Tanner & Tanner, 1995; U.S. Department of Education, 1991). The developers do not recognize that the standards themselves may need to be modified as educators discover problems and also unexpected potentials. Unless initial goals are broad and planning is a continuous process, the plans will not be implemented.

DEPARTMENTALIZATION: LESSONS FOR TODAY

A departmentalized elementary school goes against the grain. One is more likely to have fixed in mind the criticism that departmentalization leads to fragmentation in the curriculum and teachers who go their own way, than the fact that a departmentalized school does not have to be compartmentalized. Dewey's school was clear evidence of this. Dewey himself did not feel that "departmental" was a fair description of his school and what went on there. In 1936, in a statement for Mayhew and Edwards, he indicated his discomfiture with the term:

> The use of the term "departmental" in describing the organization of the school is unfortunate. It suggests a kind of compartmentalizing and isolation of forms of work that should be integrated with one another. But experience has convinced me that there cannot be all-around development of either teachers or pupils without something for which the only available word is departmental teaching, though I should prefer to speak of lines of activity carried on by persons with special aptitude, interest, and skill in them. (p. 372)

If one is going to have a departmental form of organization, it had best have cooperation among teachers built in. As indicated, cooperation was inherent in the way the Laboratory School curriculum was organized. Lack of cooperation and interaction among the school staff must of necessity lead to compartmentalization. As Dewey explained:

> It is the absence of cooperative intellectual relations among teachers that causes the present belief that young children must be taught everything by one teacher, and that leads to so-called departmental teaching being strictly compartmental with older ones. (Mayhew & Edwards, 1936, p. 372)

The "present belief" is still present.

What, precisely, happened that convinced Dewey to move quickly to a departmental form of organization? (There was no hemming or hawing; he just did it, and over others' objections.) We may never know what he or others saw that reflected the teacher's lack of subject matter knowledge. If there were written records, they disappeared. But the fact that the idea of a generalist as teacher proved inadequate to a purpose of the experiment—helping children make a good start in the major subject fields—comes through clearly in the citations from people who were there. Thinking is merely refined common sense, and common sense dictated another form of school organization. The parents were not pleased with the change. According to Mayhew (1934):

> We had to meet the objections of both parents and teachers to the change but it seemed better to face the difficulty of possible strain for classes in moving from

one teacher to another rather than the strain of mental confusion which comes from mis-statement, or vague guessing at the facts. (p. 26)

The teacher initially selected for the school was, in Dewey's words, "an all-round teacher" (1897c, p. 75; Mayhew & Edwards, 1936, p. 35). She took all 15 children as one group and taught several subjects. She had student assistants from the University who worked with small groups and individuals as needed under her direction. A child might, for example, wish to continue "some special line of effort alone" (Mayhew, 1934, p. 24). Dewey thought that a good teacher could plan activities that were intellectually valuable and would supply the roots from which organized knowledge would grow later. It was not necessary for the teacher to have specialized knowledge in the concepts and methods that constitute the various disciplines. This assumption quickly proved to be erroneous. Dewey followed his own precept of learning from experience and experimentation, and acted on what he had learned.

The process of specialization in all fields and the rapid growth of organized knowledge had made the "all-round teacher" inappropriate at the end of the nineteenth century. About a month before his experimental school reopened under the new organization, Dewey (1896a) wrote that "one of the difficulties in introducing scientific methods and materials in the lower grades is that 'facts' are taught which are not facts" (p. 355), and

methods are used which are out of date. The child should be started on the most advanced plane, with the least to unlearn and to correct; with the maximum of attainable accuracy and with a selection of ideas and principles in some ratio to their importance and future fertility. (p. 355)

In his school, Dewey recognized a problem that today we often fail to see.

The Myth That Will Not Go Away

Is it a myth, a false assumption, or just pretending? Whatever it is, our education system continues to operate as though elementary teachers have studied enough of each subject to teach them all well. According to Battista (1994), who brings the eye of the teacher educator to the problem, this is far from the case, and he cites an example that is relevant to Dewey's theory of curriculum: mathematics. Many elementary teachers view mathematics as a set of rules to be followed, rather than the way Dewey did, as a means to solve problems (p. 463). Perhaps this is because they have no special interest in mathematics and have no conceptual foundation. Whatever the reason—and instances differ—they do not teach it well. Bearing directly on Dewey's concern is a report from the National Research Council (1989):

The United States is one of the few countries in the world that continues to pretend—despite substantial evidence to the contrary—that elementary school teachers are able to teach all subjects equally well. It is time that we identify a cadre of
teachers with special interests in mathematics and science who would be well
prepared to teach young children both mathematics and science in an integrated,
discovery-based environment. (National Research Council, 1989, p. 64)

The need for specialists in the early grades who know how to develop concepts and positive attitudes in their subjects is still an unlearned lesson.

When Dewey (1896b) learned that an all-round teacher was not the answer, he appointed two teachers who were specialists: Katherine Camp, who
had been in charge of science at the Pratt Institute, would be in charge of "the
science work," and Clara Mitchell, a former teacher at the Chicago Normal
School, "of history and literature particularly" (p. 417). When school started
in October 1896, there were 32 pupils, two teachers, an instructor in carpentry and woodwork, one in music, and a number of assistants from the classes
in pedagogy. Moreover, the children had instruction in physical education by
a University faculty member, as well as the use of the University gymnasium.
Obviously, Dewey was under no illusion that a teacher without specialized
knowledge in a given field could develop concepts and positive attitudes toward
those subjects. The point is oddly missed, amid all the present-day calls for
school reform. We like to cherish our illusions.

SUPERVISION: THE GREAT UNLEARNED LESSON

Unfortunately, the problems of leadership in the 1890s are still the problems
of leadership today. Not that we lack an improving knowledge base for school
supervision. In the literature are ideas that were put to use in Dewey's school;
for example, faculty meetings were devoted to the improvement of the educational program. This practice is regarded as necessary for the professionalization
of teaching. Unfortunately, there are also unheeded warnings dating back to
Dewey and Young. Still opposed in the literature and still a problem is the
relegation of teachers to a servile class. According to Ann Lieberman (1995),
who has spent much time with teachers in schools and university courses:

Teachers have been told often enough (or it has been taken for granted) that
other people's understandings of teaching and learning are more important than
their own and that their knowledge—gained from the dailiness of work with
students—is of far less value. (p. 592)

In striking contrast, the Laboratory School was built on the idea that school
improvement depends on teachers' knowledge gained from their work. The

function of supervision was to provide supportive conditions for teachers to work out a curriculum that connected with the original theories of the school. The valuing of teachers' knowledge gained from their work is implicit in this view.

Our Problems of Supervision: Looking to Dewey and Young for Ideas

Teachers' vitality and interest in school improvement are sapped when they must work within an administrative structure that contradicts their efforts. Despite the interest in restructuring schools, various elements of autocratic control systems, better suited to robots than thinking men, women, and children, continue to persist in many school systems. This is one problem that Dewey, his wife Alice, and Ella Young addressed and about which we can learn from them.

However, there are new problems that they did not have to address, at least not in their present form; for example, the separation by policy makers of professional learning and teaching. Professional learning, teaching, and curriculum improvement were all present in Dewey's school, but they were not dealt with separately. The question can be raised as to whether this separation might weaken present-day school improvement efforts. Dewey's experience as an administrator can give perspective to current problems in the supervision of teachers. Three that seem particularly critical for school improvement are examined in this section. They are as follows: (1) an administrative structure that is incompatible with the wider educational goals of schools, (2) isolation of teaching and professional learning, and (3) too much or too little supervision.

Incompatible Administrative Structure. At the heart of Dewey's concept of supervision lies his respect for the intellectual processes of the teacher as an individual. He regarded it as a given that teachers will reflect on their work, individually and collaboratively, and modify their plans accordingly. This was fine in his school because the administrative structure promoted rather than prevented this activity on the part of teachers. In most other schools, however, there was a problem: The administrative structure was still suited to rote and recitation, although that approach to learning had lost its "theoretical supremacy" (Dewey, 1904a, p. 22).

A renewed interest in reflection emerged in the 1980s and 1990s after it had become clear once again that unless teachers considered, or thought, or reflected on their work in light of a set of ideas about learning, school improvement was unlikely (Fullan, 1991; Kliebard, 1988; Murphy, 1991; D. Tanner & L. Tanner, 1987, 1995). According to Kliebard (1988), school administrators could take a good lesson from Dewey; the administrative structure still "ultimately crushes curriculum reform" (p. 23). If teachers are to provide students with the kinds of experiences that lead to responsible self-direction, teachers should work with each other and their supervisors along participative-group lines. They should reflect on the extent to which they feel that their instructional approaches have been effective in meeting the needs of individual children. Their responsibility is to individuals as well as groups. Present in Dewey's school, few programs today focus on the goal of developing in teachers what Fox and Singletary (1986) aptly call "a reflective orientation" (p. 12). Obviously this is a supervisory lesson unlearned.

Isolation of Teaching and Professional Learning. Leaders like Darling-Hammond and McLaughlin (1995), Grossman (1992), and Lieberman (1995) take a professional learning perspective on school improvement. Lieberman, for example, looks to the creation of "a culture of inquiry wherein professional learning is expected, sought after, and an ongoing part of teaching and school life" (p. 593). Such a culture was, of course, created in the Laboratory School, and professional learning was a part of school life. Having said this, I must hasten to add that the focus was on the work of the school not on "professional learning" per se, even though Dewey's (1904b) theory on teacher education was developed as he conducted his school. In Dewey's school, professional learning was a byproduct. The difference is an important one. If professional learning—sometimes called "teacher learning" (Grossman, 1992, p. 179)—is the central focus of school improvement, rather than the job to be done or the question to be answered by the school staff, supervision still has a deficit orientation. Focusing on the work of the school conveys—without having to say so—that teachers' knowledge is valued, whereas focusing on professional learning (as leaders and policy makers do) conveys a feeling that the teachers are not quite up to dealing with the problem or question.

We can hardly go wrong in homing in on the work to be done, as Dewey did. Progress may be made toward solving a problem and teachers will feel like professionals because they are treated like professionals. This approach can have a remarkably salutary effect on professional learning. It is questionable, however, what a primary focus on professional learning can accomplish. People who have made genuine contributions in their fields were attracted by the problem they helped to solve or the question they answered. These are the kinds of people we need in education. If we expect to attract and keep them, telling them we value their knowledge, but sending a different message will never do the trick.

Finally, scholars sometimes separate professional learning from teaching for the purpose of talking about a problem in school improvement, such as insufficient time for teachers in restructuring schools. For example, in proposing some "useful theories about time" for schools that are being restructured, Cambone (1995, p. 513) separates [teacher] learning time from what he calls "curricular time"—"planning, development and instructional time combined" (p. 520). However useful such a distinction may seem in theory, it leads to conceptual and practical difficulties. One thing that no one wants is to wall off teachers' knowledge from their actions. This possibility was abhorrent to Dewey (1916), who warned "every divorce of end from means diminishes by that much the significance of the activity" (p. 124). Thus, to separate teacher learning from the work of curriculum improvement, even for the purposes of discussion, may be of doubtful use.

Too Much or Too Little Supervision. Whether in a small school or a big city school system, whether today or yesterday, the destruction of the teacher's intellectual freedom and creativity is implicit in close supervision. This was Young's concern as supervisor in the Laboratory School and as superintendent of the Chicago schools. Supervision had to facilitate, not fetter, the teacher.

In her doctoral dissertation, Young (1906) found that large city school systems had created a machine that was out of control: excessive supervision. According to Superintendent Maxwell of New York, for example, who had headed up the Brooklyn public schools, there was "much harmful interference with the work of class teachers" (p. 29). Superintendent White of Cincinnati found it deplorable that

> even the methods of teaching are definitely and authoritatively prescribed. As a result the teacher is not free to teach according to his "conscience and power," but his high office is degraded to the grinding of prescribed fineness—to the turning of the crank of a revolving mechanism. (quoted in Young, 1906, pp. 25–26)

Young concluded that there had "evolved an extensive 'business of supervision' because of the effort to have uniformity in teachers and methods" and, interestingly enough, "because of the desire of the strong administrative character to guide others rather than to be in the treadmill" (p. 27). Young did not hesitate to tell it like it was. She noted that there was a "strong tendency at the present time to get away from the active work of teaching children" (p. 31), and that "so closely associated with drudgery is the ideal of teaching the young, that trained minds and cultivated personalities shrink from entrance into the direct work" (p. 42).

The question was, why? Young believed that she had the answer: the isolation between the school and the real world. This was manifested by a gap—a chasm, really—between the curriculum and the living world of people with practical problems and practical solutions. The gap had widened steadily. As if that were not enough, there was the problem of supervision. Since schools clung stubbornly to outdated instructional approaches, the matching supervisory approaches persisted, driving away desirable young men and women from teaching.

Yet, the belief that schools were fine the way they were—that most people would not care for schools as miniature societies—persisted. According to Young:

> The isolation between the theory of the school and the theory of life is so great that the general consensus . . . advocates the retention in the school of subject-matter and forms of work which it will not tolerate in the commercial world or at home. (pp. 42–43)

The Chicago schools had thousands of teachers, the Laboratory School, only a few. The faculty numbered about 16 when Young was general supervisor. Yet, during the period when she served as Superintendent of Schools in Chicago, she followed the same principle of cooperation. The reason has currency. In her doctoral study, Young found that American teachers had virtually no policy-making voice for the profession in which they played the dominant role. She recommended that teachers' councils be organized in each school "for the consideration of questions of legislation" (p. 107). The councils would be similar to such organizations in universities (the faculty senate, for example). Not the least of the councils' functions was to end the darkness in which teachers worked out matters of concern to them: "So little does the teaching corps know about the origination of thought on questions concerning education" (p. 108). As reported by Donatelli (1971), "Such councils were organized" (p. 177).

Close supervision of the hovering sort is less common in schools today. Yet, bureaucratic control of teaching does not necessarily require physical proximity. It can occur from some state capitol as a part of a high-stakes standardized testing program (Madaus, 1988; Tanner & Tanner, 1995). A number of states also have developed observation instruments for evaluating teachers "with varying degrees of prescriptiveness" (Darling-Hammond & Sclan, 1992, p. 12). Thus, supervision of the sort that Dewey and Young wanted to get away from still continues, often "under the banner of professionalism" (p. 9).

The opposite extreme is leaving teachers on their own without help. Today many school districts have all but dissolved their departments of curriculum and instruction. It is argued that the departments are bureaucratic rather than professional and that teachers alone must develop curriculum and seek better instructional approaches for children. Is there a lesson to be drawn from Dewey's school about too little supervision? There is, from his own experience. Dewey concluded that "individual teachers were, if anything, not given enough assistance either in advance or by way of critical supervision. There might have been conditions fairer to teachers and more favorable to the success of the experiment" (quoted in Mayhew & Edwards, 1936, p. 366). As was pointed out earlier, he was certain that the teachers and supervisors would still prefer to err in that direction rather than prescribing too definite plans for teachers to follow. Today everyone would like supervision to be error free; errors have dire consequences for teachers' morale and children's learning. But there are uncertainties to overcome. How much supervision is too much and how little is too little? This is an issue of immense and continuing importance.

Evaluation of Teachers in Dewey's School

Today's proposals for teacher evaluation have definite elements of what went on in Dewey's experimental school. In fact, if they could get together for a day as in the story of Brigadoon, Linda Darling-Hammond, Eileen Sclan, John Dewey, and Ella Flagg Young probably would find the main features of their approaches astonishingly similar. According to Darling-Hammond and Sclan (1992), professional supervision "is not based on an inspection system featuring supervisors bearing checklists on brief visits to classrooms" (p. 8). They describe a different approach:

> Instead, organizational strategies for team planning, sharing, evaluating, and learning may create methods for peer review of practice. These strategies—like those used in other professional organizations and restructured businesses—may better fill the needs previously addressed by traditional supervisory functions. (p. 9)

Peer Review. There were no formal approaches to peer review in Dewey's school. Yet a form of peer review was built into the administrative structure and was a substitute for teacher evaluation. In the school, teachers had daily contact and talked over their work; the school had a cooperative organization—today we would call it an organic form of organization as opposed to a mechanistic form. According to Dewey, this kind of organization "makes unnecessary the grading and judging of teachers by the devices often used. It soon becomes evident under conditions of genuine cooperation whether a person has the required flexibility and capacity of growth. Those who did not were eliminated because of the demonstration that they did not belong" (quoted in Mayhew & Edwards, 1936, p. 371).

Professionalism, like the other approved practices in education that we have discussed, was already at work in Dewey's school in the late 1890s. Although the primary task of this school of long ago was the acquisition of knowledge about how children learn, rather than the application of such knowledge, the basic criterion for a review by peers should be the same in our schools: the ability to work with others in an emergent situation, which education clearly is.

Cooperation and Collaboration—
Separating the Significant From the Superficial

Cooperation can be of a practical nature but it also should be intellectual if programs are to be improved. In Dewey's view, in the early days of his school at least, it was overweighted with the first type of cooperation. He explained:

> Cooperation must, however, have a marked intellectual quality in the exchange of experiences and ideas. Many of our early failures were due to the fact that it was too "practical," too much given to matters of immediate import and not sufficiently intellectual in content. When the school grew larger, there was more definite departmental organization and more definite discussion of programs; in 1901 this tendency was further supplemented by the appointment of Ella Flagg as general supervisor and Alice C. Dewey as principal. Their personalities and methods were such as to introduce more intellectual organization without impeding the freedom of individual teachers. (Mayhew & Edwards, 1936, pp. 371–372)

Cooperation as an Intellectual Quality: The Contribution of Ella Flagg Young. Cooperation, evaluation, and the intellectual growth of teachers and pupils were all related, rather than contradictory, in the school. Knowledge about what cooperation really is took a step forward with the appointment of Young. For Young, cooperation meant more than spontaneously following someone else's lead. It was the opportunity for developing one's own intellectual and social power. A reaction is an individual matter, after all, "initiated by the self and terminating in creative intelligence" (Young, 1906, p. 44). The point of importance is that we tend to think of cooperation from the standpoint of the organization—as the way for schools to move forward. It is. What we often fail to recognize, however, is its basically individual character: It is an individual who initiates or reacts to an idea and can grow in the process.

Cooperation Versus Coercion in the Setting of the School. Young concluded in her doctoral research that the organizational climate of schools was unhealthy because the parts of the system were isolated. Human relationships were not recognized in the administrative system, which was similar to that in industry: mechanistic, autocratic, and exploitive. Things were worse, in a way, than in industrial organizations, because education is a social process and each child is unique. Teachers should exercise professional judgment if individual children are to learn, and if American education is to be improved. Thus, Young proposed the teachers' councils to provide a professional climate.

Dewey and Young pioneered in the development of a democratic-participative school climate. They thought that it was important to have such a climate or environment for two reasons. First, schools are responsible for preparing children for membership in a democratic social order, and this requires an environment where the conditions for a democratic spirit are present (Dewey, 1897a; Young, 1902). Second, if schools are to be improved, expertise on problems must be tapped at all levels in the school (Young, 1906).

These ideas continually recur in the literature on supervision. As Bolin and Panaritis (1992) pointed out in their incisive examination of the field's history, "In some instances, teacher freedom and involvement in curriculum making was seen as a crucial part of teachers' supervision" (p. 35). In the 1920s, for example, Denver's school superintendent, Jesse Newlon, not only proposed that teachers participate in curriculum improvement but put his model into action (Newlon & Threlkeld, 1927). According to Cremin (1971), Newlon's program of curriculum revision was "probably the first in which classroom teachers participated significantly in a system-wide effort at reform" (p. 213). Harold Rugg and George Counts (1927) outlined an approach to curriculum improvement in which teachers figured prominently.

The work on democratic-participative approaches was continued by Hollis Caswell and Doak Campbell (1935), Gordon Mackenzie and Stephen Corey (1954), Alice Miel (1946), Hilda Taba (1962), and a number of others. Their purposes were remarkably alike. They all were seeking a process that was *inclusive* (administrators and supervisors, students, and community members as well as teachers) and *professional* (based on the best available knowledge). Unhappily, over the years there have been proposals that were *exclusive* (*either* teachers or supervisors) and *technological* (decisions made at higher levels and teachers viewed as deliverers of instruction). These always failed. We tend to ignore what our professional forebears learned in their work. (Or perhaps we never even knew about it to begin with.)

The striking fact about the administrative approach in Dewey's experimental school is that it was not baseless. What Dewey thought to be the wisest way to work with teachers, and was confirmed as so in his own experience, has turned out to be valid as knowledge about administration has grown. The research of Likert (1977), for example, shows a pattern of superior performance in various settings—industry, education, government—as the organizational structure moves toward the participative-group system. The work of Nobel Prize winner Herbert Simon (1976) supports Young's (1906) conclusion that in a society such as our own where the wider culture emphasizes democratic values, control by sheer authority in the work or school setting (if it were possible in the first place) is sure to have unproductive outcomes. In Simon's words:

> Administrators have increasingly recognized in recent years that authority, unless buttressed by other forms of influence, is relatively impotent to control decision in any but a negative way. The elements entering into all but the most rou-

tine decisions are so numerous and so complex that it is impossible to control positively more than a few. (p. 227)

Thus, concludes Simon, individuals in the work setting must themselves "supply most of the premises of decision" (p. 227). This certainly applies to teaching, which must respond to human variability. Behind the classroom door, the emergent nature of the teaching–learning situation (Goodlad, 1984; Jackson, 1968) requires autonomy if the teacher is to function effectively. Good supervisors are aware of this. "Functional supervision necessarily takes the form of advice rather than authority," pointed out Simon. Young undoubtedly would have agreed. As Lagemann (1996) pointed out, Young believed that the attempt to supervise too closely worked against school reform.

Restructuring Efforts Along the Lines of the Dewey School. In the 1990s educational restructuring was a popular idea for improving schools. American industry already had become cognizant of the need to move away from technocratic management toward more participative-democratic approaches, but schools were continuing to adhere to the superannuated production efficiency model as reflected in the emphasis on accountability, competency-based education, management by objectives, and the like (Wirth, 1980). Thus, restructuring had its origins in business (and is a code word for slimming the organization down), but the point of importance is that proponents of restructuring in schools frequently advocated changes in the distribution of power. Moorman and Egermeier (1992) explain:

> More managerial discretion close to the action, or less hierarchical domination, or more participation in decisions are held to lead to better management and decision making, to instructional choices in line with the school's intended mission, and to more whole-hearted implementation of the decisions. (p. 32)

The irony is that educational administration does not have to look beyond its own literature to find the participatory model. Democratic school administration (Campbell, 1952) was the approach of choice in the years following World War II and is well entrenched as an approved practice in educational supervision (D. Tanner & L. Tanner, 1987).

Yet, shared decision making is still an unlearned lesson. While it is true that many schools involve faculty in making decisions, those decisions often involve matters that bear little relation to the instructional program (Malen & Ogawa, 1992; Tanner & Tanner, 1995). Some school districts require that teachers and principals assume certain responsibilities or tasks rather than allowing school staffs the freedom to identify instructional problems and make decisions. The prescribed tasks tend to be superficial: putting out a newsletter, for example (Malen & Ogawa, 1992). This is not the intellectual type of co-operation that Young argued for and that surely would be more stimulating for teachers. Malen and Ogawa found, in reviewing the literature and case studies on the effects of plans to democratize decision making, that "partici-pants rarely address subjects central to the instructional program in their school council or school committee meetings" (p. 200). There are, of course, stun-ning exceptions, but these authors detected a pattern that was set early in the restructuring movement. The distinction between the participatory approaches of today's schools and the Dewey school is this: Collaborative programs today often involve teachers in activities that are at best peripherally related to cur-riculum content and approaches to instruction and, as Malen and Ogawa found, even may impede curriculum improvement. In their words: "It diverts atten-tion from teaching and learning as site participants take on activities and re-sponsibilities only remotely related to the instructional component of the school" (p. 200). In the Dewey school, teachers under the leadership of super-visors and the school director engaged in continuous curriculum development. The instructional program *was* central in deliberation and planning.

It is too early to call restructuring a failed movement; in fact, there can never be such a time. Faculty decision making focused on the instructional program is an approved educational practice found by research to be effec-tive. Professionals know this; it is not a secret. What Philip Jackson (1981) has written is true:

> Good schools, unlike the manufacturers of perfumes or other exotic concoctions have few, if any, secrets to divulge. What their teachers and administrators know about how to educate, most other educators know as well. The determination to act on that knowledge is another matter entirely, of course, and is surely one of the major qualities distinguishing truly outstanding schools from those that are less so. (pp. 94–95)

Until schools act on their knowledge, the cooperative-collaborative approach will remain an unlearned lesson.

DEWEY'S SCHOOL AS A LEARNING COMMUNITY

Today there is much interest in schools as "learning communities" (Oakes & Quartz, 1995). Although Dewey's school did not carry this label, it was none-theless a community of learners whose interactions led to socially constructed knowledge. Proposals for learning communities reflect once again Dewey's emphasis on the social character of learning and his stress on democracy. (Not that they were ever really absent, but there have been times when they got relatively little attention.)

The players in our day and Dewey's are essentially the same. According to Lieberman, Falk, and Alexander (1995), "Everyone is viewed as a learner . . . students, staff and families alike" (p. 117). In Dewey's school the directors were learning as were the children, parents, and teachers. The emphasis was on creating a cooperative atmosphere. Dewey (1899) was sharply critical of "the prevailing atmosphere" where "for one child to help another in his task has become a school crime" (p. 16). Cooperation is an element in the learning community idea. According to Quartz (1995), "New norms of reform" move from "individualistic and competitive modes of interaction toward norms of care, trust and common purpose" (p. 244). Dewey probably would have liked that. However, there are differences—both subtle and striking—in the way that Dewey's school functioned as a learning community and present-day prescriptions. The Laboratory School had no slogan and did not wave the banner, "a community of learners." It just was one. It was as though it never gave a thought to a label for what it was doing.

There is a difference a century later; the idea in the present has a manufactured sound. Avoiding slogans is a problem and perhaps there is no solution in a society where slogans constantly rain down on our heads. Perhaps just knowing who we are and what we are about can counter the shaping and, sometimes, misshaping effect of slogans. Let us see how a community of learners worked in Dewey's school, sans slogan.

Leaders as Learners

Leaders learn just like anyone else, by picking up ideas from others in a social situation. Some leaders find this difficult to do or admit; perhaps they think that it is unbecoming for a leader to admit that he or she doesn't already know everything—that it makes them in some way vulnerable. Leaders who employ a democratic-participative approach are apt to pick up a few tidbits because they tap the expertise of others. Dewey picked up more than a few, and they were not always tidbits. He was not shy about saying that he learned a great deal from Ella Flagg Young.

Dewey Learns from Young—and Vice Versa. In order for leaders to learn from one another there must be mutual respect, and admiration is even better. Both were present—for each other—in the case of Dewey and Young. As seen through the eyes of Dewey's daughters: "Contact with her supplemented Dewey's educational ideas where his own experience was lacking in matters of practical administration, crystallizing his ideas of democracy in the school and, by extension, in life" (J. M. Dewey, 1939, p. 29). In Dewey's own words:

> I was constantly getting ideas from her. In the reorganization of the laboratory school after certain weaknesses in its original scheme of administration had become apparent (due largely to my inexperience in administrative matters) her influence together with Mrs. Dewey were the controlling factors. It is due to these two that the laboratory school ran so much more systematically and defi-nitely—free from a certain looseness of ends and edges in its last three or four years. (quoted in Donatelli, 1971, p. 150)

Young translated Dewey's ideas into something more concrete and prac-tical—a service to him of immeasurable value. However, the learning was not one-sided; she was gaining a philosophical basis for her own ideals and faith in human intelligence. In Dewey's words:

> Apart from the suggestions which were so numerous that I couldn't name them, what I chiefly got from Mrs. Young was just the translation of philosophic con-ceptions into their empirical equivalents. More times than I could well say I didn't see the meaning or force of some favorite conception of my own till Mrs. Young had given it back to me—I am referring even more to association with her as a colleague than when she was a student. I think what Mrs. Young chiefly got from her philosophic courses was an intellectual, systematized justification of her prac-tical and experimental belief in and respect for the intellectual procedures of the pupil as a person. I have to confess that I never appreciated that aspect of my own logical theory till I found it so emphasized by her. Putting it in another way, it was from her that I learned that freedom and respect for freedom meant regard for the inquiring and reflective process of individuals, and that what ordi-narily passes for freedom—freedom from external restraint, spontaneity in expres-sion, etc., are of significance only in their connection with thinking operations. (quoted in Donatelli, 1971, p. 150)

Young was an assistant superintendent in Chicago from 1887–1899 and in 1895 she enrolled in Dewey's seminar. She was 50 years old—older than the other students, which made her apprehensive at first. (She need not have worried; she had plenty of energy and brains and a huge backlog of experi-ence.) There is no evidence that they had known each other before then, although they had mutual friends, Jane Addams, for one (Donatelli, 1971). It may seem strange in a way that Dewey could learn anything from Young about administration when her experience was in Chicago. If any school system could be called infamous for utilizing the methods that Dewey condemned as out-moded and impeding children's education, it was Chicago's. To be sure, the

Chicago school system had gotten some bad publicity in Joseph Mayer Rice's (1893) famous series on the state of American education. Rice's was a loud voice calling attention to teaching in Chicago that "violated all laws of scientific pedagogy" (p. 205). Rice's words left no doubt about the character of education in Chicago's elementary classrooms:

> In several instances, when a pupil stopped for a moment's reflection, the teacher remarked abruptly, "Don't stop to think, but tell me what you know." Most of the pupils while speaking were trembling from head to foot. She never smiled or offered the slightest encouragement; she sat in her chair as sober as a judge trying a criminal case. (p. 205)

What Rice saw in Chicago is of particular importance for us now. As Katherine Paterson (1995), the writer of books for children, has observed, there is an oddly popular myth that the nineteenth century was "a golden age in the past when people didn't abuse or neglect their children," but, "this is a romantic dream" (p. 32). Rice's series read today makes this terribly clear, and it also helps us to understand one of the seldom-discussed appeals of progressive education: People wanted their children treated kindly.

Frightening children and making thinking impossible did not represent Young's idea of good educational practice any more than it did Dewey's. The reactions of Young and Dewey to the kind of teaching described by Rice were much the same. Young actually had observed how the teachers' values of docility and submission reflected their own treatment by autocratic administrators. In 1897 Young delivered a speech before the Pedagogical Club, reportedly "one of the most suggestive given" ("Isolation in School Systems," p. 41). In it she made the bold proposal that teachers be involved with principals and superintendents in working out the school program and courses of study. This was a Laboratory School practice that she thought all schools should emulate. Despite the fact that central administrators from the Chicago schools were in her audience, she minced no words about the effects of undemocratic school administration: "Since teachers are put in a subordinate position instead of one of interdependence and since their individuality is not respected, why should the children's be?" (p. 42).

Central in her speech was the importance of intellectual freedom, which she viewed as the freedom to think and act on one's thoughts and ideals. As it was, teachers were being motivated by fear rather than moved by an ideal. Young further declared that "children are often treated so that thought is impossible and then told to think" (p. 42). This idea would appear some 13 years later in Dewey's book, *How We Think* (1910). As noted earlier, he acknowledged her contribution.

Young's ideas and experiences became a part of Dewey's day-to-day experiences with students and colleagues and were refined as he wrote about them. Young, too, was similarly influenced. The intellectual energy being generated in the fields of ethics, philosophy, and psychology at Chicago during this period (James, 1904) was stimulating for Young and helped her to understand and act on the fundamental problems of her school system, which were basically philosophical and ethical in nature. What she understood and did affected far more than Chicago. As Dewey's daughters wrote:

> Her respect for the moral and intellectual personality of the individual, two things she did not separate, developed through her own experience into an insistence upon respect by teachers for the integrity of the mental processes of students and a constant protest against school administration from above which had an enormous influence upon school methods, first in Chicago and then throughout the country. (J. M. Dewey, 1939, p. 29)

The kind of learning that Dewey and Young experienced was natural because it occurred in the course of a friendship. Everyone has experienced this kind of learning and ideally it should be possible to construct an educational setting so that learning occurs naturally in the course of social experiences with others. This was what Dewey had in mind when he planned his school as a miniature community. A century after the formulation of this idea, we are still experimenting with it. The problem seems no less urgent today.

Parents as Learners

The parents of the students at the Laboratory School learned from Dewey and his colleagues at the University, the teachers, and each other. It was the parents who kept the school going and rescued it from such disasters as being merged with the model (practice) school of Francis Parker, a school with quite different purposes, and being unable to carry on due to lack of funds. A "staunch" (DePencier, 1967, p. 23) parent gave $2,500 at one point to make the school's continuance possible. Moreover, Dewey had decided on the departmental form of organization in the face of objections by parents. Support in these circumstances is little short of amazing. There was uneasiness about the curriculum and still the support continued. In 1904 a parent, Nellie O'Connor, wrote, "The transfer of 'the three R's' from a position of primary importance to a secondary one could not be made without many struggles; the familiar arguments must be gone over, the parents must be reconciled and educated" (p. 534).

Parents have changed little since Dewey's day—not all of them want curriculum reforms. Particularly intriguing in this regard is a finding gleaned from nine case studies of schools engaged in curriculum reforms, specifically, moving away from memorization and teaching-to-the-test toward problem solving, projects, and portfolios: "The higher the socioeconomic level and the greater the college aspirations of the students in a particular community, the greater was the resistance to the reforms" (Anderson, 1995, p. 35). In schools serving low-income minority children, the problem is not so much resistance as it is a lack of involvement.

Since the 1960s there have been many efforts to involve low-income minority parents in their children's education, and not infrequently "an important lesson learned" from such efforts is "that parent education was one necessary precondition for parent involvement" (Silvestri, 1991, p. 24). If we peel the labels off—high socioeconomic and low-income minority—we find that the problem is the same for all: the need for parents and the school to work together in the child's education. So is the often-overlooked solution: parent education. Parent education can lead to understanding, constructive involvement, and bonding with the school. Dewey had a compelling sense that educational change depended greatly on the presence of parental bonding with the school. Today, the literature bears him out, pointing unequivocally to the importance of understanding between homes and schools in order for school improvement to occur (Anderson, 1995; Comer, 1988; Elkind, 1995, Epps, 1992).

It is worth our while in a time of parent resistance to changes—or at any time at all—to examine what went on in the Laboratory School that enlisted parents' support for the radical changes in ideas and approaches.

The Parents' Association. Sending one's child to the Dewey school was not without its problems. First, there were the raised eyebrows. We can almost see them go up in the account of Ida DePencier (1967):

> Allow the pupils freedom to move around the room, to investigate and talk with one another about their investigations, to get help from one another as well as give help? No competition? No prizes for giving the teacher back what he [or she] had given them? It was almost unthinkable. (p. 22)

Parents had to defend their choice of such a strange school.

Another constant concern was the school's value to the child: Would children really learn to read and write through an interest in history and literature? Could they learn science and arithmetic through cooking, gardening, and the manual arts? Since the parents really, at heart, desired this school for their children, how could they ensure its continuance? It was clear that the parents would have to band together; thus the Parents Association came about. As one member pointed out, it "differed from most other parents' associations in that the incentive for its organization as well as its development came almost entirely from the parents" (O'Connor, 1904, p. 532). The teachers were not members. However, they were "invited by card to each meeting and urged to take part in the discussions" (p. 533).

As in so many other ways, the Laboratory School was in the vanguard in regard to relations with parents. As Butts and Cremin (1953) pointed out, until well into the 1930s public schools often were run as though ideas from parents and teachers were an encroachment upon the administrator's job. Then views started shifting and the idea was advanced that teachers, parents, and community agencies should be consulted about curriculum changes. "Parent–teachers associations grew by leaps and bounds" (p. 574).

Becoming more common today, especially in our large cities, are local school councils composed of parents, neighborhood residents, teachers, and the principal. For example, the Chicago School Reform Act of 1988 trans ferred power from the central board of education to parents at each of the city's 595 schools, granting them the authority to select, evaluate, and dis miss principals; make budgetary decisions; and make recommendations on curriculum and books. Each local school council was composed of six par ents, two neighborhood residents, two teachers, and the school principal. Certainly, smaller units encourage parents to get involved and one could find no better example than Dewey's Laboratory School.

Having said this, there are striking differences in the rationales for local school councils and the Parents' Association of the Laboratory School. The rationale for the school councils was parent power: that parents should have a stronger voice in what is taught and by whom (Wilkerson, 1989; Wong & Rollow, 1989). In contrast, the rationale for the Parents' Association was parent education. The old cliché that knowledge is power obtained here: Being able to positively influence one's child's education is the outcome of education, of being "correctly acquainted" (O'Connor, 1904, p. 532) with what the school is doing and why. In the Laboratory School where the ideas and approaches "were radically opposed to the old and familiar ones . . . knowing the why and wherefore for each change" (p. 532) was important. In addition to just keep ing in touch with their own children's work, the parents should "be able to correct misconceptions formed in regard to the school by the outside world" (pp. 532–533).

According to its by-laws, the Parents' Association had two purposes. The first was "to promote in general the interests of elementary education by dis cussing theories and their practical applications" (O'Connor, 1904, p. 533). This is a purpose that, by all odds, would be considered unusual today. The underlying assumption here was parental responsibility for improving educa tion, not only for one's own child but for all children. A parent who under stood progressive ideas and their implementation was in the best position to advance education. Such a parent was Dewey's (1899) famous "best and wisest" (p. 7).

The second purpose was to advance the Laboratory School's work. Parents were important in an experimental school: They could witness at first hand "the influence of some method, when the teacher himself is oblivious to it" (O'Connor, 1904, p. 532). Parents were particularly important in this school, which was based on the idea that "there cannot be two sets of ethical principles, or two forms of ethical theory, one for life in the school, and the other for life outside of the school" (Dewey, 1897a, p. 7). Principles of conduct are the same, argued Dewey, whether the child is at home, in school, or in the community. The child should evidence the same cooperative spirit and developing independence at home as in school.

Parents also could be, and were, critical. From her experience as an Association officer, O'Connor (1904) found that "parents who are interested in the mental welfare of their children are necessarily severe critics" (p. 533). She noted that although "narrow-minded" criticism could impede the school's work and block progress, helpful criticism and suggestion from parents "might become invaluable in the development of a system of education along psychological lines" (p. 533).

The Laboratory School parents had plenty of concerns as well as suggestions, but the Association met only once a month. To make its work more "effective and intimate" (p. 534), a standing committee was formed, and to this committee

> the parents came with their criticisms and suggestions, and the committee, in quiet consultation with the teachers, was often able to correct a bad habit unconsciously formed in a teacher; or by revealing a teacher's plan to the parent, remove his objections and reconcile him to the particular method in question. (p. 535)

Such an instructional approach was field trips. Although Dewey did not invent the idea—it was an innovation in the Quincy, Massachusetts, schools in the 1870s (Tanner & Tanner, 1990)—field trips were still very uncommon. They were probably not part of the parents' own experience. It was unclear to parents whether the trips instructed, yet they occurred often. For instance, as DePencier (1967) wrote:

> During 1896–97, an hour and a half was set aside on Monday mornings for trips to the Field Columbian Museum. This building, constructed for the 1893 Columbian Exposition, was located where the Museum of Science and Industry now stands and had a great variety of exhibits. The younger children had a plot of ground on the Wooded Island in Jackson Park where they often went to observe seasonal changes in nature. Older children went to the University labo-

ratories to see such instruments as the interferometer and spectroscope. There were also longer trips—to the quarry on Stony Island where glacial markings were observed; to the cotton mills in Aurora to see the spinning of cotton, and others to Ravinia to see the clay bluffs, to Miller Station to see the sand dunes and desert, and to Sixty-Third Street and the city limits to see a typical prairie area. (pp. 33–34)

DePencier continued: "Some of the parents criticized the field trips as being too tiring and time consuming, but the trips remained an integral part of the curriculum" (p. 34).

They remained for the same reason they were there in the first place: Dewey and the teachers believed that the trips served the needs of intellectual and social growth. But the parents did not understand. Nor could they be expected to. There was a worrisome communication gap.

The nature of the problems that they had to straighten out led the committee to conclude: "The parents must in some way become better acquainted with the real purposes of the school" (O'Connor, p. 535). Thus Dewey, Young, and Dewey's colleague and friend, James Tufts, gave a course at the University for the parents who wanted "to study more thoroughly educational questions and the work of leading educators" (Harding, 1903, p. 208). The course was presented for 3 successive years and was open to all Association members. There was ample opportunity for discussion and questions. Through education about education, the parents were brought in close touch with the school. There was, as O'Connor (1904) put it, "a greater sympathy between parents and teachers" (p. 535), thus more effectively uniting the efforts of both.

A major point of interest is how the Parents' Association got started. In the school's first year the parents were sometimes invited to meet to discuss topics concerning the home and the school, and early in the second year they felt that there was a need to formally organize. The programs for each meeting were arranged by the officers and various committee chairpersons. The presentations were by outside specialists, teachers of the subject being discussed, or the parents—from their own point of view.

The crucial question is, Does the Parents' Association of the Laboratory School offer any guidance for our present policies and school improvement efforts? I believe that it does. One of the national goals of U.S. governors, president, and Congress is that parents become more closely involved in their children's schools (National Education Goals Panel, 1994). The Goals Panel would like every schools to "improve the ties between home and school" (p. 10) and to "increase parental involvement and participation in promoting the social, emotional, and academic growth of children" (p. 11). Thus parent involvement is a present policy. (One can almost see the Parents' Association of a century ago brightening and nodding in assent with these purposes.)

However, it has been observed "that parent involvement may already be at a fairly high level" (Elam & Rose, 1995, p. 54). For example, a staggering 94% of public school parents indicated that they read or discussed a school assignment with their children, and 80% read a book to or with their children; 90% had met with a teacher or administrator about their children, and 95% said that they made certain that their children completed homework assignments.

This is involvement, but it has nothing to do with the quality of the school. There is a big vacuum here; one would hope, for example, that parents would look at the homework assignment to see if their child's curiosity and interest were being stimulated and thinking habits being built up. Homework should not be mechanical drudgery. Parents are not likely to do so, however, unless they know that critical thinking is a criterion of a good school. This is where parent education comes in. Parents should be able to judge the quality of their child's school, and their insights concerning the curriculum should be represented in educational legislation.

Our national goal is a "partnership" between the school and parents that supports the school's efforts "at home and shared educational decisionmaking at school" (National Education Goals Panel, 1994, p. 11). It cannot be overemphasized that the decision making should be informed decision making. (The omission by the panel is odd.) The Parents' Association understood this very well, which is why they sought so vigorously to become informed about education. The point of importance here is that parents should have an idea of what to look for in a good school, regardless of whether they think that the school attended by their child is doing a good job.

Parents may well think that their child's school is doing a good job. An observation in this regard is interesting. People give the schools in their communities higher ratings than they give American schools as a whole. "The closer people get to the schools, the higher the ratings. Almost two-thirds (65 per cent) of public school parents assign a grade of A or B to the school their child attends" (Elam & Rose, 1995, p. 41). Thus, distance seems to lend disenchantment, at least where the schools are concerned. This is onerous for the public's collective responsibility for educating millions of children.

Today, as a century ago, knowledge about education is power. We have a model for parent education that is worth thinking about and may make sense in our own situation. If it does, the effects may go well beyond a specific situation. What is needed now is to transcend the notion that because the nation's schools are not our schools, they deserve something less, or possibly even punitive. If parent education is organized by parents, as in the Dewey school, so much the better. What is needed is not for someone outside the school who is anti-teacher to come in and organize the parents. This is not parent education but a means of dividing parents and teachers through "empowerment."

Usually such persons have their own agenda. A parent association should be home grown.

It is indeed fascinating that Dewey's counsel concerning the best for all children was given to the Parents' Association. It was the association of learning parents to whom Dewey spoke of an ideal school and their responsibility to all children. The ideal and the responsibility both go on. *The School and Society* (1899), which was based on the parents' effort to learn about education, has been called "the most influential of all his many books" (Commager, 1951, p. 586). This was the view of the noted historian in the mid-twentieth century and it is my own view. Dewey's book continues to serve as an ideal, as Philip Jackson (1990) reminds us so beautifully.

Thus education *was* education in Dewey's school. There really was no lower or higher education; it was a learning community. Children learned at University laboratories, and teachers did not feel that parents who learned about education were trespassing on professional prerogatives. While it might be tempting to dismiss these qualities as artifacts of a simpler time, to do so would be in error. For there is still a need for parents to make sound educational decisions; in fact, the need is probably greater than ever. Children need to know how others seek reliable knowledge so that their own imaginations and critical powers will develop.

It is clear that Dewey set the tone for the school, and that it was natural and unprepossessing. He had developed his own administrative philosophy, which was inseparable from his philosophy of learning.

❖ 7 ❖

The Approach to Discipline

So-called discipline or individual difficulties of children were met by more
or different activities which might engage their attention, release creative
expression, and thus change their attitudes.
—Katherine Camp Mayhew and Anna Camp Edwards, *The Dewey School*

WHEN ONE IS ENGROSSED in an activity or a project, time seems literally to evapo-
rate. Whether reading or writing a book, refinishing a piece of furniture, or
following the precise steps in a new Maida Heatter recipe for chocolate-chip
cookies, one resents interruptions and persists until the project has been completed. In short, one is disciplined. The discipline is not imposed by someone
else but more rigorously by oneself. The outcome of the project has a hold on
the person, which is relevant to Dewey's conception of discipline. According
to Dewey (1916), discipline is "the deliberate or conscious disposition to persist
and endure in a planned course of action in spite of difficulties and contrary
solicitations" (p. 150).

Dewey wrote up his ideas on discipline in *Democracy and Education*
(1916). Actually, Dewey's conception of self-direction runs throughout his
works, but *Democracy and Education* was a "direct" (J. M. Dewey, 1939,
p. 151) result of his experience in Chicago. The Chicago years were also the
Laboratory School years, and that makes what he had to say about discipline
in *Democracy and Education* of great importance here. When he talks about
discipline as a "power to endure in an intelligently chosen course in the face
of distraction, confusion, and difficulty" (p. 151), he is talking about a conception that took shape in the Laboratory School. The ideas on discipline are
stated with firmness; there are no qualifications. We can conclude justifiably
that he felt that the children developed self-direction as an outcome of their
planning, persistence, and engrossment in activities.

A certain possibility troubles me here. There is a danger that we might
write off discipline in Dewey's school as a just-so story: The Laboratory School

120

staff had their ways (and small classes) and we have ours (and overcrowded classes), and lucky for them that they had happy children who were absorbed in their work, while we have growing numbers of troubled children who are not involved in the work.

Part of what the Laboratory School teachers did was to give each individual child a healthy dose of attention. There is absolutely no way that a teacher can do this when there are too many children in a class. It is not uncommon in these days of burgeoning enrollments at the elementary school level to find first-grade teachers facing classes of 30 or more children. The Laboratory School provides a demonstration of what is possible when teachers can study children as individuals—possible in the way of interesting children in their work and giving them a good start in becoming self-directing, socially responsible people. These approaches are tremendously important today when so many schools seem to consign children's behavior to forces beyond their control. These approaches are the subject of this chapter.

INTEREST, ATTENTION, AND HAPPINESS

As everyone knows, learning is best when children are interested in their work. This is absolutely nothing new; even the august curricular conservative, William T. Harris, said practically the same thing in 1896 in a discussion of Dewey's paper on interest and effort (Dewey, 1903). They did not see eye to eye on how pupil interest should be obtained, however, Harris saying that the teacher should contrive to make the material interesting. Didn't he know that the contrivance is apparent to even young children, who view it as a kind of game in which they cheerfully participate? Children become less cheerful and more impatient with the game as they grow older. One wonders how this escaped Harris's attention.

Over the years those concerned with poor discipline in the schools have tried everything short of alchemy. Behavioristic approaches (behavior modification) have been particularly popular despite their striking inconsistencies with the goal of developing children's power of judgment. Behavioristic approaches treat the learner as a mechanism to be conditioned. The purpose is to put the child *under* control rather than *in* control. The popularity of behavioristic approaches in a democratic society is a genuine cause for anxiety. What is puzzling is why they continue to be so popular when they seem not to be very effective. According to a study by Emmer and Aussiker (1987), cited in Rogers and Freiberg (1994), such programs did not result in fewer discipline referrals, and "students like schools least when behavioristic discipline programs are used" (p. 235).

Today, lack of discipline is viewed by the public as the biggest problem confronting local public schools (Elam & Rose, 1995). Discipline consistently is identified as a leading problem by teachers and supervisors (Stark, 1922; D. Tanner & L. Tanner, 1987; Teeter, 1995; Veenman, 1984). Understandably, one of the first things a teacher or supervisor might want to know about Dewey's school is whether anything was learned about this problem that might be truly helpful. I believe that a great deal was learned and that anyone concerned about improving discipline could do no better than examine these ideas.

Interest and Discipline

Interest and attention have two beneficial effects: They make it more likely that children will learn, and they result in a class that is controlled naturally. All the better if the interest comes from the child's inner self rather than from fear or some external reward. About this Dewey was adamant and it was the basis for discipline in his school. The idea that interest should be intrinsic for the child's intellectual and moral development challenged basic values, and in our time still is unacceptable to many people.

The Debut. When Dewey's paper, "Interest in Relation to Training of the Will," was read before the Herbart Society in 1896, there were no applause meters to measure audience reaction. Perhaps that was a good thing for Dewey, but the coolness to his ideas was, nonetheless, evident in the discussion afterward. A considerable number of those who attended had read the paper and were troubled by his analysis, first by his insistence that genuine interest is intrinsic, never something added to make learning palatable, and second by his conception of the educational use of interest. One can imagine easily the chilly reception given the following statement about the child's natural interests:

> These *are* relatively crude, uncertain and transitory. Yet they are all there is, so to speak, to the child; they are all the teacher has to appeal to; they are the starting points, the initiatives, the working machinery. (1896/1903, p. 30)

Those who found it hard to come to grips with this idea probably stopped listening or reading. If so, they missed a point that Dewey would have to repeat again and again to those who had already tuned him out, including all-too-eager teachers: The child's existing interests are not to be accepted as final. In Dewey's words:

> Does it follow that the teacher is to accept them as final; to take as a standard; to appeal to them in the sense of arousing them to act for their own satisfaction

just as they are? By no means. The teacher who thus interprets them is the only serious enemy the idea of interest really has. (p. 30)

The importance of interest is in what it can lead to, said Dewey. The child's interests should be interpreted by teachers whose broader experience and knowledge enable them to see the possibilities. "Interest," said Dewey "in its reality is a moving thing, a thing of growth, of richer experience, and fuller power. Just how to use interest to secure growth in knowledge and efficiency is what defines the master teacher" (p. 31).

We come now to the relation between interest and discipline. Dewey addressed that relation. In true interest the self is actively identified with some objective or idea because it is essential for self-expression. Children's own activity so engrosses them that discipline, in the sense of both attention and being able to plan and work toward an outcome, is achieved naturally.

Dewey (1903) was up against a wall of tradition—what he rather generously called "the theory of effort" (p. 6). According to this theory, children who devote themselves to uninteresting work develop real moral fiber. Dewey attacked the belief in his paper:

> Practically, the theory of effort amounts to nothing. When a child feels that his work is a task, it is only under compulsion that he gives himself to it. At the least let-up of external pressure we find his attention at once directed to what interests him. The child brought up on the basis of the theory of effort simply acquires marvelous skill in appearing to be occupied with an uninteresting subject, while the real heart and core of his energies are otherwise engaged. Indeed, the theory contradicts itself. It is psychologically impossible to call forth any activity without some interest. The theory of effort simply substitutes one interest for another. It substitutes the impure interest of fear of the teacher or hope of future reward for pure interest in the material presented. (pp. 6–7)

Dewey questioned the kind of moral training obtained when the child develops "habits of internal inattention" (p. 10), and he went on to drive the point home:

> While we are congratulating ourselves upon the well-disciplined habits which the pupil is acquiring, judged by his ability to reproduce a lesson when called upon, we forget to commiserate ourselves because the deeper intellectual and moral nature of the child has secured absolutely no discipline at all, but has been left to follow its own caprices, the disordered suggestions of the moment, or of past experience. (p. 10)

Dewey's paper approached interest and discipline from two vantage points, the psychological and the educational. As he pointed out, whichever of the perspectives one started with, the conclusion was the same: External approaches to learning and discipline, such as bribery and punishment, lead to doing things in an external manner and create habits of duplicity rather than moral character. "Normal interest and effort," on the other hand, "are identical with the process of self-expression" (p. 25).

The Discussion. Since we still are wrestling with the same issues, we will join the Herbartians for a moment. After complimenting the paper as "a very able production," William T. Harris (Dewey, 1903) said that Dewey was wrong: "When the materials of instruction have been selected it is up to the teacher to make them interesting" (pp. 35–36). On the face of it, this hardly seems debatable. But looking more closely, we can see the problem. What Harris meant by instructional materials was abstract knowledge—the systematic knowledge of adult consciousness (Harris, 1898; Tanner, 1991). In Dewey's view, children who were taught Harris's way were able neither to translate abstract knowledge into the more concrete form required for practical life, nor to deal later with more complex concepts in the subject area (Dewey, 1897b).

Some members of the audience began to discuss "the will of man as related to the will of God" (Dewey, 1903, p. 36). This was a preview of Christian fundamentalist arguments, in our time, against teaching children to be independent thinkers (Bradley, 1995; D. Tanner, 1988).

Superintendent Emerson White thought that interest was a vague term. "The idea of interest is a soup theory," he said. "Children should not be allowed to run in the direction of their interests. In all the real efforts of life and of experience, at least, we are called upon to sacrifice pleasure to duty" (p. 36). Harris also remarked about the "ambiguity" of the term.

Toward the end of the discussion, Charles McMurry, a professor at the Illinois State Normal School at Normal, brought the focus back to education. "We need an answer to this question," he said. "Shall we accept Dr. Dewey's analysis of the psychology of interest? He has given a full and masterly analysis. . . . Shall we accept the place and value given by Dr. Dewey to interest in the process of learning? The pedagogical problem is a simple and direct one" (Dewey, 1903, p. 37).

The last statement was not exactly true. Developing a curriculum that starts with children's natural interests is no simple matter. As Dewey (1903) said in his paper, it involves more than knowing the principles of child development: Leading children from their present tasks and needs to facts and concepts in the major fields of knowledge "is to tax to the utmost the wisdom of the adult, knowledge of history, science and the resources of art" (p. 31). Yet the Laboratory School teachers did it and they furnish us with a demonstration of what is possible in the way of learning and discipline.

Redirection of Children's Activities

Teachers can use interests to prevent and deal with discipline problems. How they do this will depend on the child's stage of development, as will be discussed shortly. To turn children loose to follow their interests is not what this is about, because that has always proved disappointing. There have been spectacular examples from the Progressive Era on, such as the free school movement of the 1960s and early 1970s (Cremin, 1974; Tanner & Tanner, 1990).

As described earlier, Dewey's Laboratory School had a definite curriculum with skills and understandings that it was felt worthwhile for every child to have. There were various ways, some very challenging, in which they could be learned. For example, older youngsters applied the problem-solving strategies that they had learned earlier to investigate scientific phenomena of interest to them. There was wiggle room in the curriculum. This was deliberate so that children could learn to make intelligent choices and carry out the solutions they had undertaken. There was room to grow, room to care, and room to develop intellectual and social power. As noted, the importance of work that immerses children because they feel a personal identification with it as a form of self-expression often is overlooked. It is no wonder that so many spirits rebel and so much time is measured as something to pass; as former children, we are all biased in favor of work that engrosses us, for we remember watching the clock. (Unless we were awfully lucky with our teachers.)

The approach of the Dewey teachers to dealing with individual behavior problems is clear from the quotation at the beginning of this chapter: Children were redirected into other activities that had the same desired goal. The activities were based on the teacher's knowledge of the child. Actually, redirection is what teachers do anyhow. Dewey addressed this very point in *Democracy and Education* (1916): "Speaking accurately, all direction is but *re*-direction; it shifts the activities already going on into another channel" (p. 32). The objective is learning as well as control. What the Laboratory School teachers wanted to develop was intrinsic change rather than mere outward compliance, and thus the child was an active participant in selecting the new activity.

Individual choices were only part of the picture in the Laboratory School and they tended to be most marked among the older groups. Younger children planned as a group enterprise; they began each day with a summary of how far their group had progressed with a given activity or activities and worked out the details of what they sought to accomplish that day. Older children were at the stage where they had made enough progress in the major fields of knowledge to become rather impatient with this approach and often went right to work on their individual and collaborative projects (Mayhew & Edwards, 1936).

The Power of Suggestion. The approaches used in redirection depend somewhat on the child's age. Dewey knew that young children have natural imaginative abilities and also are highly suggestible. As discussed, approaches to learning capitalized on these natural qualities, focusing on fundamental human concerns. The point here is that children's natural suggestibility, combined with imagination, resulted in their engrossment in activities. Children learned to develop habits of control and precision because of natural skills and teacher guidance. However, sometimes changing the activity was necessary for a particular youngster; children, like adults, have individual tastes and needs. Children's high level of suggestibility was a boon here and still is. Many parents and teachers instinctively use the technique of redirection.

Generative Versus Restrictive Approaches. Redirection generates constructive energy and activity. Restrictive discipline tells a child what not to do. It creates a vacuum and, as everyone knows, nature abhors a vacuum. Schools where discipline is a problem tend to have restrictive discipline. Respect for students is reflected in generative approaches such as those followed in Dewey's Laboratory School. For example, a group the age of today's seventh graders were studying how humans comprehended the principles of geological science. Most of the group were interested in how scientist-philosophers were able to explain the effects of the planetary system on the earth's climate. As Mayhew and Edwards (1936) recount:

> There were in this group, however, and in several of the older groups a number of boys who were irked by the historical approach and who seemed to require a shift in method. Their interests were not in line with those of the rest of the children; their attention was divided or entirely lacking; and their efforts, in accord with their interest, either retarded or interfered with those of the others. These boys were finally taken out of the class and allowed to follow their own diverse and individual lines until the general trend of their interests could be determined. (pp. 213–214)

An account of what the teachers did at this point is fascinating; some of our solutions may lie in similar approaches. The boys' interest was found to be in science, related to their work in the shop where they were making things "such as pile-drivers, stands for their microscopes, heat engines, or the simple astronomical or surveying and navigating instruments of the early discoverers and inventors" (p. 214). The teacher worked with them as a small group on a simple general topic, gradually leading back to their individual choices. By starting with the topic of the measurement of time and seasonal change, the teacher guided the youngsters into individual projects in which they constructed two different kinds of instruments for measuring the sun's altitude.

Science and mathematics were correlated in the project, which required many geometrical constructions. In the process, the children worked out a number of original propositions and the use of geometrical terms. According to Mayhew and Edwards, "The interest and vigor with which the boys worked out these problems was such that for two weeks it seemed best to drop all other experimental work" (p. 216). Actually, the time involved in this project was about one-and-a-half hours a week for 3 quarters. (The school, like the University, was on the quarter system.) Mayhew and Edwards (1936) listed the ideas that the former recalcitrants dealt with:

[a] study of the various theories of the nebular hypothesis, of the position of the fixed stars relative to the earth's yearly motion, and a brief summary of the theory of the comets, meteorites and the character of the larger planets. (p. 217)

Mayhew and Edwards (1936) reported that the boys were greatly interested in a lecture given at the University by Thomas C. Chamberlain on his theory of the origin of the solar system and a lecture by a visitor to the University, Sir Robert Ball. "Many of the technical terms were beyond their understanding but they were able to give a fairly good account of Mr. Chamberlain's meteoric theory and the formation of the continents and ocean basins" (p. 219).

The original plan had been to follow these ideas with the work that the rest of the group had been doing on geological history. The experimental science would have illustrated the formation of rocks. "However, these boys' vivid interest in their first taste of astronomy and the concentrated attention given the geometrical construction seemed to make it worth while to go on with this work" (p. 217).

In their experimental efforts to reconstruct measurement instruments that had been of such incredible value to humankind, the boys not only grew intellectually but experienced emotional satisfaction. There was more constructive energy. That is what we want: destructive energy redirected so that it becomes constructive energy for learning and personal satisfaction. Redirection can pay dividends, and of importance here is the teacher's role. As the teachers themselves said:

This work with a difficult group of boys also illustrates the necessity of great care and insight on the teacher's part in the choice of subject matter and the use of methods that are in accord with the individualized interests and varying abilities and attitudes of children. (p. 217)

The idea of redirection has been restated from various perspectives (Jones & Tanner, 1981; Prescott, 1934; Tanner, 1978) In the 1930s Daniel Prescott, the child developmentalist, proposed that schools permit children "to work off their emotion by engaging in socially useful projects" (1934, p. 460). The projects would emerge from their inquiries into civic and social problems. "If the public would permit this," Prescott wrote, "school would not involve so much of frustration, of boredom, or of active antagonism in pupils" (p. 460).

Some schools did give children firsthand experience in identifying and ameliorating social problems. In those schools, children learned social responsibility in a manner that is not possible through merely reading and discussing community problems (Tanner, 1978). Prescott was right that in teaching social responsibility through socially useful activities, we have a rich opportunity to provide a satisfying outlet for activity and convey to children that their actions do make a difference. We also are improving the curriculum.

The redirection of negative or destructive behavior into socially useful behavior is one perspective on redirection. As Prescott stressed, the goal is not to eliminate emotional energy but to rechannel it toward growth.

Nevertheless, redirection is basically an instructional procedure and this is the way it was used in Dewey's Laboratory School. The purpose was to find activities that would engage a particular child and at the same time meet the instructional objectives that were the same for all. A century later, we have the objectives, but the individual attention is a rare and precious commodity. Without it, this approach to discipline is not possible.

The Lost Individual (Child)

We turn now to a problem that was mentioned just briefly before: the focus on groups rather than individuals in current educational literature. Perhaps it would be stating the case too strongly to say that this is at the root of our problems, but it certainly has not made things better for either discipline or learning. Meeting the needs of individuals is more than a lofty ideal; there are practical reasons for doing it. Whatever the approach to reform, the possibility that groups will learn decreases, rather than improves, to the extent that the needs of individual children in the group are not met. Somehow we cling to the notion that general instructional approaches will meet the needs of all. Dewey learned otherwise in his school.

Attention and Success. A child who has moved to the United States from Haiti has become a successful young adult: She is a finalist for a National Book Award. To what does she attribute her success? That she attended a specialized high school in New York City (Clara Barton) where "the classes were small and challenging" (Purnick, 1995, p. B3). When classes are big, "you don't get much attention," she said in a newspaper interview. Since her parents always stressed the importance of education, she might have done well in another school. However, her parents "wanted her to get as much attention as possible" (p. B3), so she applied to and was accepted into a program where the class size was 22 students. The interviewer's thoughtful conclusion is really an unanswerable question: "One thing led to another, as in most lives. Did one program or school or connection make the difference? Maybe. Maybe not. But she got her chances."

The best and wisest parents want their children to have chances. Dewey believed that it was the public duty in a democracy to furnish such chances to all children.

Dewey (1904a) saw what many pretend not to see—that a child's chances to develop optimally are reduced when classes are big and it is impossible to give children individual attention. A teacher may never get around to the child who does not understand. This hurts children's chances. Listen to a school dropout: "The teacher didn't show you too much. If you didn't get it the first time, the teacher didn't have much time to show you" (Nelson, 1988, p. 241).

On the other hand, youngsters can really blossom under good tutoring conditions (more leisure, less stress), even when they have shown no interest in class. Dewey (1903) noted in his Herbart Society paper:

> I have it argued in all seriousness that a child kept after school to study has often got an interest in arithmetic or grammar which he didn't have before. As if this proved the efficacy of "discipline" *vs.* interest. Of course the reality is that the greater leisure, the opportunity for individual explanation afforded, served to bring the material into its proper relations in the child's mind—he "got a hold" of it. (p. 17)

Every teacher has had similar experiences.

Still Believing in Magic. According to Bloom (1984), the teacher's problem is to teach individuals in classes as well as they can be taught under good tutoring conditions. The idea has always been seductive. There is no magical program or approach that can make this happen. In the words of Ralph Tyler (1957), who was Bloom's teacher, "No mechanical procedure can guide the educational efforts of every child" (p. ix). Bloom never gave up trying, however, and the result was the mastery learning approach, a procedure in which pupils progress through hierarchically ordered learning tasks. Mastery systems reduce opportunities for the teacher to vary the curriculum to meet individual needs. They are as mechanical an approach as one might find. In the 1970s and 1980s, for many teachers programmed instruction was synonymous with individualized instruction. This was not their fault; they were generations away from a time when the teacher's role included studying individual children— their interests, talents, and problems—and translating what was learned into action (Prescott, 1957; White, 1958).

Bloom was not the first to attempt to individualize instruction and have it turn into a convergent-group model; Frederick Burk and Carleton Washburne were before him (D. Tanner & L. Tanner, 1987). He will not be the last, unless educators finally come to this understanding: "To search for a perfect individualized program fitted to the needs of each person is a fantasy that diverts our attention from ways we can realistically respond to individual differences" (Talmadge, 1980, p. 21).

Inadequacy of General Knowledge. As Tyler (1991) pointed out:

> Dewey found that every child in his school was, in some respects, unique. He found that a child's problems were not solved by applying generalized knowledge alone. He had to study each individual child to identify his or her particular strengths, difficulties, and supporting environment in order to understand the basis on which the student could be helped to learn effectively. (p. 7)

One needs only to leaf through the tables of contents in recent educational journals to discern that the individual child is not the focus of educational reform. In fact, the focus has left the classroom and is on teacher leadership and shared decision making at the school level. The effect has been teacher overload. The individual child seems lost indeed. Gary Griffin (1995) writes:

> Although the intention that teachers should not assume school leadership in the absence of ongoing interactions with students was a bold and theoretically sound one, teachers who are engaged in the new dual roles of school *and* classroom leadership appear to be caught in a situation where the demands of teaching are not reduced to compensate for the *added* demands made by engaging in school leadership. (p. 44)

Griffin investigated the effects of school-level decision making on elementary teachers' classroom interactions with students as indicated by conversations with the teachers. Five schools were involved in his study. Not surprisingly, the first item on the agendas of all five schools was how to deal with student behavior problems. In each of the schools, "there was a group of boys and girls who appeared to need considerably more teacher and school attention than was being exerted" (p. 36). As Griffin points out, the development of school-wide discipline policies appears to be a justifiable focus for newly empowered teachers in collaborative decision-making situations.

Yet the approaches tended to be regulatory (and, eventually, punitive) and were not centered on or even linked with ways that teachers approach instruction. This is unfortunate. Studies have found that experienced teachers of disturbed and difficult children consider improving the educational program to be the best approach for controlling students (Tanner, 1978). This certainly makes sense since discipline must be connected with its purpose, the improvement of learning.

Why, one is led to wonder, do the school-wide policies fail to link behavior problems with pedagogy—at least in the five schools Griffin studied? According to Griffin, the answer appears to lie in school cultures: Teachers stick together rather than raise dangerous issues of pedagogical expertise. In one school this began to happen. According to a teacher, "It took all the diplomatic skill some of us possessed to relieve a potentially bombastic situation" (Griffin, 1995, p. 36).

Sooner or later, as Griffin observes, school critics are going to begin to carp that school-level decision making is stealing time that should be devoted to the classroom. Indeed, perceptive educational leaders like Griffin already are concerned because teachers' classroom responsibilities have not been reduced commensurately, while they are expected to assume additional school-wide tasks. School organization policies, including the work assigned to teachers, are bound to affect children's present education and future lives. Dewey (1904a) warned:

> We forget that it is precisely such things that really control the whole system, even on its distinctively educational side. No matter what is the accepted precept and theory, no matter what the legislation of the school board or the mandate of the school superintendent, the reality of education is found in the personal and face-to-face contact of teacher and child. The conditions that underlie and regulate this contact dominate the educational situation. (p. 23)

It hardly seems necessary to say that instructional approaches to student behavior problems require face-to-face contact. Restructuring or reorganization that results in fewer teacher–child contacts or contacts of lesser quality is not good for either learning or discipline. Even before school-level decision making became the focus for improving education in the 1990s, many schools were overcrowded and teachers were unable to provide the help to individuals that is tacitly understood in the educational literature to be their obligation.

Recent literature on instruction also emphasizes cooperation and collaboration. The marked attention given to ways that children can learn to work together, is evidenced in the emphasis on cooperative learning approaches; the literature is filled with these.

Dewey would welcome the emphasis on cooperation but might have reservations about the ways it is being carried out, which have been discussed in this book. Dewey's idea of having the school represent a community life is well known. Unfortunately, what retreats into the background is a distinguishing feature of the school: the study of individual children so that activities truly reflect their needs.

The very idea of teaching implies that individuals will be helped to overcome their individual learning problems and that their particular talents and potentialities will be cultivated. Individuals are linked irrevocably with groups, or more largely, with the human community, to which they can bring sorrow or happiness. Every artistic talent, for example, is a possibility of pleasure for untold numbers of other humans. In 1995, the huge Monet exhibit at the Art Institute of Chicago attracted millions—a sign of the limitless possibilities of pleasure. But individuals must have attention and opportunity if they are expected to bring happiness to others as well as themselves.

After the 1950s, study of the individual child literally fell out of the literature. One is led to wonder why, and certain possibilities come to mind: nationalizing influences on the curriculum after Sputnik, followed by the War on Poverty. The culture of poverty concerned educators in the 1960s and 1970s, and the very term culture means alikeness. More than this cannot be said here, but the reader who is interested might pursue these possibilities and others in attempting to understand why the individual child has become lost.

The individual child, with special problems, potentialities, and needs, is waiting. One cannot imagine a physician giving the same prescription to every patient in the waiting room; the idea is simply ludicrous. But this essentially is what has happened in our schools.

DISCIPLINE AND DEVELOPMENT

Dewey's (1916) definition of a disciplined individual is simplicity itself: "A person who is trained to consider his actions, to undertake them deliberately" (p. 151). For Dewey, the power that fuels the stick-to-itiveness in discipline, the thing that makes a person persist despite distractions, is interest. This is true for both children and adults. Since discipline and intellectual development are inseparable, it comes as no surprise that in the Laboratory School, healthy growth in discipline meant children's increasing ability to plan and undertake an activity and to use the work that they had to do as a behavioral standard. Only in this way does the child "have a normal and healthy standard," making it possible "to appreciate his [or her] failures and to estimate them at their right value" (1897a, p. 14). The idea that the activities themselves should furnish the standards for behavior is natural and normal. We do it ourselves in the real world of life and work outside the school.

Dewey's concept of discipline was always positive, with emphasis "upon forming habits of positive service" (p. 14) in the miniature community, rather than negative, with emphasis on violations of school regulations. Of course, there were rules and procedures that children might not yet appreciate but that still had to be enforced. For example, teachers had to promote cooperation and help children understand its reason. Children could come to comprehend through practice. As Richard Hersh and his colleagues so wisely pointed out: "Children must have practice in democratic living . . . in order to discover its intellectual justification on their own terms" (Hersh, Miller, & Fielding, 1980, pp. 6–7).

In this section of the chapter Dewey's developmental stages are considered and put in a contemporary form that I believe may be helpful to teachers.

Developmental Stages: The Problem of Classroom Usefulness

In modern times, the best-known stage theories are Piaget's and Kohlberg's. The developmental psychologist James R. Rest (1983) reported that Piaget's book, *The Moral Judgment of the Child* (1932/1948), continues to be "one of the most influential and seminal works" (p. 570). Piaget's work was picked up and pursued by other psychologists. Kohlberg arrived at his own version of moral development, which was essentially "a repudiation" (Youniss & Damon, 1994, p. 275) of Piaget's theory. On the psychological scene, there is no doubt that Piaget's work was influential. However, the usefulness of Piaget's and Kohlberg's developmental theories for teachers is another matter entirely and that which concerns us here. Both have been cited for being of limited use in improving education (Biggs, 1992; Elliot, 1982). Kohlberg's work seems especially vulnerable in this regard. Indeed, the "theoretical weaknesses" of Kohlberg's approach spilled over onto Piaget and "implausible claims and assumptions about moral behavior forever became associated with Piagetianism in the public mind" (Youniss & Damon, 1994, p. 276).

Classroom Applicability of Piaget's Stage Theories. According to Elliot (1982), teachers find it hard to link Piaget's cognitive and moral development theories with practice and "there remains doubt in some quarters about the direct relevance of the theory for classroom practice" (p. 244). In one sense, the criticism is justifiable. Piaget's theory of moral judgment is concerned only with that, not with moral behavior. There was nothing deceptive in this on Piaget's part; he was not trying to fool anyone. "It is the moral judgment that we propose to investigate," he wrote in the "Foreword" to his famous work on child morality, "not moral behavior or sentiments" (1932/1948, p. vii).

But teachers are concerned with behavior. So, for that matter, are psychologists. Investigating the relation between moral judgment and behavior, Damon (1977) discovered that there was little predictability between youngsters' justice solutions in an imagined situation and their real behavior in matched settings. Rest (1983) proposed "components" of morality that include moral behavior. However, the behavioral aspect is given short shrift in his proposal and is not related to real problems, which, of course, Dewey insisted upon.

In another sense, however, the criticism that Piaget's theory lacks relevance for teachers' professional work is unjustified. Piaget's moral theory is concerned with the development of children's understanding of cooperation and its benefits for the individual and society. This is a "general, programmatic direction" (Rest, 1983, p. 571) with applicability for teachers. As Youniss and Damon (1994) point out, Piaget's work anchors moral development "firmly in the social relations that engender morality" (p. 418). Here one finds an unmistakable affinity with Dewey, who also emphasized the social nature of intellectual and moral development. Unfortunately, the importance of the child's social world in Piagetian theory often has been blurred, as he has been confused with Kohlberg, who ignored the social factor in moral development and took the stance that an individual's reasoning stage was predictive of action. (Kohlberg would later realize the error in his own reasoning.)

Piaget on Instruction: A Remarkable Likeness. While it is true that Piaget's best-known works are concerned with individual cognitive development rather than the life of the school and approaches to teaching, he did write and speak about these matters elsewhere. The similarity between Piaget's ideas about instruction and Dewey's is remarkable and deserves more than passing mention. For example, Piaget, in a speech to a group of European educational reformers in 1932, made the suggestion that instead of instilling information in children, educators instill a "tool" or "intellectual instrument" that children could use to develop coherent knowledge (Youniss & Damon, 1994, p. 269). The tool chosen by Piaget was the scientific method; the benefits of scientific thought were that it diminished egocentric thinking and encouraged consideration of diverse viewpoints. Piaget told the New Education Fellowship that the instrument could be developed through schools that stressed "group work, common study, [and] self government" because

> [o]nly a type of education founded upon a social relationship which is of a kind to succeed in uniting adults, will allow of the development of sane moral and international attitudes, and make of our children a finer generation than ourselves. (quoted in Youniss & Damon, 1994, p. 279)

For Piaget as for Dewey, the ways that children construct knowledge were influenced by social communication and cooperation and had a wider social influence. This was enormously important because of the social, economic, and moral interdependence of humankind—here to stay (but often unfaced) in 1932. "The economics of isolation, purely internal politics, intellectual and moral reactions limited to one group, no longer exists," said Piaget (quoted in Youniss and Damon, p. 269).

As Youniss and Damon point out, Piaget's ideas were common among the intelligentsia at that time. It should be noted that groupwork and student government were observable by then in the best American schools. The educational literature of the 1930s contains a multitude of studies designed to compare the newer practices with traditional textbook learning (Tanner & Tanner, 1990). The point of importance here is that like Dewey, Piaget argued that children must learn to use in school the collaborative approach to problem solving that we expect them to use as adults. In a world full of dangers where "all important events in the world are international" (Piaget, quoted in Youniss & Damon, 1994, p. 269), this is simply necessary. While it might be argued that the world has continued to limp along since Piaget, one might add, not very well. In the theories of both Dewey and Piaget, the child constructs knowledge in a social milieu and how the knowledge is constructed has wider social implications.

There are remarkable similarities between Dewey and Piaget. Both pointed out that there is a qualitative difference between the child's and the adult's cognitive processes. The failure of traditional education, noted Piaget (1970), resides in its treatment of the child as "a small adult being who reasons and feels as we do while merely lacking our knowledge and experience." He continued, "Since the child viewed in this way was no more than an ignorant adult, the educational task was not so much to form its mind as simply furnish it; the subject matter provided from outside was thought to be exercise enough in itself" (pp. 159–160).

At times it has been tempting to adjust the view of the child so that it more nearly matches national needs. During the Cold War and space-race, children often were viewed as miniature scientists. The psychologist of the moment was Jerome Bruner (1960), whose thesis was that "intellectual activity anywhere is the same" (p. 14). But as Dewey warned in his lectures to parents, the child is not a miniature adult capable of engaging in scientific inquiry. "There is no distinction between experimental science for little children and the work done in the carpenter shop," and "such work as they can do in physics or chemistry is not for the purpose of making technical generalization or even at arriving at abstract truths. Children simply like to do things and watch to see what will happen" (1899, p. 44). Dewey subsequently proposed three stages in intellectual development, which will be discussed later as they relate to discipline.

Returning now to problems with Piaget's theory, one difficulty for teachers is that the relationship between moral and conceptual development remains vague. Helen Weinreich Haste (1982) made this very observation:

[Piaget] hypothesized a parallel relationship between moral and conceptual development, which his later studies could have elaborated, but he never integrated
his moral and his conceptual studies. . . . It has been left to others to do this.
(p. 181)

What she and many others have failed to note is that this had already been
done by Dewey, before the turn of the century. The integration was complete,
and what made it useful to teachers is that it was inseparable from the curriculum and the life of the school.

Kohlberg's Morality Lesson. Kohlberg saw himself as a Piagetian but differed
from Piaget in a way that is important for us here. Piaget (1932/1948) found
in his study of children's moral development that there were two different and
simultaneous sets of values in the child: adult and peer. They coexisted during
much of childhood but there was a gradual change to peer-centered values.
This was the outcome more of changing circumstances in the child's life than
of stage-type cognitive changes. Kohlberg (1963) believed that it was not
possible for two sets of values to exist at the same time in the child. There was
only one morality structure in childhood; it was adult-focused, mindlessly
obedient, and unyieldingly loyal to persons in charge. Kohlberg (1970) identified three levels and six stages of moral development. At the lowest level the
child obeys authority simply to avoid punishment, and at the highest is ori-
ented to choice and conscience. An examination of Kohlberg's stage descriptions will show that only after childhood do peer-centered kinds of morality
such as those described by Piaget—fairness, for example—appear. This just
does not jibe with reality. As everyone knows who has watched young children at play, they have peer-centered standards of morality. In the words of
Youniss and Damon (1994): "Even at a very early age, children express—and
act on—rich and robust notions of kindness, sharing, fairness, reciprocity, and
other peer-oriented moral standards" (p. 276). At the same time, children
affirm respect for adult authority. It is not unusual "to hear a child say in one
breath that he would always do whatever mom tells him, and then in the next
breath that he would share his bike with his friend even if mom said not to,
because his friend had always been generous with him" (p. 276).

Kohlberg eventually acknowledged the importance of the social factor in
moral development. The way this came about is just fascinating. Kohlberg,
Kauffman, Scharf, and Hickey (1974) tried moral education with prisoners.
Relatively quickly in this experiment, they found that asking inmates to improve
their reasoning abilities by discussing hypothetical dilemmas was not a sufficient force for moral development and personality change. Prisoners often come
from disordered families and dangerous neighborhoods and have no good
memories of cooperative persons. Moreover, community life in prison is less

than a model of regard for others. Their social experience is likely to go against higher concepts in Kohlberg's schema.

Kohlberg and his colleagues decided to change their intervention program so that it went beyond mere discussion groups to the establishment of just communities within the prison. Prisoners needed to have experience in a just community where people lived harmoniously. Rest (1983) summarized the implications of Kohlberg's experiment:

> (P)eople who are cynical, self-protective and brutalized need to have more than just the cognitive awareness of the possibility of harmonious living; they need concrete experience in a just community in actual operation, they need to experience that their contributions to the community are reciprocated and that support from others is really there; they need confirmation and reconfirmation that cooperation is a workable—and even preferable—way to live. (p. 568)

Dewey's conception of the school as a social community was a recognition of this need. Some children who came to Dewey's school had already begun to understand the benefits of cooperative social arrangements. This kind of learning had occurred at home. The teachers thus had a foundation to build upon, and children were led gradually to discover new possibilities of cooperation. Often, however, children learn cooperation at home but schools do not teach it. Mayhew and Edwards (1936) noted that children whose experience was in schools where youngsters were not trained in cooperative and mutually helpful living had a hard time adjusting to the Dewey school—and it to them.

Some homes are very good in providing a foundation in cooperation. However, one need not be a social scientist to know that there are many children whose background is tied to chaos and abuse. Such cases are uncovered every day in the media. Cooperation for these youngsters is motivated by fear rather than mutual respect. The equilibrium that they have with their environment may be based on reciprocity with other individuals for offensive acts (or acts perceived as offensive) rather than seeking the benefits of cooperation emphasized by Piaget as vital for development.

Dewey's idea of the school as a community that "reproduces, within itself, the typical conditions of social life" (1897a, p. 14) seems woefully inadequate in view of the other influences that play upon and prey upon children. It is the school's job to teach the possibilities of cooperation; specifically, it is our responsibility to society and can make life for a child richer and happier. If consciously done, it could be enough. As Kohlberg found, probably to his surprise, not living and learning in a just community interferes with the process of moral development, at a terrible cost to individuals and society. Thus the application of Dewey's idea seems unquestionably wise.

As Rest (1983) pointed out, it is of importance that Kohlberg, a leading proponent of the pure cognitive viewpoint, "changed his views about the singular efficacy of pure cognitive advancement after becoming involved with people lacking in positive social experiences" (p. 568). That Kohlberg himself no longer believed that discussion of hypothetical situations was the primary instrument of acquiring morality is significant. Meanwhile, some teachers continue to regard Kohlberg's levels and stages as a complete approach to moral education.

Dewey's Developmental Stages

Dewey's Laboratory School was based on the idea that the curriculum should have an "effective influence upon conduct" (1900d, p. 230). For this to happen, schools would have to abandon out-of-date notions about the human mind, for example, that mind is mind whether in child or adult—the only difference being that of quantity. Unhappily, most schools adhered to this conception. Content was divided into child-size portions of logically organized facts, to be digested and committed to memory. The theory was that the process itself had a positive influence on behavior and character. Since the curriculum (including approaches to instruction) was divorced from the child's life experience and the life of practice, it was unlikely to have a long-term effect on behavior or even a short-term effect.

In contrast, the curriculum that Dewey and the teachers worked out was based on concepts of growth and change. Mind developed when schools recognized children's natural equipment or uninvested capital. Dewey believed that if his developmental conception was applied to education, school subjects could "become integral parts of the child's conduct and character" (1900d, p. 224). In studying children's learning, Dewey identified stages of development.

It is interesting that Dewey had two formulations of growth stages. They occurred at different times in his work and have a different scope, although they are not substantially different. The two formulations fit together and have a great deal in common, not surprisingly since they both came out of the Laboratory School. The second one is more refined and represents a further development of his thinking.

The First Formulation.   Dewey unveiled his stages of growth as a painter would a masterpiece. When the school had been in existence for 5 years, he wrote: "In coming now to speak of the educational answers which have been sought for the psychological hypotheses, it is convenient to start from the matter of the stages of growth" (1900d, p. 226). Dewey's article, "The Psychology of the Elementary Curriculum," not only started with the stages but was entirely about them. It appeared, fittingly enough, in the final issue of the *Elementary School Record* (Dewey, 1900d). Dewey obviously saw the stages as the center-piece of his school's work.

There are three stages of growth. Dewey believed that by being true to these stages, teachers could present the school subjects with the least resistance and in the most productive way. The implication for discipline is clear—not to mention learning. Dewey, of course, viewed discipline and learning as inseparable.

The first stage is manifested by direct personal and social interests and an immediate relationship between ideas and action. There is a need for a motor outlet. Activities dominate the curriculum for these reasons: (1) to provide an immediate outlet for expression, (2) to maintain "the connection between knowing and doing, so characteristic of this period of the child's life" (1900d, p. 227), and (3) to enrich and enlarge the child's experience outside of school. The objective is for children to view the school not "as a place apart" (p. 227), but as one where they engage in human activities performed by adults in the real world. As described earlier, subject matter was presented not as lessons, but through activities.

In Dewey's first stage, the guiding principle is the child as an active being. The activity program is not to be confused with letting children run loose to follow their impulses of the moment. It is carefully planned, always with what comes later in mind.

One of the world's most unfortunate problems is the inability of people to get along with one another. This can have painful repercussions in the workplace and, indeed, in every situation where social interaction is required. (There are few where it is not.) The first stage is manifested by the child's natural sociability. The school begins to invest this capital with activities that are characterized by interest in the companionship of others and sensitivity to the rights of others.

The second stage, from ages 8 or 9 to 11 or 12, is manifested by children's increasing sense that there are more permanent and objective results and that they need to develop the skills necessary to attain those results. Dewey's second stage is manifested as follows:

> When the child recognizes distinct and enduring ends which stand out and demand attention on their own account, the previous vague and fluid unity of life is broken up. The mere play of activity no longer directly satisfies. It must be felt to accomplish something—to lead up to a definite and abiding outcome. Hence the recognition of rules of action—that is, of regular means appropriate to reaching permanent results—and the value of mastering special processes so as to give skill in their use. (p. 227)

The educational problem in this stage as far as subject matter is concerned is to differentiate the unity of human experience into fields of knowledge, selecting material that illustrates the importance to humankind of command over certain methods of thinking and action in realizing its highest purposes. The problem regarding instructional approaches is analogous: to bring children to recognize the need for a like development within themselves—the need to gain for themselves "practical and intellectual control of such methods of work and inquiry" that will enable them to "realize results" for themselves (p. 228).

Throughout history humans have exercised patience, courage, and ingenuity along with continual judgment when confronted with novel conditions, even in the face of hazard. American history was selected in the Laboratory School as a typical example of these qualities. No attempt was made to cover the whole ground in chronological order. "Rather, a series of types is taken up: Chicago and the northwestern Mississippi valley; Virginia, New York, and the Puritans and Pilgrims in New England," for "the aim is to present a variety of climates and local conditions; to show the different kinds of obstacles and helps that people found, and a variety of historic traditions, and customs and purposes of different people" (p. 228). While in Dewey's first stage there is dramatic identification of the children with the social life being studied, in the second stage there is additionally an intellectual identification: Children put themselves in the position of confronting the problems that were met and rediscovering for themselves ways of meeting the problems. In Dewey's second stage the guiding principle is the relation of means to ends. This encompasses all curriculum areas, not just history.

In science, for example, the child attempts to find out how various materials are manipulated to produce a given result. Yet this is applied science rather than pure science. Dewey both clarifies and cautions:

> It is thus clearly distinguished from experimentation in the scientific sense—such as is appropriate to the secondary period—where the aim is the discovery of facts and verification of principles. Since the practical interest predominates, it is a study of applied science rather than of pure science. For instance, processes are selected, found to have been of importance in colonial life—bleaching, dyeing, soap and candle making, manufacture of pewter dishes, making of cider and vinegar, leading to some study of chemical agencies, of oils, fats, elementary metallurgy. In art, attention is given to practical questions of perspective, of proportion of spaces and masses, balance, effect of color combinations and contrasts, etc. (p. 229)

Dewey was concerned that as the various subjects began to be viewed as independent, the separation would leave "the child without definite command of his own powers, or clear consciousness of purposes" (p. 230). It was not until the school's fifth year of existence that the educational principle for

Dewey's second stage manifested itself. This was relatively late in the school's life and points again to the fact that positive results in any laboratory are not always immediate. Our history is littered with the aborted fetuses of educational experiments. Dewey's words convey an unlearned lesson in this regard, but they are also encouraging:

> It is perhaps only in the present year that the specific principle of the conscious relation of means to ends has emerged as the unifying principle of this period; and it is hoped that emphasis of this in all lines of work will have a decidedly cumulative and unifying effect upon the child's development. (p. 230)

The means–ends principle, if consistently followed in all schoolwork, can have an influence on conduct. The child who is concerned with what is needed to produce a given result, is behaving appropriately insofar as the school is concerned and is developing intellectual and social power.

In Dewey's second stage, schools arrange their programs so that children feel the need to go to books and other forms of the experience of others and to have command over the social symbols of language and quantity. Dewey wrote that command of these symbols (the three Rs) is "one of the most important means in extending experiences" but that "certain conditions should be observed in their introduction and use" (p. 230). Unfortunately, in most schools the approach was "wholesale and direct" without recognizing the conditions and making the necessary curriculum adaptations. Dewey identified two. First, children should have in their own personal experience a background of contact with social and physical realities. This is necessary so that symbols do not become "a second-handed" (p. 230) substitute for reality. Second, children's direct experience should supply problems and interests that require turning to books "for their solution, satisfaction and pursuit" (p. 230).

Because they are social, the three Rs must always have "a highly important place in education," Dewey said. In fact, "these subjects are social in a double sense" (p. 230):

> They represent the tools which society has evolved in the past as the instruments of its intellectual pursuits. They represent the keys which will unlock to the child the wealth of social capital which lies beyond the possible range of his limited experience. (p. 230)

Yet the child's intellectual and moral individuality should "not be swamped by a disproportionate amount of the experience of others" (p. 231). This could be avoided by furnishing children with plenty of personal activity in expression, construction, and experimentation so that the tools add to their powers "instead of [creating] a servile dependency" (p. 231). Dewey argued that when reading, writing, and mathematics are introduced as part of children's experience, these subjects have more vitality and meaning and the time devoted to learning them is considerably reduced.

Dewey (1900a) noted that while in the first stage children act out images rather than projecting them into the future as ends, the conscious relation of means to ends is not entirely absent in this stage. "On the contrary, even with 6-year-old children consciousness dawns of a certain sort of ends somewhat remote, and consequently the child is interested in regulating his acts so as to reach the end" (p. 49). In observing a group playing a game, he noticed that about half of the children planned their moves to get to the goal first, but the others were carried away with what they were doing; "if the one who was it got to running away from the goal, he kept on running, in spite of the fact that the others were making for the goal" (p. 50). The activity was so satisfying that it was impossible to guide it by a result to be reached. For Dewey, there were three points to be made here: (1) not all children go through stages at the same time, (2) the transition in developing power or skill is not abrupt, and (3) stages should be anticipated and planned for. Dewey stressed that the change from the first to the second stage comes about more easily when children are engaged in an activity that is practical rather than abstract. It comes more naturally, for instance, in cooking cereal for lunch than in learning to calculate for some distant use. A good activity will present difficulties that suggest the need to find an effective way of dealing with them.

In Dewey's second stage, children's activities are investigative rather than "directly productive" (1900c, p. 229). Skills mastered in this fashion rather than mechanically give intellectual power, and "books and all that relates to them take the important place to which they are entitled" (p. 231). A point of attention here: The skills can be taught in the earlier stage. "[I]t is possible, in the early years," wrote Dewey, "to appeal in teaching the recognition and use of symbols, to the child's power of production and creation; as much so in principle as in other lines of work seemingly more direct" (p. 231). The advantage is that children have a "definite result" by which to measure their progress.

Dewey and the faculty found that they had postponed some of this work so that it was below the child's intellectual level. "The effect," wrote Dewey, "is that the child, having progressed to a more advanced plane intellectually feels what earlier might have been a form of power and creation to be an irksome task" (p. 232). The implications for discipline are obvious. When children exhibit little enthusiasm or interest in their work, the problem may be that the work is below their intellectual level. Children can be tolerant, but only for a while; then the urge to grow manifests itself.

There are lost children at any stage, but for a youngster in the 8–12 age group this can be a disaster. Children know that there are more permanent outcomes than when they were in the play period and they feel the need to attain the necessary skills to reach them. If time progresses and the need is not met, they may begin to feel that they are on the sidelines rather than an actor or shaper in the saga of humankind. No child should feel this way and it is costly if one does.

The work of third-stage children (12- and 13-year-olds) measures strikingly against their beginnings. In Dewey's words:

> It comes when the child has a sufficient acquaintance of a fairly direct sort with various forms of reality and modes of activity; and when he has sufficiently mastered the tools of thought, inquiry and activity, appropriate to various phases of experience, to be able profitably to specialize upon distinctive studies and arts for technical and intellectual aims. (p. 232)

Children at this stage know how to work both collaboratively and independently. As noted by Mayhew and Edwards (1936), there has been a slow but steady shift in the youngster's mental outlook "from the psychological approach of the learner or mere observer of facts to the logical one of the adult, who observes to an end and classifies what he has observed with the purpose of its further use" (p. 223). As described earlier, children in Dewey's third stage are encouraged to work on independent projects in a given subject field rather than a thematic activity or problem that involves the entire group. The ability to work independently on a specialized project is important today when so many high schools are offering college-level courses that require this kind of work. We can see that the third-stage children in Dewey's school would have been well positioned in this regard.

Interestingly enough, Dewey's article on the growth stages was reprinted in the second edition of *The School and Society*, attesting to its continuing importance in the author's eyes. By then, as Dewey noted, the *Elementary School Record* had long been out of print. *The School and Society* had already been reprinted 22 times and certainly could have stood on its own without the article.

The Second Formulation. In 1910, Dewey proposed three stages of intellectual development. This formulation specifically concerned how teachers could direct children's natural endowments—the most important being curiosity—"into habits of critical examination and inquiry" (p. 29). For Dewey, intellectual development was learning to think well. Children can be taught to think only by appealing to and cultivating their natural capacities, and this is not possible unless teachers understand what these capacities are. Once again, Dewey was talking about investing uninvested capital, but this time the yield is, specifically, effective habits of thinking. Interestingly, although Dewey's conception of thinking as problem solving and the steps in the complete act of thought are well known, his theory of child development relative to teaching thinking has received little attention. It is neither the basis for commercial thinking programs nor widely circulated in the literature. One must go directly to Dewey's book, *How We Think.*

Judging from their materials, program developers have not done this. Programs for teaching thinking fail to recognize children's natural capacities and present thinking as discrete skills. For example, Sternberg (1986) suggested that problem solving be taught through "performance components"—such as encoding, application, and so on. "Separation of the performance components used in solving problems is critically important for diagnosis and remediation of problem-solving performance" (p. 27). Taking a similar tack, the Developmental Activities Project (for developing thinking) "bases its framework on Piaget's 46 concrete operational mental structures" (Phillips & Phillips, 1994, p. 50). Thinking is divided into "structures" that turn out to be skills such as classification or measurement. No one would argue that children should not be able to perform tasks such as those found in Bloom's taxonomy of educational objectives, Sternberg's performance components, and Piaget's structures; however, the separate skills should not be confused with the whole act of solving a problem. Developers of commercial materials have so imposed their products on schools that it is hard for teachers (and supervisors) to think straight about teaching thinking. Teachers, however, can ask this question: Where is the sense of the whole and a sense of wonder? For if all our children learned were discrete skills, real thinking would be impossible.

Now to the stages: Dewey's first stage, in earliest childhood, is evidenced by a curiosity that gets the child into everything—reaching, pounding, and manipulating objects until they stop revealing new properties. "Such activities," Dewey (1910) wrote, "are hardly intellectual, and yet without them intellectual activity would be feeble and intermittent through lack of stuff for its operations" (p. 32). The second stage develops through social interaction when the child learns to turn to others to add to personal experiences. When objects no longer respond in an interesting way to the child's manipulations, and the child appeals to persons to supply interesting information, a new era begins. The incessant "whys" at this second stage are not demands for scientific or technical information but for more and bigger facts. Yet the child senses, however dimly, that the facts are not the entire story. In the feeling "that there is more behind them and more to come from them, lies the germ of *intellectual* curiosity" (p. 32). Dewey's third stage is evident when the child's curiosity is no longer satisfied by asking someone else the question. "When the child continues to entertain it," Dewey wrote, "and to be alert for whatever will help answer it, curiosity has become a positive intellectual force" (p. 33). Dewey stressed that the child's interest in a question or problem is stimulated by observing things and collecting material; no one has handed the problem over to the child.

Stage three will not unfold of its own accord, but teachers have an ally—in Dewey's words, "the open-minded and flexible wonder of childhood" (p. 33). The trouble is that this natural gift is easily lost. If "not used and cultivated at the right moment" (p. 33), Dewey warned, the wonder that germinates problems tends to disappear or weaken. Although there are individuals whose intellectual curiosity is not easily discouraged, "in most its edge is easily dulled and blunted" (p. 33). According to Dewey, schools cannot create this natural resource, but neither should they allow it to wane. The teacher's task is

> to keep alive the sacred spark of wonder and to fan the flame that already glows. His problem is to protect the spirit of inquiry, to keep it from being blasé from overexcitement, wooden from routine, fossilized through dogmatic instruction or dissipated by random exercise upon trivial things. (p. 34)

The implications for discipline are clear. The youngster whose curiosity has become a positive intellectual force is engaged in looking further and is, thus, behaving appropriately. Control is natural. On the other hand, the youngster who is discouraged by the curriculum from looking further into problems or questions stimulated by personal interest or observation, may be bored silly by so-called "developmental activities." Boredom has always been the greatest enemy of discipline.

Some schools and homes have done an excellent job of fanning the flame of wonder, and children have become so interested in a question that they will engage in an uphill struggle to discover the answer. In some high school science programs, for example, students must find a laboratory for their research and may have to endure being turned down repeatedly before they find one. This excerpt from a newspaper item is illustrative:

> Matthew has been collecting rocks since he was 4 years old, amassing a collection that has overtaken his room at home. As he got older he read voraciously about rocks and talked to other rock collectors. When he was in the eighth grade he discovered fluorescent rocks, which glow under ultraviolet light. No one knew what caused the glow, and his curiosity was piqued.
>
> He went to several laboratories in the Los Angeles area, but was turned away by many of them for his high school research. . . . At one university, they told him their equipment was too expensive to "let just anybody off the street" use it, a reaction many high school students get.
>
> Then he went to the Gemological Institute of America, a gem grading organization in Santa Monica. They welcomed his research. (Newman, 1996, p. B8)

Matthew McCann, a high school senior from California, was a finalist in the Westinghouse Science Talent search, for his project on the mineral calcite (the rock that glows). For most of the students in this high school science competition, winning was not as important as experiencing "the greater joy of asking a question and discovering the answer" (p. B8). Dewey (1916) pointed out that "the mass of pupils are never going to become scientific specialists" (p. 258), yet it is important that they learn what scientific method is, so that they can use it not just in science but in a wider context—as the way, for example, of treating everyday problems.

Obviously, students should investigate a problem because they are curious. "And it is safe to say," Dewey wrote, "that the few who go on to be scientific experts will have a better preparation than if they had been swamped with a large mass of purely technical and symbolically stated information" (p. 258). This is the "psychological" (p. 258) approach and requires time—more than is needed merely to memorize material from texts. According to Dewey, the time "is more than made up for by the superior understanding and vital interest secured" (p. 258). In this connection, it is interesting but hardly surprising that the Westinghouse contest winners "tend to be from the schools that permit students the time and resources to pursue such work" (Newman, 1996, p. B8).

All of this bears directly on Dewey's third stage. School programs can breathe life into learners' longtime interests and questions. Beginning as a rock collector, Matthew looked further; his school provided appropriate conditions for Dewey's third stage. As Dewey (1933a) characterized this stage: "A distant end controls a sequence of inquiries and observations and binds them together as a means to an end" (p. 39). Finally, the curriculum itself should generate new interests and problems that pique children's curiosity.

STAGES OF DISCIPLINE

Figure 7.1 presents a developmental sequence of three stages of discipline. The figure represents an extension of the ideas in Dewey's stages and also is based on approved practices in education. In this proposed model, both children and teachers have specific responsibilities at each stage of discipline. According to Tyler (1991):

> Personal and social responsibility were expected of every person and group involved in the Dewey School operation. When a student believed that he or she was responsible for learning what the schools were expected to teach much more of the desired learning took place than when the student believed that it was the teacher's responsibility to make him or her learn. When the teacher believed that he or she was responsible for stimulating and getting student learning much more of the desired learning took place than when the teacher believed that his or her responsibility was to make assignments and hear recitations. (p. 5)

FIGURE 7.1 Developmental Stages of Discipline

Stage	Child's Responsibility	Teacher's Role
Stage I (Personal and Social Interest Stage)	Listens to teacher and to other members of the group; exchanges information and experiences with others, and helps others to understand a new idea; shares in planning the day's work and in delegating responsibilities; shares in reviewing the results; when dissatisfied with something he or she has made or done, asks the teacher for guidance; knows how to share materials and resources; channels energies constructively	Draws out each child's viewpoint about procedures for carrying out activities; ensures that the daily plan is workable and sufficiently different to supply a new experience involving a group problem; is alert for opportunities for development; provides expert and specialized direction; helps child to judge behavior in terms of the work to be done; is a good role model
Stage II (Means–End Stage)	Recognizes the needs and rights of others; understands the basis for all reasonable organizational rules and procedures; has formed habits of working in an orderly way (as with a series of steps) to accomplish something; asks for help in getting skills in a particular direction; sees that his or her part of an activity is accomplished; helps others when asked; treats furniture and other equipment with care; appreciates difficulties that people who lived in earlier times had	Provides opportunities to solve real problems, past and present; allows children enough flexibility to go on with work in which they have a vivid interest; is alert for opportunities for the necessary use of skills; does not rely on general procedures to meet the needs of all children; uses redirection as an instructional procedure and to rechannel energy; uses incidents of daily life and the curriculum to develop the concept of justice; is a good role model
Stage III (Generative Stage)	Is personally and socially responsible, and demonstrates leadership; upholds the concept of justice; conceptualizes a problem, generates and tests solutions, continues with the project despite confusion and difficulty; takes responsibility for directing his or her own learning	Fans the flame of curiosity; provides opportunities to observe persons whose life work is discovery; helps students to conceptualize a problem and develop plans of action; provides students with the ego strength needed for autonomous principled action; is a good role model

The purpose of the model proposed here is not to present an exhaustive list of child and teacher roles and responsibilities, but to provide examples. The child's responsibilities are matched with teacher functions at each stage of development. The idea is to answer in some measure an important teacher need: knowledge of what teachers should emphasize or provide in their classrooms to help children get to each stage. One point of importance: The ideas in this book are all of a piece. Dewey's conception of discipline (the capacity for sustained attention) should be considered together with his theories on the nature of the child (whose interests supply the energy for learning), instruction (centered on the problem to be dealt with), and the total school environment (including school organization). These ideas underlie the responsibilities of child and teacher described in this section.

As seen in the figure, the three stages in the developmental sequence are the *personal and social interest* stage, the *means–ends* stage, and the *generative* stage.

Stage I: Personal and Social Interest Stage. Children in this stage begin to develop "the power for continuous attention" (Dewey, 1916, p. 162) by having interests. In a sense this is the child's responsibility, but it is one that a child can't help having. Children are naturally interested in the real world; the attention demanded by engaging in it is also natural. Dewey does not call this self-control because it is a giving out rather than a holding in. As Baker (1955) pointed out, in Dewey's school control was also the outcome of "daily, even hourly interchange of ideas among teachers and children, where purposes were formed and plans were made to execute them" (p. 152). As shown in the figure, control also stemmed from a workable daily plan. One did not—and should not—leave this to chance. According to the teachers, a daily plan that worked was best ensured by answering questions and a "skilful [*sic*] refreshing of the children's memories" (Mayhew & Edwards, 1936, p. 305).

These ideas still make good sense. Plans are not likely to work out unless they are on everyone's front burner and there is constant checking to see if they are working out or, maybe, need to be revised a bit. (The alternative is an unmet purpose, and possibly a group that is out of control.) Moreover, children's minds are most likely to grow if plans are weighed against earlier experiences. The plans, after all, spring from the spirit of inquiry. Children are learning habits of control and getting experience in the fundamentals of reflective thinking. The two are, of course, inseparable.

Finally, everyone's viewpoint counts in a democratic society. Drawing out a child's point of view about procedures for carrying out a plan enfolds the child in the community group and provides focus.

Stage II: Means–Ends Stage. A child in the means–ends stage has formed the habit of judging his behavior in connection with the work that he has to accomplish. This is a healthy standard for the child, on which the teacher should put emphasis. Stated somewhat differently, acts that are concerned with the problem to be met and solved are the right ones. Problem behavior can stem from an inflexible schedule, where children are well into the procedures for reaching a goal but are torn away by the school program. As the figure indicates, a teacher's (and school's) role is to provide flexibility. The idea of consciously relating means to ends should be emphasized throughout the curriculum. There are rules for reaching a result in any field, whether art or science, and this general idea can be useful as the child progresses through a curriculum that becomes increasingly differentiated and could leave the child without a sense of being in control.

Asking for help is not always easy for a child and yet that is perhaps the most vital communication in the face-to-face contact of teacher and child— vital for learning and behavior. Although children should help one another, they must receive expert guidance from their teacher. There are at least two reasons for this: The teacher is—or should be—a specialist and, more important perhaps, the child's questions or problems are developmental clues to be acted upon. The child may need a new skill or may even have dawning interests that can enrich the child's life. Surely the teacher should know about them, for this is what it means to be a teacher.

Finally, how much more stimulating for children to approach material as original thinkers than to feel that all there is to know has already been found out. As everyone knows, there are two kinds of problems: those that have been solved and those that have not. As Dewey pointed out, to put oneself in the place of someone long ago who had a problem to solve does not make the solution less original. It is still the child's. "All thinking whatsoever," Dewey (1910) wrote, "so be it *is* thinking, contains a phase of originality" (p. 198). We do not want children to feel that the answers are already in for any field of study, and that is what happens when material is presented "with dogmatic finality and rigidity" (p. 198). Dewey warned that when that happens, children "may continue as docile pupils, but they cease to be students" (p. 198). Docility is not what we are after, thinking is. To be a student is to think and to think is to approach material with originality. In Dewey's words:

> Originality means personal interest in the question, personal initiative in turning over the suggestions followed by others and sincerity in following them out to a tested conclusion. (p. 198)

As discussed earlier, some schools have rediscovered (or reinvented) this instructional approach, but it still has not been widely accepted. Meanwhile, much instruction is finalities handed down. It is flat—like soda with all the bubbles gone out.

However, the opportunities to practice problem solving should include unsolved problems, too. To make sure that the process and the spirit of demo-

cratic citizenship are instilled in children, they need practice with real school
and community problems. It cannot be emphasized enough that this includes
the action and testing phases. "Test and see" was, in a sense, the motto of the
Dewey school (for teachers as well as children). It still speaks to us, if we will
but listen. Children feel that the school is theirs and treat it with care. It is
interesting that while we stress the importance of not spoiling our world, things
like school furniture are rarely mentioned in the same breath. In Dewey's
school, making over and repairing chairs (an activity of interest to children)
had great transferable value.

Stage III: Generative Stage. As shown in the figure, individuals at the generative stage are self-directing. They focus their attention on an end in view
and what needs to be done to attain the result. Here the difference compared
with the means–ends stage is in degree rather than kind: Children in both can
follow the steps to solve a problem. But this is not the whole story: While
children at the means–ends stage can solve a problem, at the generative stage
they can conceptualize a problem. The teacher's matching responsibility is to
furnish experiences and materials that generate real problems. Reaching the
generative stage is a growth process requiring certain kinds of activity for the
earlier stages. "Only when thinking is constantly employed in using the senses
and muscles for the guidance and application of observation and movements,
is the way prepared for subsequent higher types of thinking," said Dewey
(1910, p. 66). At the generative stage, the child's original, natural gifts have
evolved through continuous use into "the trained power of thought" (p. 66).

A problem observed by teachers (including university teachers) is that
students often fail to suspend judgment until all the possibilities that arise are
consecutively followed up on and the evidence has been examined. Again,
Dewey's counsel bears upon a present problem. "The only way to achieve traits
of carefulness, thoroughness, and continuity," he said, "is by exercising these
traits from the beginning, and by seeing to it that conditions call for their
exercise" (p. 66). One conclusion to be drawn here is that we will not help
children's development if we rest content with the notion that sloppy and
inaccurate work represents an early stage of development. It is often better
seen as a bad habit in the making. Development in discipline—close and patient
attention to details—should start early as it did in Dewey's school. It starts
with the confidence in one's own powers that comes from face-to-face contact with a teacher who conveys care and interest in the child. As we all know,
it takes just one adult to make a difference in a child's life, and how much
better if that teacher treats discipline and learning as a single process.

❖ 8 ❖

Lessons Learned

The everyday work of the school shows that children can live in school as out of it, and yet grow daily in wisdom, kindness, and the spirit of obedience—that learning may, even with little children, lay hold upon the substance of truth that nourishes the spirit, and yet the forms of knowledge be observed and cultivated; and that growth may be genuine and thorough, and yet a delight.

—John Dewey, *The School and Society*

"THE LESSON OF KINDNESS surpasses all." So wrote a father in a poem of appreciation to his daughter's second-grade teacher at the close of the 1936–37 school year. As he recognized, simply urging children to be kind will not teach the lesson; if children are to grow in kindness, they need models. An important social contribution of progressive schools was the kind treatment of children. I was that little girl—I attended a public school in Grand Rapids, Michigan.

Each of the lessons from Dewey's school, as described in the previous chapters, stands on its own but they all fit together. In fact, one thing seems quite naturally to lead to (or require) another. For example, a problem bedeviling many schools today is how to connect the child with the subject. Based on their reports, the Dewey teachers would say that the connection starts with experiences that reflect subject matter as the outcome of human activities and problems. There should be a human connection simply because there is one. In many schools today it is still not being brought out; there is a curtain of mystery separating the child from the subject. The interest of children in an activity with which they can connect leads to problem identification. Children learn to think through practice in solving problems, but children must be allowed to do their own thinking in their own way and not according to the teacher's rigid scheme prepared in advance. This requires that children be treated as individuals. If this is to happen, the flexibility that is supposed to be accorded to children should be accorded to teachers. Policies that view teachers as technicians are incompatible with the reality of children's individual differences. Children's social sensitivity can be developed or improved by learning to live with others in a miniature community, but this idea will not suffice; the curriculum should be geared to the social experience of humankind. Dewey's curriculum was focused on the common problems and experiences of all people, and it is time—the dangers of divisiveness having shown themselves—that we give consideration to his way.

A good curriculum is developmentally appropriate and developmental. It begins with the way that children see the world—in a unified fashion—and becomes more specialized as they learn facts and concepts in various subject fields and the subjects gradually emerge in their minds as entities. Even when this happens, learners should be encouraged to find relationships between various subjects of study. Good teachers plan so that youngsters systematically are led to do so and they imbue the material with a feeling of reality "by being intermingled with the realities of everyday life" (Dewey, 1916, p. 192).

In a good elementary school, the teachers are specialists in the subject fields so that children have accurate and up-to-date knowledge and can draw upon teachers' expertise in solving problems. (As noted, this idea of Dewey's has long been resisted.) Subject matter is not isolated because the school has a definite and prominent vertical theme that holds the curriculum together. This is as necessary for the curriculum as a spine is to a person. A civilizational theme provides opportunities to progressively acquaint youngsters with human problems and possibilities and gives them a sense of being constructive participants in the continuing saga of humankind. This feeling of kinship and future possibility comes from reproducing life situations, and if the teaching is good, the concepts in the school subjects are seen in their proper everyday life setting. The connection between the child and the subject is strengthened.

An organizing theme is absolutely necessary but it is not enough to unify the curriculum. Teachers should be in continual contact with one another. They should be free to say that a certain approach did not work out so that they can begin again with a different tack. Inflexible plans are the enemy of school improvement. Likewise, a poor fit between the child and a learning activity is the enemy of school discipline. The teacher may have to redirect the child's activity. This is one reason why a child is not the teacher; although children can learn from one another, they (obviously) do not have the professional knowledge to substitute one activity for another having the same purpose, nor are they in a position to identify emerging talents and do something about it. (Today we set great store in children as teachers, but this idea does have its limitations.)

In any book, one's last chapter is one's last chance. I will discuss the lessons that seem to have priority, and make some suggestions based on Dewey's school and its underlying ideas as they seem to relate to our present problems and possibilities.

HANDS-ON ACTIVITY IN THE ELEMENTARY SCHOOL

One thing that made Dewey's Laboratory School a wonderful school was the hands-on activities. They forged a tactile link between the child and the curriculum. What better connection could there be than a three-dimensional one? The hands-on activities were also a curriculum unifier; when children made things, they learned history, science, and mathematics through invention. Science, art, and culture were one. There was thinking involved of the most fundamental kind: continuous observation of materials, planning, and use of the hands. The thing that was cultivated was the mind's eye. There were appreciations as well, for beautiful objects and inventions, because one learned at first hand how hard it is to make them and the thought involved.

Technology and the Curriculum

Today children just punch the computer—they do not make anything. It is just a single-dimensional, flat screen. Hands-on activity, when it does occur, tends to be in science only, whereas in Dewey's school it was across the curriculum—related to the organizing theme. Technology, as Dewey (1897a) clearly recognized, continues to evolve and children must have the kind of education that will enable them to understand its impact on society—the problems as well as the possibilities. Today many educators have allowed themselves to fall into thinking that the main curriculum problem presented by technology is whether teachers successfully can "integrate technology into their curricula" (Apple Computer, Inc., 1995, p. 1), as advertised by the computer companies. Granted that, as one writer has pointed out, "no one seems quite sure how to weave such an amorphous mass of unedited information into teaching" (MacFarquhar, 1996, p. B1), the curriculum problem of greater import is technology's influence, for better or for worse, on social life. This is absolutely the same problem that Dewey dealt with in his school. Understanding the influence of industrial change was important for the child's education and still is because people continue to invent marvelous things.

In the closing years of the twentieth century, concern has been focused on how to use technology in teaching; currently the other problem is almost buried in the razzle dazzle of making schools high tech. Yet, there are voices calling attention to the problem, much as it was diagnosed by Dewey in *The School and Society* (1899). In words recalling Dewey's of a century ago, the English educator, John Abbott (1995), wrote:

> The Industrial Age, by mechanizing production and reorganizing the workplace into large factory units, effectively destroyed this pattern of life that had evolved over millennia, and that saw living, working, and learning as a single interconnected entity. (p. 6)

As Abbott pointed out, "this earlier world is hard to imagine. Yet its achievements were immense" (p. 6). The problems created by the achievements were also immense; children in Dewey's Laboratory School learned about both. According to Abbott, young people in the early years of the nineteenth century, before the industrial revolution, "were imbued with the importance of trusting their own judgment . . . [and] sought to make themselves and their products ever better." Further, there was "an underlying philosophy that if a job is worth doing it is worth doing well" (p. 6). Dewey tried in his school to capture these values from the earlier world.

However, according to Abbott, being "creative and personally enterprising" cannot be learned in the classroom. "Instead," he argued, "[these attributes] largely grow from experiences of an active life, and require a far broader base than a classroom" (p. 8). Needless to say, Dewey would disagree. His idea of a good school was one that permitted a child to lead an active life. Children could develop the same values and competencies that Abbott wrote about, by rediscovering and carrying out an industrial process step by step in light of historical background and effects on community life. Such was the approach followed in children's study of the textile industries in Dewey's school. There is no reason why it could not be followed today—going beyond the industrial age, of course, through our own age of science and technology. There are good reasons why it should be followed.

Curriculum Balance. One reason is simply the need for a balanced curriculum—something that is all too easy to forget when test scores are the first priority, and how technology can be used more effectively in classrooms, a close second. Interest and achievement are not improved by an unbalanced curriculum—one without hands-on activity. In fact, they can be the casualty of such a curriculum. Dewey was deeply concerned with curriculum balance; his concept of balance is interesting. In his school, children took a variety of subjects. Along with the major fields of knowledge, they studied modern foreign languages, music, dramatics, and the fine and manual arts—nor were they shortchanged when it came to physical education. One could call it a balanced curriculum and one would be right. For Dewey, however, there was more involved; not only should the curriculum as a whole be balanced, but there should be balance within topics; for example, in the study of occupations, children's activities were intellectual and practical (hands-on). Based on his school's experience, Dewey (1900c) stressed the need to keep "a balance between the intellectual and practical phases of experience" (p. 82). From the teachers' reports, it is evident that there was a balance. Today there is a definite need to bring in industrial arts—hands-on work—in the elementary school. It is developmentally sound and a way of generating lasting interests of the healthful kind.

Return of the Mind's Eye. Another reason is that hands-on activity is a thinking tool. In the final decades of the nineteenth century, there was much interest in manual training or hand education. What is enormously important is that it was considered by its originators to be a fundamental part of everyone's education. This was very different from training for a certain trade. Furthermore, it was thought to be helpful in improving intellectual ability—"quite as much as the conventional symbols of language and quantity improved motor activity" (Butts & Cremin, 1953, p. 383). The interest in manual training fit well with Dewey's idea that the child's impulse to construct is uninvested capital for learning facts and concepts in the subject fields. Although in the Laboratory School manual training was part of general or cultural education in that children learned to use tools, it was first and foremost a thinking tool.

As Ryan (1995) pointed out, "Dewey's main intellectual concept was that of a 'problem.' Individuals and societies alike are stirred into life by problems" (p. 28). Children in Dewey's school were stirred into constructive activity by problems; it was natural and developmental and they learned how to think. What is more, they actually acquired new concepts and generalizations in the subject fields, something that even the most avid manual training enthusiasts did not often advertise as an outcome. (They mostly spoke of intellectual development in general.)

Over the years the mind–body dualism that Dewey did away with in his school persisted in other schools and the ancient prejudice against handwork prevailed. "When schools are equipped with laboratories, shops and gardens," wrote Dewey in 1916, "where dramatizations, plays, and games are freely used, opportunities exist for reproducing situations of life, and for acquiring and applying information and ideas in carrying forward of progressive experiences" (p. 191). Today elementary schools with shops and gardens are as rare as if Dewey's Laboratory School had never existed. In secondary schools there has actually been a reduction in opportunities to develop practical problem-solving skills through hands-on activities. In teaching industrial arts, schools are using software instead of real hands-on experiences. Enrollments in such courses have declined steeply—as much as 40% in some schools (Davis & Reid, 1996). Academically talented students also should have opportunities to develop problem-solving skills through hands-on projects. Such projects should be a part of everyone's education. A teacher from a school district that closed its high school power technology/metal shop predicted that educators and policy makers would recognize again that all children need to develop "three-dimensional problem-solving and practical skills" (Rannels, 1991, p. 457).

There is evidence of this recognition, although it has in no way coalesced into a movement. There is in some fields, engineering, for example, renewed interest in the "mind's eye" and its importance in designing a system. According to Ferguson (1992), engineering design begins with visualizing an idea that the designer carries out with the mind's eye. The point of interest to us is that the models and drawings are thinking tools and also means of communication. This would be as true in the elementary school as in the engineering school—it certainly was in the Laboratory School. In fact, Dewey (1900b) made a similar point in his article on the educational use of occupations almost a century earlier. One does not think for its own sake; there must be a difficulty or a need to be met. One reflects on what might be the best way to overcome it—leading "to planning, to projecting mentally the result to be reached" (p. 83). The idea that is manipulated with the mind's eye is tried. In Dewey's school these activities were carried out collaboratively; children made various suggestions to facilitate whatever the process happened to be. A point made by Ferguson is of interest here: The computer cannot substitute for intimate (firsthand) knowledge of the system being designed. Translated to the elementary school, punching buttons on a computer is no substitute for carrying out a process, if children are to truly learn to think.

Expanding Intellectual Horizons and Improving Behavior Through the Manual Arts

One of the most remarkable contributions of the school was to show how children's hands-on activity can expand their intellectual horizons. Dewey (1900b) had a powerful outcome in mind. He wanted the child to recognize that people have, through necessity and ingenuity, improved and enriched the conditions of living and in the course of their work "have been awakened to the sense of their own powers—have been led to invent, to plan, and rejoice in the acquisition of skill" (p. 84). Actually, the hoped-for outcome was more than intellectual—it had to do with the child's outlook on life, with character. Dewey believed that human nature was the outcome of experience, and the hands-on experiences for individual youngsters could bring out the appreciations that are inseparable from constructive social power. He wanted children to develop this power.

Manual Training in Dewey's School. Dewey and his gifted teachers showed us what is possible; children learned by theme-related activity in which they had to think out their own model and work plan. They engaged in collaborative inquiry—working out difficulties and figuring out through experimentation how something could be done. This was manual training—the problems were three-dimensional. Hands-on activity that is tied to a theme is vastly different from manual training with an emphasis on the physical skills involved: mastering the use of tools or producing an object. The difference was clarified by Dewey (1900b) for educators in his day. Although manual training was offered in Dewey's school, it was never simply to teach children to use tools. The work in the shop correlated with the other departments; it was an integral part of the curriculum. "I am sure that weaving is more interesting to the children because they can make their looms and spindles in the shop," wrote Frank Ball (1900, p. 184), who headed up the shopwork. "Their history does not become dull because they have made in miniature the same things that the people they have been studying about made. They encounter and appreciate the difficulties that the early people had" (p. 184).

The teachers made good use of the shop. In their book, under the heading "manual training," Mayhew and Edwards (1936) described such activities. For example, in connection with the theme "progress through invention and discovery," a group of children the age of today's third graders became interested in the development of navigation:

> In the shop, a rude boat was made. The principle of how to overcome friction as much as possible by a pointed bow and stern was worked out, and the boat contrasted with the flat one made the year before by burning a dugout. The question of how a sail worked, especially in sailing against the wind was solved. (p. 123)

Another year, children studying the problems that the Phoenicians had to solve to improve the comfort of their lives discussed the kinds of houses that they would build as a tribe. Mayhew and Edwards (1936) relate:

> [It] was decided that stone might be used, since there was such an abundance. The question of how it could be made to stick together was brought up and led to a discussion of lime in its native state and its use as mortar. The children then turned into masons, made mortar boxes, trowels, and a sand sieve in the shop. Lime was procured, and experiments were carried on to demonstrate the effect of water upon it. Mortar was made and used to build a typical house of that time and region. (p. 123)

We are left with the impression that the activities for which the school was justly famous would not have been possible without the shop. A second impression is the striking realness of the curriculum—something that is lacking today in most elementary schools and, unfortunately, that few are looking for. Problem solving tends to remain at the discussion level for most children in school. In Dewey's Laboratory School, however, information was put to use. Children raised questions that were answered by experiments. Mayhew and Edwards wrote about children of this age (7- and 8-year-olds): "From this time on, the child can realize that an experiment is a definite question, the answer to which is to be used in the process out of which it arose" (p. 126). The point is an important one and concerns something that most educators recognize as an approved practice but many do not practice. (As

Philip Jackson (1981) pointed out, the application of professional knowledge is what separates the good schools from the bad.) Children should develop a consciousness of the use of knowledge to improve a process or a situation, and good schools provide such opportunities. Without them education remains lifeless, and holding children's interest and attention is less likely.

Gender and Hands-on Work: A Lesson from Dewey's School. In the closing decades of the twentieth century great gains were made in creating equity in the curriculum. Yet, the gender gap continues in technology education. Despite efforts to increase the enrollments of girls in high school technology courses, the percentage of girls is very low—often less than 10%. The fact that technology "is a major key to success in America" (Gloeckner & Knowlton, 1996, p. 47) makes the major enrollment differences unacceptable in a democratic society that is obligated to provide all students with access to the curriculum—including equitable treatment in all subjects.

Researchers have identified a number of factors in the career choices of females. Some have to do with expectations about competency. In her work, Linn (1994) found that "all members of the group with a larger membership are expected to be more competent than all members of the group with a smaller membership" (p. 766). Thus, since more men are in technology, they must be better than female technologists, or so the argument would go. Expectations have a reinforcing effect on enrollments; many girls also believe that male technologists are better—when they stop to think about it at all. Therein lies the problem: Many high school girls never think about technology as a field because they have no background or experience in this area.

What does our knowledge base in the field of curriculum tell us about developing interest in technology? It should begin in kindergarten with constructive and expressive activities that are related to the curriculum. Throughout their elementary school experience, children should have opportunities to develop practical problem-solving skills through hands-on projects. As Charol Shakeshaft (1995) pointed out, this is particularly important for girls; boys have more out-of-school experiences in making things, which gives them familiarity with tools and the sciences. All children need these experiences, but in the case of girls the effect of not having them shows up later in lack of interest and confidence. If curriculum-related manual training is brought into the elementary school, there is less likelihood that the courses will be segregated by sex in middle school and high school, because a foundation will have been laid for later technical education.

In Dewey's school a century ago, girls as well as boys took manual training in the lower grades. Their teacher wrote when the program had been in operation for 5 years:

There is no reason why girls should not have this training as well as boys, and experience has proved that in this, as in the other departments of the school, they are as expert and often more painstaking. (Ball, 1900, p. 178)

INTEREST AND MOTIVATION

In his Laboratory School, Dewey found that if children were interested in something, they would go very far with it. Today, to talk about the relation of interest and effort seems to belabor the obvious. The same may be said about individual differences; the fact that each individual differs from every other is so well established that it seems almost too embarrassing to point out—it isn't, because both of these ideas still meet with resistance. Dewey noted that these two ideas are "still temperamentally abhorrent" to many teachers and parents, and that "[a] great many others are willing to admit them when stated in general terms, but feel the strongest emotional reluctance to giving children the benefit of them by applying them to teaching methods" (1933b, p. 443). Unfortunately, this is also the case today; however, now as then, there are teachers who apply them.

Why are these ideas not more widely applied? There are many reasons, but I will mention only three here. First, teachers still do not have the necessary supporting conditions—one of the most obvious being class size. Oddly, the next two reasons also have to do, at least indirectly, with support for teachers. The second reason is that until recently researchers have shown little interest in the relation between children's interests and motivation to learn. In fact, in the 1970s and 1980s the word *motivation* all but dropped out of the teacher education literature. Interest as a concept did not fare much better. On the other hand, the term *behavior modification* did appear often (motivation and interest are beside the point in operant conditioning theory.) As Krapp, Hidi, and Renninger (1992) pointed out, many researchers "under the influence of behaviorism chose . . . to avoid the interest concept entirely" (p. 4). Third, our national and state policies for improving education have not been concerned with making children more interested and able to learn. The preferred strategy has been to set goals and standards for achievement.

In 1989, national goals were set by the nation's governors in terms of "will learn," as if learning can be ordered and it will happen automatically. The target was the year 2000. By early 1996, it was acknowledged that the goals would not be met by the year 2000. Feeling that the goals were not specific enough, the nation's governors and corporate leaders decided to "move from broadly defined goals to rigorous, specific standards for student achievement" (Applebome, 1996a, p. B8). The idea was given endorsement by President

Clinton, who advised that the rigorous standards be enforced with state competency tests (Applebome, 1996b, p. B10). Whether goals are stated broadly
or there are specific standards for proficiency, the problem remains the same:
how students can learn. One cannot simply order achievement; this approach
has never worked and I see no reason to expect that it ever will. As the educator Richard Gibboney pointed out, education is not "a factory with tightly
fitting gears and a big handle outside the walls that you wind up" and "you
turn the handle faster and more widgets come out. Well schools don't work
that way" (quoted in Applebome, 1996a, p. B8). "Individual effort is impossible without individual interest," Dewey (1933b, p. 444) warned. It is individuals we are talking about here as well as schools. No one expects government and corporate leaders to have professional knowledge in the field of
education, but a group of policy makers should be representative concerning
the needs and problems of schools—for example, problems of student motivation and teacher morale.

The point is that one of the reasons why teachers have not applied ideas
about the relation of interest and effort more widely is because demands on
the schools have supported a different model of the student—the automatic
learner. This has left the teacher to wrestle with the awful truth: There is no
such thing. What results when a child is uninterested in work is an energy-
consuming struggle. As Dewey (1993b) pointed out, these youngsters do not
put forth their "best efforts" because they cannot:

> However hard [the child] may work at it, the effort does not go into the accom-
> plishment of the work, but is largely dissipated in a moral and emotional struggle
> to keep the attention where it is not held. (p. 444)

Whatever the pressures on schools, educators can avoid the energy-
consuming struggle and help children by applying the ideas from Dewey's
school. One is that if a child is interested in her work, she is likely to know
what is going on and, what is more, to proceed in that work without picky
and sometimes distracting orders from the teacher. Dewey wrote:

> Psychological investigations have proved that learning is better and faster when
> the learner understands his problem as a whole and does his work under his own
> motive power rather than under minute, piecemeal dictation from a boss. (1933b,
> p. 446)

Recent investigations have continued to confirm these early findings
(Mitchell, 1993; Snow, 1989; Vispoel & Austin, 1995). Whatever the agenda
of policy makers outside the school—and it may be political, "showing a commitment to keeping education on the nation's agenda" (Applebome, 1996a,

p. B8)—in good schools teachers improve learning by making the work interesting.

Finally, as Ralph Tyler (1986) so wisely observed, some people "are able to translate external pressures into constructive responses . . . into forces supporting far-sighted educational improvements" (p. 78). Applying Dewey's discovery about the relation between interest and effort, since confirmed by others, would be a constructive response with lasting benefit for children and our society.

The Return of Interest in Interest

With the rediscovery of Dewey (Ryan, 1995), there has been a growing interest and respect for his concept of interest. Dewey's book, *Interest and Effort in Education* (1913), has been a gold mine for researchers and is widely cited in their work. Clearly, it is still the definitive study of this subject. Dewey expected that others would build and, hopefully, improve upon the work of his school (Mayhew & Edwards, 1936). *Interest and Effort in Education* was based on that work.

Research on Interest

Researchers have approached Dewey's conception from both theoretical and practical vantage points. On the theoretical side, some have sought to move away from the general concept of interest and have proposed distinctions between different kinds of interests. Practically, they wonder how teachers can be more successful at interesting their students and have sought to identify instructional approaches used by teachers who are successful. In general, the latter studies simply have confirmed the soundness of the procedures followed by Dewey and the teachers. For example, in his study involving high school mathematics students, Mitchell (1993) concluded that "the more students perceive themselves as active learners rather than as passive absorbers of knowledge, the more a classroom environment will persist as a mathematics interest holder" (p. 434). Mitchell found that the students in his study "felt involved when they got to do activities in order to learn new material, rather than sitting and listening" (p. 428). He stressed that doing so means that "students are active participants in the learning of new material . . . working on a project, writing book chapters, learning new concepts with carefully structured group work" (p. 428) rather than mechanical drill. This is an echo from Dewey's Laboratory School, where the teachers were careful to see that children continually were learning something new—that the day's activities did not repeat what was done the day before but built on it. Those were elementary school children, but the idea is the same at any level. The importance of Mitchell's work for us here is that he empirically tested Dewey's ideas that interest stems from the students' active involvement with what is to be learned and that learning is a dynamic and moving process—fresh experiences connected with previous experiences—and found them to be valid.

Unfortunately, the interpretations and extensions of Dewey's concept of interest often differ markedly from the original and may be of little use to anyone who wants to apply lessons from the Laboratory School. For example, some researchers have put forward the proposal that there are two kinds of interests—personal or individual interests, which the learner brings to school, and "situational" interests, which are intentionally developed in a planned educational environment (Hidi, 1990; Hidi & Baird, 1988; Krapp, 1989). According to Andreas Krapp of the Universitat der Bundeswehr (Munich), since the teacher has no influence over children's incoming interests, the teacher's concern is situational interest. As Mitchell (1993) points out, the idea of categorizing interests in such an arbitrary fashion is in itself open to question—indeed, there is no basis for "the tenability of this proposal" (p. 425). Even if there were, there is a serious problem with dividing interests along the lines of in-school and out-of-school: The exact same dichotomy is created that Dewey was trying to break down in his school. Also, there is the matter of a developmental curriculum, which begins with the child's natural interests and activities; these are neither individual nor situational, but universal. The young child is a unitary being, and so are the child's interests. Dewey sought to maintain the unity of self—no small order—but splitting the concept of interest is not the way. What we inevitably get is first-class and second-class interests—school interests being the preferred ones. There is yet another problem here: To get into dichotomies (or create them) is to enter dangerous territory where education in a democratic society is concerned. In the United States, the development of children's individual interests is or should be a concern of the schools, for such interests can have social value as well as contribute to individuals' happiness. As Dewey suggested, it is up to the teacher to determine which interests are prized by the wider community and worthy of cultivation by the school.

For older students as well, it would be impossible to categorize some interests as either personal or situational. Take, for instance, a finalist in the Westinghouse Science Talent Search for her project in astronomy. She had always been curious about the stars but the curiosity was brought to a focus by a school-related activity, a trip to an observatory (Newman, 1996). This was the approach to interests in Dewey's school; children were not asked to leave their worlds at home, but those worlds were systematically opened into a universe of interests and understandings. The proposal for a distinction between personal and situational interests is not based on ideas that were applied in the Laboratory School.

As Lee Cronbach (1981), who was a pioneer in the field of educational evaluation, pointed out, Dewey "said some things that were fairly clear as a guide for the elementary school" (p. 49). What is needed now is to find ways of helping teachers to apply them in their classrooms.

THE TEACHER: WHAT HAVE WE LEARNED FROM DEWEY'S SCHOOL?

The teacher's role was to improve instruction by gearing it to children's growth stages—an entirely new approach to school improvement in the 1890s. The stages themselves did not take shape until the school's fifth year, but working out a curriculum that harmonized with and facilitated growth was the problem that occupied the teachers from the beginning. The curriculum development roles of the Dewey teachers and teachers today, although they have somewhat different purposes, have much in common. It is true that the main interest of Dewey and the teachers was a new curriculum organization based on child growth, while that of teachers today is improving student learning. Yet, are these purposes really so different? A curriculum based on knowledge about various periods of a child's life most certainly would serve to improve learning. We, like the Dewey teachers, are concerned with curriculum reconstruction because of the vast increase in knowledge. In the closing years of the nineteenth century, Dewey observed that "the accumulation of knowledge has become so great that the educational system is disintegrating through the wedges of studies continually introduced" (1896a, p. 354). Society was exerting pressure on high schools and colleges for more subjects and more time for them. Nor were elementary schools exempt. "It is finding its way into the primary grades, partly from social infiltration—partly from the continued pressure from above for such training below as will relieve the difficulties of the situation above," Dewey (p. 354) wrote. Again, we note a remarkable similarity with the educational situation today. In truth, the situation has not changed.

Dewey's plea that if the "increased demands" (p. 354) in all fields were to be met in secondary and higher education, approaches to instruction must be changed beginning in kindergarten, still begs to be heard. Dewey's response, as we know, was the developmental curriculum. Dewey's curriculum thought was vertical—there is no doubting this—and the teachers followed suit. We need more vertical thinking about the curriculum on the part of teachers today.

In the last analysis we, like our fascinating forebears from a century ago, are trying to make school a richer and more satisfying experience for every child. It is in the process that we differ quite strikingly.

Centrality of the Curriculum

The Dewey teachers were not loaded down with all of the paraphernalia of school improvement with which we often burden teachers and that distracts them from their main charge of educating children. The present-day involvement of teachers in making decisions at the building level that rarely concern the instructional program (but consume plenty of time nonetheless) was mentioned earlier. Such activities funnel off attention from instructional problems, such as how a child is led to recognize a problem as his own so that his attention is self-impelled, and how to create a coherent curriculum with a cumulative effect. The curriculum is the missing element in too many of our efforts at school reform. It is the thing that we *will* get to after the organizational change is made—but never do. In Dewey's Laboratory School, the curriculum was central. It was discussed by each teacher in weekly typewritten reports and it was also the main topic of discussion at meetings.

Getting Teachers to Think Vertically. The Dewey teachers had a clear sense of what came next in the curriculum. Perhaps this is because their curriculum development responsibilities made them think vertically, or because they were experts in their fields, for as Dewey (1904b) pointed out, a body of knowledge is by its own nature

> organized subject matter. It is not a miscellaneous heap of separate scraps. . . .
> Even if (as in the case of history and literature), it be not technically termed
> "science," it is none the less material which has been subjected to method—has
> been selected and arranged with reference to controlling intellectual principles.
> There is, therefore, method in subject-matter itself—method indeed of the highest order which the human mind has yet evolved, scientific method. (p. 22)

It is evident that a clear picture of the curriculum in its cumulative sense is necessary if we want the curriculum to have a cumulative effect. Indeed, there is something almost perverse about teachers who cannot see beyond their own grades or courses and who may be concerned, at best, with horizontal curriculum integration. Such teachers might be compared with a pedestrian who sees only a few feet ahead. Such people cannot be trusted to guide others; indeed, we fear for their own footing.

A need about which many persons in positions of educational leadership are not conscious (or appear not to be) is for teachers to have a longitudinal (consecutive) view of the curriculum. According to Dewey (1904b), the development of a longitudinal view will require changes in the preparation of preservice teachers, particularly as regards student teaching.

What is needed is the habit of viewing the entire curriculum as a continuous growth, reflecting the growth of mind itself. This in turn demands, so far as I can see, consecutive and longitudinal consideration of the curriculum of the elementary and high school rather than a cross-sectional view of it. The student should be led to see that the subject-matter in geography, nature-study, or art develops not merely day to day in a given grade, but from year to year throughout the entire movement of the school; and he should realize this before he gets much encouragement in trying to adapt subject-matter in lesson plans for this or that isolated grade. (p. 26)

This is still necessary for the professionalization of teaching.

A sense of the development of a subject comes from experience. Thus the student teacher's experience should be

intensive in purpose rather than spread out miscellaneously. . . . It is much more important for the teacher to assume responsibility for the consecutive development of some one topic, to get a feeling for the movement of that subject, than it is to teach a certain number (necessarily smaller in range) of lessons in a larger number of subjects. What we want, in other words, is not so much technical skill, as a realizing sense in the teacher of what the development of a subject means. (p. 28)

Dewey was arguing for what he called "the laboratory point of view" as opposed to the "apprenticeship" (p. 9) approach in the professional preparation of teachers. The objectives of each are very different. The apprenticeship idea has the purpose of giving teachers immediate skill in classroom management and instruction, whereas the laboratory idea (similar to training persons in other professions) provides intensive practice so that teachers have "*control of the intellectual methods* required for personal and independent mastery of practical skill" (p. 11). In other words, helping prospective teachers relate theory to practice comes first; developing skill in classroom routines, second—according to Dewey, after graduation. The point of importance is that the competence of teachers will never be ensured unless they are given responsibility for the consecutive development of a topic at the preservice level and understand how a subject develops year by year. Such experiences and understandings are rare.

As an educational leader, Dewey was in a position to make these suggestions based on the experience of his own school. Today in schools where the curriculum is of high quality, teachers and supervisors are engaged in continuous and systematic curriculum development to articulate the curriculum. Curriculum articulation is developed horizontally (between and among subject fields) and vertically (from grade level to grade level). It gives us pause for thought that these activities were carried on informally as well as formally in

Dewey's school in the 1890s. I, for one, appreciate the importance of his contribution of a powerful organizing vertical theme—the possibilities of which have yet to be realized. (Of course, the thought that they might be realized is one reason why I wrote this book.)

Starting Reform with the Curriculum. As noted earlier, Dewey's purpose in his school was to develop a curriculum that harmonized with child growth. His ultimate goal, as stated in the famous lines about the best and wisest parent, was to make America a land of opportunity for every child within its borders. The practical way to accomplish this was to provide children with an introduction to the best in the way of reliable knowledge and culture, and to do so in the active setting of a miniature society. Dewey stressed in his *Plan* that children's work "be so directed" that they will recognize its value for them "at the time, and not simply as a preparation for something else, or for a future life" (1895a, p. 2). The ideas were both stunning and seamless in their execution. Although Dewey was never so sure, they continue to be confirmed in their soundness by scholars and present-day events.

The point that is so important is that he began with an idea for a curriculum. Whatever stood in the way of the curriculum, was neatly discarded, or perhaps not so neatly. (We never learn from the record what happened to the unfortunate woman who was the "all-round teacher" but taught facts that were not facts.) Reform should start with the curriculum if we expect it to happen at all. Cooperative learning, portfolios, nongraded classrooms, and other segmental reforms will never do much if there is something not right about the curriculum. Ralph Tyler (1949), who built on Dewey's work, suggested that curriculum developers select "a small list of important objectives that are feasible of attainment" (pp. 43–44).

Multiage Grouping. Multiage grouping also was discarded for curricular reasons; that is, it did not appear to facilitate children's cognitive development. Dewey (1895a) started out with the view that children of various ages should be grouped together, but, as he explained in a talk to the Parent's Association in February 1899:

> We believed there were mental advantages in the give-and-take thus secured, as well as the moral advantages in having the older assume certain responsibilities in the care of the younger. As the school grew, it became necessary to abandon this policy and to group the children with reference to their common capabilities or store of knowledge. (1900d, p. 126)

"In various ways," Dewey continued, "we are attempting to keep a family spirit throughout the school, and not the feeling of isolated classes and grades" (p. 127). Children of all ages still attended school assemblies for singing and to hear what the groups were doing. Older youngsters devoted a half-hour a week to helping some of the younger groups with their work, especially constructing things. But that was a far cry from multiage grouping. The principle had not worked in practice.

There were, of course, no reviews of research for Dewey to consult; he based his decision on experience, and once again it seems to have been on target. In our own time, the results of studies that focused on the cognitive effects of multiage grouping "do not favor the multi-age classroom" (Veenman, 1995, p. 362). More to the point, it seems clear that Dewey found vertical grouping more in keeping with the developmental curriculum and vertical theme. As noted earlier, each age group had a topic reflecting the increasing capability of humans to find ways of solving problems, and sometimes creating new problems. The curriculum lent itself to single-age grouping. Dewey's stages of growth, however, were multiage—an interesting difference that cannot be explored here but begs investigation.

Dewey and the Teacher: A Pragmatic Faith

Dewey's faith in the teacher has become legendary. It was not sentimental but firmly anchored in common sense and followed from what he saw as the reality of things, pedagogically speaking. Dewey (1904a) insisted that whatever the instructional theory of the moment, mandate from above, organizational innovation, it was in the contact of teacher with child and children with each other where "the real course of study" (p. 23) was found. To believe otherwise is to delude ourselves, and, therefore, one has to have faith in the teacher, but that faith need not and should not be blind. In his school, Dewey found that some teachers were more competent than others and had a better grasp of his school's underlying ideas and purposes. In retrospect, he wished that more effort had been made in the school's later years to shore up the teachers' theoretical knowledge, so that they could better relate practice to theory (Mayhew & Edwards, 1936). Nevertheless, in his words, "the development of concrete material and of methods of dealing with it was wholly in the hands of the teachers" (p. 367). What really helped in this regard was the school's underlying hypothesis that learning is connected with active work. This clean and simple concept guided instruction and lay at the heart of the teachers' meetings, which were, in effect, seminars. In fact, it ruled the roost, so to speak.

School organization followed the curriculum organization. When the school became larger, department heads worked with teachers in each special field as well as with all other heads to ensure that the curriculum was articulated and was revised as the children's attitudes indicated problems.

Supervision and Curriculum Improvement—A Unitary Process. The field of curriculum had not yet been developed; that came later (Cremin, 1971; Tanner & Tanner, 1990, 1995). However, Dewey's school pioneered a guiding principle that continues to serve us well: Supervision and curriculum development are an integral process. This idea has since been developed further by others. The work of Hilda Taba was particularly notable in this regard and was discussed earlier.

What might we find for ourselves in Dewey's faith? Two things stand out in particular. First, the reality of the teacher is here to stay; a teacher is no less real than a mother or a father. This is not something that we would wish to change, considering the value of the modeling effect alone. However, the more we deny that reality—the essential face-to-face contact—the less likely we are to reform our schools. No one is suggesting anything that parents do not want for their children. They want small classes, catch-up help, and teachers who support the child's aspirations. Anyone who doubts this need only ask the parents.

Second, one should never take for granted that all teachers are equally intimate with theoretical principles. (While this point may seem obvious, like so many obvious things, it often is ignored.) My own experience is that teachers often are expected to master the instructional approaches without any understanding of the reasons behind them. This is certain death for school reform. However, the solution is out there waiting, if we will but take our cue from Dewey's school: seminar-type discussions where problems are considered in their theoretical as well as practical relations.

Reflection. In a session of the American Educational Research Association annual meeting in 1996 in New York, a teacher educator commented that she was tired of hearing about Dewey's problem method. "What about reflection?," she asked the speaker, who happened to be the noted Dewey biographer Alan Ryan (1995). Ryan's response is worth quoting here. "Do not sell the problem short," he said. "Reflection is really part of problem solving. What it says is stop—stop and think." Teachers need to be able to stop and think—collaboratively and individually. The thinking always concerns a problem, what comes next. Dewey's teachers stopped and thought, and this was a part of the curriculum development (and supervision) process.

LOOKING AT REFORM THE DEWEY WAY

We come back now to the beginning—Dewey's purpose in starting his school, which was to show what was advisable. The questions that concerned Dewey concern us today. Should classes be smaller? Should there be a different approach to learning and discipline in our schools? If so, there needed to be some school to demonstrate this. Dewey's school did this and more: It showed not only what was advisable but what was possible—given certain circumstances, of course, about which he pulled no punches.

Dewey looked at reform in a very simplified way; reformers today tend to look at reform in a very complicated way, thereby obscuring some of its most essential features: smaller classes, a developmental curriculum that begins with children's natural abilities and interests, and opportunities for children to give of themselves through their own creativity. The idea that teachers must communicate and parents must communicate and all must be able to talk with each other is really very simple, as is the point that Dewey would continue to make long after he left Chicago: The human character is shaped by what goes on outside of school as well as in school.

Building Character—The School and Its (Sometimes) Allies

Dewey (1897a) had plenty to say about schools' moral work, and his school was based on these ideas: (1) the school as a social community, which by its nature provides experience in community life; (2) formation of positive habits of perseverance, precision, cooperation, and service to the community (instead of emphasis on wrongdoing); and (3) teaching each and every subject in a way that brings out and makes central how people are affected by it.

There is emotion involved here as well as intellect. According to Dewey (1897a), the interest in community welfare that he wanted his school to instill in children is "an interest which is intellectual, practical as well as emotional" (p. 15). Dewey's moral individual has an interest in "perceiving whatever makes for social order and progress, and for carrying these principles out." This, Dewey said, "is the ultimate ethical habit to which all school habits must be related if they are to be animated by the breath of moral life" (p. 15).

Models of Behavior. Dewey's moral individual has the courage of his or her convictions. What is the role of the school in developing such a risk-taking person? As Sidney Hook (1975), who was one of Dewey's students and contributed the preface to the 1975 reprint of *Moral Principles in Education*, pointed out, "Dewey does not say" (p. xvi). Hook asks whether perhaps it might be done by providing youngsters with models of behavior in history, literature, and art. This was done in Dewey's school; we know from the teachers' reports that the models were there from past and present real life. Each topic studied in connection with the vertical theme had its share of models—who might not be worth emulating in all respects (who is?), but at least stood up for what they were committed to as the right in the conflicts of life. Learning and doing models were provided by means of contact with the heroes of another cloth—university researchers who were immersed in finding the answers to the world's secrets (and those of other planets) and whose enthusiasm was inescapably contagious.

Thus, although Dewey may not have described it in his moral education book or the earlier Herbart yearbook article (1897a) on which it was based, the curriculum of his school was peopled with marvelous models who did things to enrich people's lives and, indeed, make them possible, and who unveiled the world's wonders, beckoning the children ever onward to do the same. They were pied pipers of a sort, but the enticement they offered was not delusive (unlike the Pied Piper of Hamelin).

As every teacher knows, children are influenced by models outside the school. If they are models that make the world a better place, the school's moral work is easier, but if they are persons whose actions create a worse world, the job is more involved. Today, as noted by Dill and Haberman (1995), many children are "surrounded by idols who admire violence" (p. 69). These youngsters are particularly vulnerable because they are growing up in poverty and "are not aware of, have not seen, and so do not value" (p. 69) socially and morally responsible behavior. Dill and Haberman then go on to offer suggestions about how schools can introduce students to "an alternative culture of nonviolent options" (p. 69). The ideas are excellent. The trouble is that they are not enough. Coming in the back door and doing their work on children's character are the other powerful influences.

Powerful outside influences were at work on the children who attended Dewey's school, too, but they were not very different from the school's culture. Does that make the Dewey school's work any less valid? No, because he and the teachers showed what is possible when the influences are on the side of social and moral responsibility. The trick, and no mean one at that, is to make the influences more favorable. Dewey understood this, just as we do. But there is a difference: He went on to do something about it. There is a lesson here.

Influences Versus Instruction. "Business and professional men . . . are in a better position than any other one class to realize what slums and bad housing do to foster criminality," wrote Dewey in 1934 (p. 8). His article on "character training for youth," written for *The Rotarian*, is a real treasure because of its bearing on present character education issues. Indeed, so striking is its contemporaneity that it gives one the odd feeling that Dewey is here observing and commenting on what is going on. In the article there are no delusions; not only does he point out the powerful influences on character, but he gives them honest weight. The issue of criminality is clarified, and because the factors persist, the analysis is useful in our day as well. Most important for ourselves, however, is that he suggests things that educators, businesspeople, and professionals can do to "stem the tide of disrespect for law" (p. 6).

In the mid-1930s, juvenile crime and racketeering were increasing and the school was being blamed for lack of attention to moral education. "There are many who demand that systematic moral and religious instruction be introduced into the schools," wrote Dewey (p. 6); the observation could have been made today. Dewey's article was a response to the criticism and the demand. Was (is) the criticism justified? What was (is) the place of moral education in schools? Those interested in the questions ought to have at least two things clearly in mind, Dewey said. First, character is deeply rooted and "its branches extend far" (p. 6). Dewey defined character as follows:

> Character means all the desires, purposes, and habits that influence conduct. The mind of an individual, his ideas and beliefs, are a part of character, for thought enters into the formation of desires and aims. Mind includes imagination, for there is nothing more important than the nature of the situations that fill imagination when a person is idle or at work. (p. 6)

If it were possible to peer into someone's mind and "see which mental pictures are habitually entertained," we would have the key to the person's character.

Second, and following from the first point, since character is so inclusive, the things that shape it "are equally extensive" (p. 6). It is important that this be remembered when asking what the school is doing and is able to do among the other influences that actively form character. "Compared with other influences that shape desire and purpose, the influence of the school is neither constant nor intense," Dewey wrote (p. 6). Children's character education is going on "every waking hour of the day." Each of the influences that modifies a child's thoughts and desires is part of the child's character development.

Compared with the power of these other influences, the school has the children for only a few hours a day (and not every day) and is concerned mainly with teaching subjects and emphasizing skills that, from the children's viewpoint, bear little relation to the things they are mainly interested in. The material is memorized for "reproduction in recitations" (today it would be for tests, high stakes and otherwise) rather than for "direct manifestation in action outside the school" (p. 6). Dewey pointed out that although schools demanded that students be painstaking, punctual, and neat, "the good habits formed in these matters are so specialized that their transfer over into out-of-school matters is largely a matter of accident." Because of the remoteness of the material, "the effect on character is also remote" (p. 6).

Dewey emphasized that character is formed; it is not a thing that can be taught as mathematics and geography are taught. Yet certain things regarding character can and should be taught. This kind of instruction tends to occur in the home and the school when something is done that is not approved of—for example, the child has lied about something or has left undone an assignment or task. Dewey warned, however, that the effectiveness "of even direct moral instruction cannot be foretold," and that "its efficacy depends upon its fitting into the mass of conditions which play unconsciously upon the young" (p. 8).

Environmental Influences. The conditions that Dewey chose for the purposes of illustration are still present, and one in particular is a major public issue: the effect of visual media upon children. In the 1930s, it was movies. As Dewey pointed out, studies had shown that many children "have been stimulated in unwholesome ways by the movies" (p. 8). Researchers had found a close association between the conditions surrounding the child and the influence of movies upon that youngster.

Dewey described the findings from the research:

> The luxury of scenes depicted on the screen, the display of adventure and easy sex relations, inoculate a boy or girl living in narrow surroundings with all sorts of new ideas and desires. . . . The things that a boy or girl from a well-do-do and cultivated home would discount or take simply as part of the show are for other children ideals to be realized—and without especial regard for the means of their attainment. (p. 8)

When a large family lives in cramped quarters in a depressed neighborhood, parents often are only too glad to have the children out of their way. As Dewey wrote, "The street is their natural outlet and the mother gets relief to the degree that they are out of the two rooms of the home." Further, "The effect of such conditions in creating a type of life in which the discipline and example of the gang count much more than that of the family cannot be exaggerated" (p. 8). This is still true, of course. The same cast of characters is on stage influencing children's character in negative ways: the violence in the movies and on television, the gangs, the bad housing, the families who let children grow up without guidance.

Television and Character. By the 1970s concern about movies had given way to concern about television. Here again what children saw was found to have an effect on behavior; children who watched violence behaved aggressively. Children lacking the prosocial influence of other contexts—peers, neighborhoods, and families—were especially at risk for becoming aggressive. In 1972 a monumental study conducted at the request of Congress concluded that "the present entertainment offerings of the television medium may be contributing, in some measure, to the aggressive behavior of many normal children" (Surgeon General's Scientific Advisory Committee, p. 30). The report's summary emphasized that exposure to violence on television very likely affected only children predisposed by many factors to aggressive behavior.

What is so important about the study is that the subjects first had been surveyed as 8-year-olds in 1960. That study found that the more aggressive the children were in school, the more violence they watched on TV. In 1982 a second follow-up study found that some of the subjects had grown up into dangerous people. At age 30, the men who had seen more TV violence at age 8 had been arrested more frequently for violent crime, were more abusive toward their spouses and had children who were more aggressive (Pearl, Bouthilet, & Lazar, 1982).

Observing high levels of violence on television can affect children in another negative way. Researchers have found that children become accepting (or tolerant) of aggressive behavior in real life (Drabman & Thomas, 1974; Molitor & Hirsch, 1994). This is not a finding to give comfort to educators concerned with character formation, or for that matter to the public.

As Dewey recognized, families, peers, neighborhoods, and schools can multiply or undermine each other's effects. It has been suggested that when prosocial behaviors are reinforced in other contexts, the negative effects of television may be countered or neutralized (Cremin, 1976; Heusmann, cited in Mortimer, 1994). There is an easier (and more certain) way of dealing with the problem: changing television. As Robert Lieber, a researcher who reviewed all the research in the 1972 study, pointed out in a newspaper interview, television is one cause of violence that can be altered more easily than a family's emotional climate or economic status. "We don't want to take the babysitter away," he said, "we just want to keep her from committing murder in the living room" (Charlton, 1972, p. 63).

The years have gone by and other than parental advisory warnings run by broadcasters when they determine that the shows are violent, things are very much the same. The babysitter is still committing murder. The television industry takes the position that parents can regulate what their children see. The position is unreasonable; many (if not most) parents cannot be with their youngsters all the time. The technology is available to permit parents to screen programs deemed inappropriate, but the question remains as to whether they will do so. Families that generally provide poor guidance or no guidance are not likely to do it. Children from these environments are especially vulnerable to what they see on the screen. According to a researcher on the effects of television, it is "unrealistic" to expect parents to be the regulators "all by themselves" (Eron, cited in Mortimer, 1994, p. 7).

However much they may ignore it, or wish they didn't have to think about it, educators are having their good efforts undermined by television. As one observer quipped, "All this is hardly news." He went on to point out:

> The elementary idea that children need the moral direction and protection of adults, backed by force of law, governs policy in virtually every sphere of Ameri-

can life—except television, the most pervasive influence of all. (Frankel, 1995, p. 42)

Most of us feel that there is nothing that we can do about the outside influences; our domain is in the classroom and/or school. Perhaps in feeling that way we are selling our children short. Dewey would not—and did not— let the outside influences off so easily.

Needed Changes. Dewey identified four factors in the improvement of character education. The first was economic change. "It is difficult to produce a cooperative type of character in an economic system that lays stress on competition," Dewey (1934, p. 58) told the Rotarians. The second factor was parent education, which was "a large element in bringing about better moral education of children and youth" (p. 58). In the course of a generation, knowledge of how human nature is developed had grown tremendously. But there were "multitudes" of parents who had not the slightest contact with this knowledge and were "totally unaware of the influences that are most powerfully affecting the moral fiber of their children" (p. 58). The humanity of John Dewey simply flowed in this proposal, for society had not helped parents to cope intelligently and needed to do so. The third factor was the provision of recreation for youth. According to Dewey, the young naturally are impelled "toward activity and toward some kind of collective association," and neither were being provided for under the changed conditions of urbanization and changes in rural life. This was contributing to the poor results in character formation.

Last but not least was the school. "If I put the school fourth and last," Dewey wrote, "it is not because I regard it as the least important of factors in moral training but because its success is so much bound up with the operation of the three others" (p. 58). What changes could schools make that would be helpful? There were two, in particular, both lessons that Dewey learned from his own school. First, schools needed to be organized as communities. Moral education through discussion is more effective if it grows from particular situations in children's experience rather than focusing on discussing "virtues and vices in the abstract" (p. 58). Explained Dewey:

> The more the school is organized as a community in which pupils share, the more opportunity there is for this kind of discussion and the more surely it will lead to the problems of larger social groupings outside the school. Moreover, such organization would give practice in the give and take of social life, practice in methods of cooperation and would require the assumption of definite responsibilities on the part of young people—adapted of course to their age and maturity. (pp. 58–59)

Second, schools should provide more opportunity for "positive action" and correspondingly less "passivity and mere absorption" than were then present, and still are to a great degree. It is the latter suppressive type of instruction that "stimulates unguided and unruly activity as compensation beyond the schools walls" (p. 59). Moreover, it does not awaken taste and interests that youngsters would follow up on constructively out of school.

Obviously, introducing a course in morals was not the way for schools to do a better job in forming character. Lest his readers miss that point, Dewey warned.

> In short, as far as schools are concerned, the present interest in more effective character education may have two different results. If it is satisfied by merely adding on a special course for direct instruction in good behavior, I do not think it can accomplish much. If it leads public attention to the changes that are needed in the schools in order that they may do more to develop intelligent and sturdy character in the young, it may well be the beginning of a most important movement. (p. 59)

Enlisting Support. Dewey appealed to business and professional organizations to exert an influence in the areas mentioned. He noted that they had already accomplished much in promoting the development of playgrounds. There were other specific things that they could do, ranging from understanding to action:

> They can determine to a great extent the treatment of delinquents, with respect to both prevention and cure. They are in a better position than any other one class to realize what slums and bad housing do to foster juvenile criminality. They can exercise a powerful influence upon the kind of movies that are shown in the community. (p. 59)

They also could influence the curriculum in generative ways for character development. Dewey had little patience with the cost-cutting measures that removed from the curriculum the things that were both developmentally sound and a constructive use of energy. He appealed to business and professional leaders:

> Instead of throwing their powerful influence for so-called economy measures that eliminate provision for activity in lines of useful work in the schools, retaining only the driest and more formal subjects they can effectively cooperate with school authorities to promote school subjects that give a healthy outlet to those impulses for activity that are so strong in the young. (p. 59)

Not only was Dewey proposing constructive ways that business leaders could help, but the suggestions themselves were—and still are—vitally important for the school's work in character education. Take, for example, the problem of television content. Doubtlessly, Dewey today would be much more concerned about television than he was about the movies. The problem is more serious, if for no other reason than the greater accessibility of TV. (Children need not turn their pockets inside out to find a nickel.) As Gilbert Seldes, the critic of popular entertainment, observed, "Entertainment entered the home," and "what was offered was virtually free" (cited in Kammen, 1996, p. 262).

As I read Dewey's article, it occurred to me that educators should not be so school-bound in their prescriptions for character education. For example, every proposal for improved housing in urban neighborhoods that have been neglected for decades should be seen as an opportunity for making the school's influence in shaping character more helpful. Those proposals should be supported by educators. Unfortunately, the ramifications for the school's work of what Dewey called "indirect forces" are not always recognized by educators. The benefits for children may seem too indirect and remote. As one elementary school principal, whose school had a program for helping troubled families get assistance, said, "My number one priority has to be toward improving achievement" (Cohen, 1996, p. 8). But indirect forces such as stressed families and bad housing are more direct than they appear to be where achievement is concerned (Schorr, 1989), and character. (We see how wise Dewey was to view them as inseparable aspects of development.)

Our efforts to create the kind of education that forms character should include all of the influences that form character instead of leaving some of them (the most powerful) out. Dewey is himself a model for improving character education in its widest, and therefore most useful, sense. As one educator observed, blaming the schools for perceived failures in character education can and should be turned to community support (Field, 1996, p. 122), but it will not happen of its own accord.

Features of a Dewey School

One may already have a Dewey school—or be trying to have one. There is much merit in this because the ideas generated from the Laboratory School and discussed in various chapters in this book are approved practices in education, and they result in effective learning. Descriptions of these practices can be found in the literature. This is not to say, however, that the practices can be found in schools—at least, not the way that Dewey had in mind. For example, there is much discussion about problem solving, but many educators talk of higher-order thinking skills as though certain skills could be separated and mastered apart from their real-world context. Still, children may be doing the real thing, the whole act of problem solving, in the school. Only the teachers and other professionals in the school can know, and it is they who can make a difference where the lessons from Dewey's school are concerned. Here are some things to look for in a school:

1. It is organized as a social community; children are learning in the active setting of a miniature community.
2. There is a developmental curriculum that begins in kindergarten with children's natural interests and abilities.
3. The curriculum has two dimensions, the child's side (activities) and the teacher's side (facts and generalizations in the major fields of knowledge).
4. The teachers are specialists in their subject fields.
5. The social significance of subject matter is brought out in instruction.
6. Children have hands-on experiences in the manual arts.
7. Children are engaged in solving real problems, past and present. The subjects in the curriculum are integrated in the way that they work and are synthesized in the real world.
8. There is a powerful organizing vertical theme.
9. Curriculum thought is vertical; teachers have a longitudinal view of the curriculum.
10. Teachers work together in planning theme-related activities.
11. Teachers confer frequently, informally and formally.
12. The school is imbued with a test-and-see (experimental) attitude.
13. The curriculum is continually being developed and plans are modified as new difficulties and potentials are found.
14. There is a close relationship with a university.
15. Classes are small enough to give individual attention to each child.
16. The child's attention is self-impelled.
17. Regarding discipline, appropriate behavior is determined by the nature of the work to be done.
18. In the case of individual discipline problems, the child is redirected into a different activity with the same objective.
19. Younger groups begin the day by reviewing what was accomplished the day before and planning the day's work cooperatively; older children start right in on their independent projects.
20. Children are free to move around in the room and seek help from others.
21. The teacher is viewed by the children as a fellow worker in the activities in progress instead of as an all-powerful ruler.
22. Children are developing habits of cooperation and service to the community.
23. Teachers support the child's aspirations.

24. The school takes advantage of cultural and educational institutions in the community to enrich the curriculum and children's lives; Dewey's idea that there is no lower or higher education, just education, is in operation.

25. The children are happy.

The theory behind the school—the idea of the school as a small cooperative society where, under wise guidance, children can solve problems at any stage of development, and where "the systematic knowledge of adult consciousness is gradually and systematically worked out" (Dewey, 1897b, p. 364)—is remarkable for it embraces all that we, who as a people demand so much of our schools, could want for our children. But there is more to be learned about children's learning. We need laboratory schools to demonstrate what is possible. Meanwhile, the lessons learned from Dewey's Laboratory School can be applied with great profit for children and pleasure for teachers. Perhaps the best part of the story is just beginning.

References

Abbott, J. (1995). Children need communities. *Educational Leadership, 52*(8), 6-10.

Anderson, R. D. (1995). Curriculum reform: Dilemmas and promise. *Phi Delta Kappan, 77*(1), 33-39.

Apple Computer, Inc. (1995). Advertisement. *Educational Leadership, 52*(8), 1.

Applebome, P. (1996a, February 21). Governors want new focus on education. *New York Times*, p. B8.

Applebome, P. (1996b, March 28). Clinton urges state action on education. *New York Times*, p. B10.

Baker, M. C. (1955). *Foundations of Dewey's educational theory*. New York: King's Crown Press.

Ball, F. H. (1900). Manual training. *Elementary School Record, 1*(7), 177-185.

Baron, J. B., & Wolf, D. P. (Eds.). (1996). *Performance-based student assessment: Challenges and possibilities* (Ninety-fifth Yearbook of the National Society for the Study of Education, Part 1). Chicago: University of Chicago Press.

Bates, S. (1995, January 8). A textbook of virtues. *New York Times*, Education Life, pp. 4A, 16-18, 44, 46.

Battista, M. T. (1994). Teacher beliefs and the reform movement in mathematics education. *Phi Delta Kappan, 75*(6), 462-470.

Beane, J. A. (1995). Curriculum integration and the disciplines of knowledge. *Phi Delta Kappan, 76*(8), 616-622.

Biggs, J. B. (1992). Returning to school. In A. Demetriou, M. Shayer, & A. Efklides (Eds.), *Neo-Piagetian theories of cognitive development* (pp. 277-294). London: Routledge & Kegan Paul.

Bloom, B. S. (1984). The 2 sigma problem: Search for methods of group instruction as effective as one-to-one tutoring. *Educational Researcher, 13*(6), 4-16.

Bolin, F. S., & Panaritis, P. (1992). Searching for a common purpose: A perspective on the history of supervision. In C. Glickman (Ed.), *Supervision in transition* (Yearbook of the Association for Supervision and Curriculum Development, pp. 30-43). Alexandria, VA: Association for Supervision and Curriculum Development.

Bowman, B. (1991). Educating language minority children: Challenges and opportunities. In S. L. Kagan (Ed.), *The care and education of young children: Obstacles and opportunities* (Nintieth Yearbook of the National Society for the Study of Education, Part 1, pp. 17–29). Chicago: University of Chicago Press.

Bradley, A. (1995, October 18). Training sessions target religious right at the grassroots. *Education Week, 15*(7), 6.

Brandt, R. (1992). On building learning communities: A conversation with Hank Levin. *Educational Leadership, 50*(1), 19–23.

Brandt, R. (1993). What can we really do? *Educational Leadership, 51*(3), 5.

Brent, J. (1993). *Charles Sanders Peirce: A life.* Bloomington: Indiana University Press.

Bruner, J. S. (1960). *The process of education.* Cambridge, MA: Harvard University Press.

Bruner, J. S. (1985). *Child's talk: Learning to use language.* New York: Norton.

Burns, T., & Stalker, G. M. (1972). Models of mechanistic and organic structure. In K. Azumi & J. Hage (Eds.), *Organizational systems* (pp. 240–255). Lexington, MA: Heath.

Buttenweiser, P. L. (1969). *The Lincoln School and its times.* Unpublished doctoral dissertation, Columbia University, New York.

Butterfield, F. (1996, May 6). Major crimes fell in '95. *New York Times,* pp. A1, B8.

Butts, R. F., & Cremin, L. A. (1953). *A history of education in American culture.* New York: Holt, Rinehart & Winston.

Cage, M. C. (1995, April 7). Re-engineering. *Chronicle of Higher Education,* pp. A16, A19.

Cambone, J. (1995). Time for teachers in restructuring. *Teachers College Record, 96*(3), 512–543.

Camp, K. B. (1900). Science in elementary education. *Elementary School Record, 1*(6), 155–166.

Camp, K. B. (1903). Elementary science teaching in the laboratory school. *Elementary School Teacher, 1*(4), 1–8.

Campbell, C. M. (1952). *Practical applications of democratic administration.* New York: Harper & Row.

Caswell, H. L., & Campbell, D. S. (1935). *Curriculum development.* New York: American Book Company.

Charlton, L. (1972, February 19). Study aides voice misgivings about report on TV violence. *New York Times,* pp. 1, 63.

Chase, F. S. (1962, Spring). Purpose of a laboratory school. *Laboratory School Administrators Association Newsletter,* p. 2.

Childs, J. L. (1939). The educational philosophy of John Dewey. In P. A. Schilpp (Ed.), *The philosophy of John Dewey* (pp. 417–444). New York: Tudor.

Christie, J. F. (Ed.). (1991). *Play and early literacy development.* Albany, NY: State University of New York Press.

Cohen, D. L. (1996, May 1). In the zone: Effort aims to link economic gains, school reforms. *Education Week, 15,* 1, 8–9.

Comer, J. (1988). Educating poor minority children. *Scientific American, 295*(5), 42–48.

Commager, H. S. (1951). *Living ideas in America.* New York: Harper and Row.

Cordeiro, P. A. (1994). The principal's role in curricular leadership and program development. In L. W. Hughes (Ed.), *The principal as leader* (pp. 161–183). New York: Macmillan.

Cremin, L. A. (1961). *The transformation of the school.* New York: Knopf.

Cremin, L. A. (1965). *The genius of American education.* New York: Vintage Books.

Cremin, L. A. (1971). Curriculum-making in the United States. *Teachers College Record, 73*(2), 207–220.

Cremin, L. A. (1974). The free school movement—a perspective. *Today's Education, 63*(1), 71–74.

Cremin, L. A. (1976). *Public education.* New York: Basic Books.

Cronbach, L. (1981). Tyler's contribution to measurement and evaluation. *Journal of Thought, 21*(1), 47–52.

Cuffaro, H. K. (1995). *Experimenting with the world: John Dewey and the early child-hood classroom.* New York: Teachers College Press.

Cushman, L. S. (1900). Principles of education as applied to art. *Elementary School Record, 1*(1), 3–11.

Damon, W. (1977). *The social world of the child.* San Francisco: Jossey-Bass.

Darling-Hammond, L., & McLaughlin, M. W. (1995). Policies that support professional development in an era of reform. *Phi Delta Kappan, 76*(8), 597–604.

Darling-Hammond, L., & Sclan, E. (1992). Policy and supervision. In C. Glickman (Ed.), *Supervision in transition* (Yearbook of the Association for Supervision and Curriculum Development, pp. 7–29). Alexandria, VA: Association for Supervision and Curriculum Development.

Darling-Hammond, L., & Snyder, J. (1992). Reframing accountability: Creating learner-centered schools. In A. Lieberman (Ed.), *The changing contexts of teaching* (Ninety-first Yearbook of the National Society for the Study of Education, Part 1, pp. 11–36). Chicago: University of Chicago Press.

Darwin, C. R. (1860). *On the origin of species by means of natural selection; or, the preservation of favored races in the struggle for life.* London: J. Murray. (Original work published 1859)

Davis, M. D., & Reid, M. J. (1996, April). *The facelift of a school subject.* Paper presented at the meeting of the Society for the Study of Curriculum History, New York.

DePencier, I. B. (1967). *The history of the laboratory schools: The University of Chicago 1896–1965.* Chicago: Quadrangle Books.

Dewey, J. (1895a). *Plan of organization of the university primary school.* Privately printed (University of Chicago Archives, Regenstein Library).

Dewey, J. (1895b). The results of child study applied to education. *Transactions of the Illinois Society for Child-Study, 1*(4), 18–19.

Dewey, J. (1896a). Pedagogy as a university discipline. *University Record* (University of Chicago), *1*, 353–355.

Dewey, J. (1896b). The reflex arc concept in psychology. *Psychological Review, 3*, 357–370.

Dewey, J. (1896c). The university school. *University Record* (University of Chicago, *1*, 417–419.

Dewey, J. (1897a). Ethical principles underlying education. In C. A. McMurry (Ed.), *Third yearbook of the National Herbart Society* (pp. 7–34). Chicago: University of Chicago Press.

Dewey, J. (1897b). The psychological aspect of the school curriculum. *Educational Review, 13*, 356–369.

Dewey, J. (1897c). The university elementary school, history and character. *University Record* (University of Chicago), *3*, 72–75.

Dewey, J. (1899). *The school and society*. Chicago: University of Chicago Press.

Dewey, J. (1900a). Froebel's educational principles. *Elementary School Record*, *1*(5), 143–151.

Dewey, J. (1900b). General introduction to groups V and VI. *Elementary School Record*, *1*(2), 49–52.

Dewey, J. (1900c). Psychology of occupations. *Elementary School Record*, *1*(3), 82–85.

Dewey, J. (1900d). The psychology of the elementary curriculum. *Elementary School Record*, *1*(9), 221–232.

Dewey, J. (1900e). *The school and society* (3rd ed.). Chicago: University of Chicago Press and New York: McClure, Phillips.

Dewey, J. (1902). *The child and the curriculum*. Chicago: University of Chicago Press.

Dewey, J. (1903). Interest in relation to training of the will. In C. A. McMurry (Ed.), *Second supplement to the first yearbook for 1895 of the National Herbart Society* (pp. 5–39). Chicago: University of Chicago Press. (Original work published 1896)

Dewey, J. (1904a). *The educational situation*. Chicago: University of Chicago Press.

Dewey, J. (1904b). The relation of theory to practice in education. In C. A. McMurry (Ed.), *The relation of theory to practice in the education of teachers* (Third Yearbook of the National Society for the Scientific Study of Education, Part 1, pp. 9–30). Chicago: University of Chicago Press.

Dewey, J. (1909). *Moral principles in education*. Boston: Houghton Mifflin.

Dewey, J. (1910). *How we think*. Boston: Heath.

Dewey, J. (1913). *Interest and effort in education*. Boston: Houghton Mifflin.

Dewey, J. (1916). *Democracy and education*. New York: Macmillan.

Dewey, J. (1930). From absolutism to experimentalism. In G. P. Adams & W. P. Montague (Eds.), *Contemporary American philosophy* (Vol. 2, pp. 13–27). New York: Macmillan.

Dewey, J. (1933a). *How we think* (rev. ed.). Lexington, MA: Heath.

Dewey, J. (1933b). Why have progressive schools? *Current History*, *38*, 441–448.

Dewey, J. (1934, September). Character training for youth. *Rotarian*, *45*, 6–8, 58–59.

Dewey, J. (1935). *Liberalism & social action*. New York: Putnam's Sons.

Dewey, J., & Dewey, E. (1915). *Schools of tomorrow*. New York: Dutton.

Dewey, J., & Runyon, L. L. (Eds.). (1900). *Elementary School Record* [a series of nine monographs]. Chicago: University of Chicago Press.

Dewey, J., & Tufts, J. H. (1936). *Ethics*. New York: Henry Holt. (Original work published 1908)

Dewey, J. M. (1939). Biography of John Dewey. In P. A. Schilpp (Ed.), *The philosophy of John Dewey* (pp. 3–45). New York: Tudor.

Dill, V. S., & Haberman, M. (1995). Building a gentler school. *Educational Leadership*, *52*(5), 69–71.

Donatelli, R. (1971). The contributions of Ella Flagg Young to the educational enterprise. Unpublished doctoral dissertation, University of Chicago.

Drabman, R. S., & Thomas, M. H. (1974). Does media violence increase children's toleration of real-life aggression? *Developmental Psychology*, *10*(3), 418–421.

Dunleavey, M. P. (1995, January 18). Hopeful start for bringing social studies to life. *New York Times*, p. B7.

Dykhuizen, G. (1973). *The life and mind of John Dewey*. Carbondale: Southern Illinois University Press.

Elam, S. M., & Rose, L. C. (1995). The 27th annual Phi Delta Kappa/Gallup poll of the public's attitudes toward the public schools. *Phi Delta Kappan, 77*(1), 41–56.

Elkind, D. (1991). Developmentally appropriate practice: A case study of educational inertia. In S. L. Kagan (Ed.), *The care and education of young children: Obstacles and opportunities* (Ninetieth Yearbook of the National Society for the Study of Education, Part 1, pp. 1–16). Chicago: University of Chicago Press.

Elkind, D. (1995). School and family in the postmodern world. *Phi Delta Kappan, 77*(1), 8–14.

Elliot, C. (1982). The measurement characteristics of development tests. In S. Modgil & C. Modgil (Eds.), *Jean Piaget: Consensus and controversy* (pp. 241–255). New York: Holt, Rinehart & Winston.

Elmore, R. F., & Fuhrman, S. H. (1994). *The governance of curriculum*. Alexandria, VA: Association for Supervision and Curriculum Development.

Emmer, E., & Aussiker, A. (1987, April). *School and classroom discipline programs: How well do they work?* Paper presented at the annual meeting of the American Educational Research Association, Washington, D.C.

Epps, E. G. (1992). School-based management: Implications for minority parents. In J. J. Lane & E. G. Epps (Eds.), *Restructuring the schools: Problems and prospects* (pp. 143–163). Berkeley: McCutchan.

Epstein, J. (1990). What matters in the middle grades—grade span or practices? *Phi Delta Kappan, 71*(6), 436–444.

Feffer, A. (1993). *Pragmatists and American progressivism*. Ithaca, NY: Cornell University Press.

Ferguson, E. S. (1992). *Engineering and the mind's eye*. Cambridge, MA: M.I.T. Press.

Field, S. L. (1996). Historical perspective on character education. *Educational Forum, 60*(2), 118–123.

Finklestein, B. (1989). *Governing the young: Teacher behavior in popular primary schools in the nineteenth century United States*. New York: Falmer.

Floden, R. E., Buchmann, M., & Schwille, J. R. (1987). Breaking with everyday experience. *Teachers College Record, 88*(4), 485–506.

Foshay, A. W. (1995). Aesthetics and history. *Journal of Curriculum and Supervision, 10*(3), 191–206.

Fox, S. M., & Singletary, T. J. (1986). Deductions about supportive induction. *Journal of Teacher Education, 37*(1), 12–15.

Frankel, M. (1995, October 8). "Alas for Hamelin!" *New York Times*, Section 6, pp. 42, 44.

Fullan, M. (1991). *The new meaning of educational change*. New York: Teachers College Press.

Geiger, B. (1994). Stimulating moral growth in the classroom: A model. *High School Journal, 77*(4), 280–285.

Gloeckner, G. W., & Knowlton, L. K. (1996). Females in technology education: Obligation of a democratic society. *Technology Teacher, 55*(4), 47–49.

Goldhaber, J. (1994). If we call it science, *then* can we let the children play? *Childhood Education, 71*(1), 24–27.

Goodlad, J. I. (1984). *A place called school.* New York: McGraw-Hill.

Goodspeed, T. W. (1916). *A history of the University of Chicago: The first quarter-century.* Chicago: University of Chicago Press.

Goodspeed, T. W. (1928). *William Rainey Harper.* Chicago: University of Chicago Press.

Griffin, G. (1995). Influences of shared decision making on school and classroom activity: Conversations with five teachers. *Elementary School Journal, 96*(1), 29–45.

Grossman, P. (1992). Teaching to learn. In A. Lieberman (Ed.), *The changing contexts of teaching* (Ninety-first Yearbook of the National Society for the Study of Education, Part 1, pp. 179–196). Chicago: University of Chicago Press.

Harding, H. H. (1903). Social needs of children. *Elementary School Teacher, 4*(4), 205–209.

Harmer, A. (1900). Textile industries. *Elementary School Record, 1*(3), 71–81.

Harms, W. (1990, Winter). Stories from the Dewey school. *Lab Notes, 11*(2), 2–4, 6–11.

Harris, W. T. (1898). My pedagogical creed. In O. H. Lang (Ed.), *Educational creeds of the century* (pp. 36–46). New York: Kellogg.

Hartshorne, H., & May, M. A. (1929–1930). *Studies in the nature of character* (Vols. 1–2). New York: Macmillan.

Hernandez, R. (1994, April 20). Group sues school districts over civic service programs. *New York Times,* p. B13.

Hersh, R. H., Miller, J. P., & Fielding, G. D. (1980). *Models of moral education.* New York: Longman.

Hidi, S. (1990). Interest and its contribution as a mental resource for learning. *Review of Educational Research, 60*(4), 549–571.

Hidi, S., & Baird, W. (1988). Strategies for increasing text-based interest and students' recall of expository texts. *Reading Research Quarterly, 23*(4), 465–483.

Honan, W. H. (1994, May 27). Schlesinger sees free speech in peril. *New York Times,* p. B3.

Hook, S. (1975). Preface. In J. Dewey, *Moral principles in education* (pp. xi–xvi). Carbondale: Southern Illinois University Press. (Original work published 1909)

Howard, M. B. (1993). Service learning: Character education applied. *Educational Leadership, 51*(3), 42–43.

Isolation in school systems. (1897, April 30). *University Record* (University of Chicago) *2,* 41–43.

Jackman, W. S. (1904). A brief history of the school of education. *University Record* (University of Chicago), *9,* 2–7.

Jackson, P. W. (1968). *Life in classrooms.* New York: Holt, Rinehart & Winston.

Jackson, P. W. (1981). Comprehending a well-run comprehensive: A report on a visit to a large suburban high school. *Daedalus, 110*(4), 81–95.

Jackson, P. W. (1990). Introduction. In J. Dewey, *The school and society and the child and the curriculum* (pp. ix–xxxii). Chicago: University of Chicago Press.

James, W. (1890). *Principles of psychology.* New York: Henry Holt.

James, W. (1904). The Chicago school. *Psychological Bulletin, 1*, 1–5.

Jones, R. S., & Tanner, L. N. (1981). Classroom discipline: The unclaimed legacy. *Phi Delta Kappan, 62*(7), 494–497.

Kagan, J. (1994). *Nature of the child*. New York: Basic Books.

Kammen, M. (1996). *The lively arts: Gilbert Seldes and the transformation of cultural criticism in the United States*. New York: Oxford University Press.

Katz, L. G. (1991). Pedagogical issues in early childhood education. In S. L. Kagan (Ed.), *The care and education of young children: Obstacles and opportunities* (Nineteenth Yearbook of the National Society for the Study of Education, Part 1, pp. 50–68). Chicago: University of Chicago Press.

Kilbridge, J. T. (1949). The concept of habit in the philosophy of John Dewey. Unpublished doctoral dissertation, University of Chicago.

Kilpatrick, W. H. (1918). The project method. *Teachers College Record, 19*(4), 319–335.

Kilpatrick, W. H. (1925). *Foundations of method*. New York: Macmillan.

Kilpatrick, W. H. (1939). Dewey's influence on education. In P. A. Schilpp (Ed.), *The philosophy of John Dewey* (pp. 447–473). New York: Tudor.

Kliebard, H. M. (1988). Fads, fashions and rituals: The instability of curriculum change. In L.N. Tanner (Ed.), *Critical issues in curriculum* (Eighty-seventh Yearbook of the National Society for the Study of Education, Part 1, pp. 16–34). Chicago: University of Chicago Press.

Kohlberg, L. (1963). The development of children's orientations toward a moral order: I. Sequence in the development of moral thought. *Vita Humana, 6*, 11–13.

Kohlberg, L. (1970). Education for justice. In J. M. Gustafson (Ed.), *Moral education: Five lectures* (pp. 57–65). Cambridge, MA: Harvard University Press.

Kohlberg, L., Kauffman, K., Scharf, P., & Hickey, J. (1974). *The just community approach to corrections*. Cambridge, MA: Moral Education Research Foundation.

Krapp, A. (1989). Interest, learning and academic achievement. In P. Nenniger (Chair), *Task motivation by interest*. Symposium conducted at the meeting of the Third European Conference of Learning and Instruction, Madrid.

Krapp, A., Hidi, S., & Renninger, K. A. (1992). Interest, learning and development. In K. A. Renninger, S. Hidi, & A. Krapp (Eds.), *The role of interest in learning and development* (pp. 3–25). Hillsdale, NJ: Erlbaum.

Krupnick, M. (1995, September 24). Liberal saint: John Dewey who "brought pragmatism into the great world." *Chicago Tribune*, Section 14, pp. 6–7.

Laboratory Schools Work Reports, 1898–1899 (University of Chicago Archives, Regenstein Library).

Lagemann, E. C. (1996). Experimenting with education: John Dewey and Ella Flagg Young at the University of Chicago. *American Journal of Education, 104*(3), 171–185.

Levin, H. (1990). *Accelerated schools: A new strategy for at-risk students*. Palo Alto: Accelerated Schools Project, Stanford University.

Lieberman, A. (1995). Practices that support teacher development: Transforming conceptions of professional education. *Phi Delta Kappan, 76*(8), 591–596.

Lieberman, A., Falk, B., & Alexander, L. (1995). A culture in the making: Leadership in learner-centered schools. In J. Oakes & K. H. Quartz (Eds.), *Creating new educational communities* (Ninety-fourth Yearbook of the National Society for the Study of Education, Part 1, pp. 108–129). Chicago: University of Chicago Press.

Likert, R. (1977). *Past and future perspectives on system 4.* Ann Arbor, MI: Rensis Likert Associates.

Linn, M. C. (1994). The tyranny of the means: Gender and expectations. *Notices of the American Mathematical Society, 41*(7), 766–769.

Lukens, H. (1901, April 20). Letter to Dewey. April 20, 1901. University Presidents' Papers. University of Chicago Archives, Regenstein Library, University of Chicago.

MacFarquhar, N. (1995, October 23). Abolishing class rank splits school. *New York Times,* pp. B1, B6.

MacFarquhar, N. (1996, March 7). The internet goes to school. *New York Times,* pp. B1, B4.

MacIver, D. J. (1990). Meeting the needs of young adolescents: Advisory groups, interdisciplinary teaching teams, and school transition programs. *Phi Delta Kappan, 71*(6), 458–464.

Mackenzie, G. N., & Corey, S. M. (1954). *Instructional leadership.* New York: Bureau of Publications, Teachers College, Columbia University.

McLarin, K. J. (1995, February 1). Curriculum or not, teachers teach values. *New York Times,* A1, B7.

McLellan, J. A., & Dewey, J. (1895). *The psychology of number and its application to methods of teaching arithmetic.* New York: Appleton.

Madaus, G. F. (1988). The influence of testing on the curriculum. In L. N. Tanner (Ed.), *Critical issues in curriculum* (Eighty-seventh Yearbook of the National Society for the Study of Education, Part 1, pp. 83–121). Chicago: University of Chicago Press.

Malen, B., & Ogawa, R. (1992). Site-based management: Disconcerting policy issues. In J. J. Lane & E. G. Epps (Eds.), *Restructuring the schools: Problems and prospects* (pp. 185–206). Berkeley: McCutchan.

Manchester GATE School. (1995). Mission Statement. Fresno, CA: Author.

Mayer, M. S. (1941). *William Rainey Harper.* Chicago: University of Chicago Press.

Mayer, M. (1957). *Young man in a hurry.* Chicago: University of Chicago Alumni Association.

Mayhew, K. C. (1934). Draft for Chapter 1, "General history." *Katherine Camp Mayhew Papers.* Special Collections, Milbank Memorial Library, Teachers College, Columbia University.

Mayhew, K. C., & Edwards, A. C. (1936). *The Dewey school.* New York: Appleton-Century.

Mead, G. H. (1934). *Mind, self and society.* Chicago: University of Chicago Press.

Miel, A. (1946). *Changing the curriculum: A social approach.* New York: Appleton-Century-Crofts.

Mitchell, M. (1993). Situational interest: Its multifaceted structure in the secondary school mathematics classroom. *Journal of Educational Psychology, 85*(3), 424–436.

Moehlman, A. B. (1925). *Public education in Detroit*. Bloomington, IL: Public School Publishing.

Molitor, F., & Hirsch, K. W. (1994). Children's toleration of real-life aggression after exposure to media violence: A replication of the Drabman and Thomas studies. *Child Study Journal, 24*(3), 191–204.

Moorman, H., & Egermeier, J. (1992). Educational restructuring: Generative metaphor and new vision. In J. J. Lane & E. G. Epps (Eds.), *Restructuring the schools: Problems and prospects* (pp. 15–59). Berkeley: McCutchan.

Mortimer, J. (1994, February). Profiles. *ISR Newsletter, 18*, 5–7.

Murphy, J. (1991). *Restructuring schools: Capturing and assessing the phenomena*. New York: Teachers College Press.

Mussen, P. (1989). *Child development and personality*. New York: Harper.

National Education Goals Panel. (1994). *The national education goals report: Building a nation of learners*. Washington, DC: U.S. Government Printing Office.

National Research Council. (1989). *Everybody counts: A report to the nation on the future of mathematics education*. Washington, DC: U. S. Government Printing Office.

Nelson, M. R. (1988). Issues of access to knowledge: Dropping out of school. In L. N. Tanner (Ed.), *Critical issues in curriculum* (Eighty-seventh Yearbook of the National Society for the Study of Education, Part 1, pp. 226–243). Chicago: University of Chicago Press.

Newlon, J. H., & Threlkeld, A. L. (1927). The Denver curriculum-revision program. In H. Rugg (Ed.), *Curriculum making: Past and present* (Twenty-sixth Yearbook of the National Society for the Study of Education, Part 1, pp. 229–248). Bloomington, IL.: Public School Publishing.

Newman, M. (1996, January 10). New York leads list of Westinghouse science finalists. *New York Times*, p. B8.

Noddings, N. (1994). Conversation as moral education. *Journal of Moral Education, 23*, 107–118.

Oakes, J. (1995). Normative, technical, and political dimensions of creating new educational communities. In J. Oakes & K. H. Quartz (Eds.), *Creating new educational communities* (Ninety-fourth Yearbook of the National Society for the Study of Education, Part 1, pp. 1–15). Chicago: University of Chicago Press.

Oakes, J., & Quartz, K. H. (Eds.). (1995). *Creating new educational communities* (Ninety-fourth Yearbook of the National Society for the Study of Education, Part 1). Chicago: University of Chicago Press.

O'Connor, N. J. (1904). The educational side of the parents' association of the laboratory school: From a parent's point of view. *Elementary School Teacher, 4*, 532–535.

Paterson, K. (1995, October 15). Family values. *New York Times, Book Review*, p. 32.

Peaceful integration. (1991, October 20). *New York Times*, Section 4, p. 16.

Pearl, D., Bouthilet, L., & Lazar, J. (1982). *Television and behavior: Ten years of scientific progress and implications for the eighties* (Vols. 1 and 2). Washington, DC: U.S. Government Printing Office.

Peterson, P. E. (1985). *The politics of school reform 1870–1940*. Chicago: University of Chicago Press.

Phillips, D. R., & Phillips, D. G. (1994). Beans, blocks and buttons: Developing thinking. *Educational Leadership, 51*(5), 50–53.

The philosophy of education. (1896, November 6). *University Record* (University of Chicago), *1*, 422.

Piaget, J. (1948). *The moral judgment of the child*. New York: Free Press. (Original work published 1932)

Piaget, J. (1970). *Science of education and the psychology of the child*. New York: Orion Press.

Poplin, M. S. (1992). The leader's new role: Looking to the growth of teachers. *Educational Leadership, 49*(5), 10–11.

Portner, J. (1994a, February 9). Educators keeping eye on measures designed to combat youth violence. *Education Week, 13*, 21.

Portner, J. (1994b, April 27). Youth service day brings new challenges to districts. *Education Week, 13*, 7.

Prescott, D. A. (1934). Emotion: Neglected factor in education. *Progressive Education, 11*(8), 459–462.

Prescott, D. A. (1957). *The child in the educative process*. New York: McGraw-Hill.

Purnick, J. (1995, October 23). Schools offered lots of help to a shy Haitian girl— but that was then. *New York Times*, p. B3.

Quartz, K. H. (1995). Sustaining new educational communities: Toward a new culture of school reform. In J. Oakes & K. H. Quartz (Eds.), *Creating new educational communities* (Ninety-fourth Yearbook of the National Society for the Study of Education, Part 1, pp. 240–254). Chicago: University of Chicago Press.

Rannels, L. (1991). The place of industrial arts in the academic community. *Phi Delta Kappan, 72*(6), 456–457.

Rest, J. R. (1983). Morality. In P. H. Mussen (Ed.), *Handbook of child psychology* (4th ed., Vol. 3, pp. 556–629). New York: Wiley.

Rice, J. M. (1893, April). The public schools of Chicago and St. Paul. *Forum, 15*, 200–215.

Rogers, C., & Freiberg, H. J. (1994). *Freedom to learn* (3rd ed.). New York: Merrill.

Ruenzel, D. (1995, February 1). In search of John Dewey. *Education Week, 7*, 23–29.

Rugg, H., & Counts, G. S. (1927). A critical appraisal of current methods of curriculum-making. In H. Rugg (Ed.), *Curriculum making: Past and present* (Twenty-sixth Yearbook of the National Society for the Study of Education, Part 1, pp. 425–447). Bloomington, IL: Public School Publishing.

Ryan, A. (1995). *John Dewey and the high tide of American liberalism*. New York: Norton.

Sarason, S. (1971). *The culture of the school and the problem of change*. Boston: Allyn and Bacon.

Schachter, J.L. (1994, November 30). Confronting Dewey. *Education Week, 6*, p. 37.

School record, notes, and plan. (1896a, November 6). *University Record* (University of Chicago), *1*, 419–422.

School record, notes, and plan. (1896b, December 4). *University Record* (University of Chicago), *1*, 460–461.

Schorr, L. B. (1989). *Within our reach: Breaking the cycle of disadvantage*. New York: Anchor Books.

Schwartz, H. (1988). Unapplied curriculum knowledge. In L. N. Tanner (Ed.), *Critical issues in curriculum* (Eighty-seventh Yearbook of the National Society for the Study of Education, Part 1, pp. 35–59). Chicago: University of Chicago Press.

Scott, C. A. (1994). Project-based science: Reflections of a middle school teacher. *Elementary School Journal, 95*(1), 75–94.

Shakeshaft, C. (1995). Reforming science education to include girls. *Theory Into Practice, 34*(1), 74–79.

Shepard, L. A. (1995). Using assessment to improve learning. *Educational Leadership, 52*(5), 38–43.

Shils, E. (1983). *The academic ethic*. Chicago: University of Chicago Press.

Silvestri, K. (1991). Parent involvement goes to school: New Jersey's public policy and public schools program. *Equity and Choice, 7*(1), 22–27.

Simon, H. M. (1976). *Administrative behavior* (3rd ed.). New York: Free Press.

Simon, S. B., Howe, L. W., & Kirschenbaum, H. (1972). *Values clarification: A handbook of practical strategies for teachers and students*. New York: Hart.

Slade, A., & Wolf, D. P. (Eds.). (1994). *Children at play: Clinical and developmental approaches to meaning and representation*. New York: Oxford University Press.

Slavin, R. E. (1989/90). Here to stay—or gone tomorrow? *Educational Leadership, 47*(4), 3.

Snow, R. E. (1989). Toward assessment of cognitive and conative structures in learning. *Educational Researcher, 18*(9), 8–14.

Sobel, T. (1993). Revising the New York State social studies curriculum. *Teachers College Record, 95*(2), 258–272.

Soltis, J. F. (1994). The new teacher. In S. Hollingsworth & H. Sockett (Eds.), *Teacher research and educational reform* (Ninety-third Yearbook of the National Society for the Study of Education, Part 1, pp. 245–260). Chicago: University of Chicago Press.

Sommerfeld, M. (1994, December 14). Foundations seek more active role in replicating successful models. *Education Week, 14*, 6–7.

Soundy, C. S., & Genisio, M. H. (1994). Asking young children to tell the story. *Childhood Education, 71*(1), 20–23.

Stark, W. E. (1922). *Every teacher's problems*. New York: American Book Company.

Sternberg, R. J. (1986). *Beyond IQ: A triarchic theory of human intelligence*. Cambridge: Cambridge University Press.

Storr, R. J. (1966). *Harper's University: The beginnings*. Chicago: University of Chicago Press.

Surgeon General's Scientific Advisory Committee on Television and Social Behavior. (1972). *Television and growing up: The impact of televised violence*. Washington, DC: U.S. Government Printing Office.

Taba, H. (1962). *Curriculum development: Theory and practice*. New York: Harcourt.

Talmadge, H. (1980). What is individualization? In J. Jeter (Ed.), *Approaches to individualized education* (pp. 5–23). Alexandria, VA: Association for Supervision and Curriculum Development.

Tanner, D. (1988). The textbook controversies. In L. N. Tanner (Ed.), *Critical issues in curriculum* (Eighty-seventh Yearbook of the National Society for the Study of Education, Part 1, pp. 122–147). Chicago: University of Chicago Press.

Tanner, D., & Tanner, L. (1987). *Supervision in education: Problems and practices.* New York: Macmillan.

Tanner, D., & Tanner, L. N. (1990). *History of the school curriculum.* New York: Macmillan.

Tanner, D., & Tanner, L. (1995). *Curriculum development: Theory into practice* (3rd ed.). Englewood Cliffs, NJ: Prentice-Hall.

Tanner, L. (1978). *Classroom discipline for effective teaching and learning.* New York: Holt, Rinehart & Winston.

Tanner, L. N. (1988). The path not taken: Dewey's model of inquiry. *Curriculum Inquiry, 18*(41), 472–479.

Tanner, L. N. (1991). The meaning of curriculum in Dewey's laboratory school. *Journal of Curriculum Studies, 23*(2), 101–117.

Tanner, L., & Tanner, D. (1987). Environmentalism in American pedagogy: The legacy of Lester Ward. *Teachers College Record, 88*(4), 337–347.

Teaching across disciplines. (1994, December). *ASCD Update,* pp. 1, 3–4.

Teeter, A. M. (1995). Learning about teaching. *Phi Delta Kappan, 76*(5), 360–364.

Tyler, R. W. (1949). *Basic principles of curriculum and instruction.* Chicago: University of Chicago Press.

Tyler, R. W. (1957). Foreword. In V. White, *Studying the individual pupil* (pp. ix–x). New York: Harper & Brothers.

Tyler, R. W. (1978). Unfinished tasks of American education. *Educational Studies, 9,* 1–10.

Tyler, R. W. (1986). What the curriculum field needs to learn from its history. *Journal of Thought, 21*(1), 70–78.

Tyler, R. W. (1988). Progress in dealing with curriculum problems. In L. N. Tanner (Ed.), *Critical issues in curriculum* (Eighty-seventh Yearbook of the National Society for the Study of Education, Part 1, pp. 267–276). Chicago: University of Chicago Press.

Tyler, R. W. (1991, March). *The long-term impact of the Dewey school.* Paper presented at the meeting of the John Dewey Society, San Francisco.

U.S. Department of Education. (1991). *America 2000: An education strategy.* Washington, DC: Author.

University elementary school. (1898, November 25). *University Record* (University of Chicago), *3,* 220–221.

University elementary school. (1899a, June 9). *University Record* (University of Chicago), *4,* 62–63.

University elementary school. (1899b, September 1). *University Record* (University of Chicago), *4,* 122–123.

Vaihinger, H. (1935). *The philosophy of "as if"* (2nd ed., C. K. Ogden, trans.). London: Routledge & Kegan Paul.

Van Hoorn, J., Nourot, P., Scales, B., & Alward, K. (1993). *Play at the center of the curriculum.* New York: Macmillan.

Veenman, S. (1984). Perceived problems of beginning teachers. *Review of Educational Research, 54*(2), 143–178.

Veenman, S. (1995). Cognitive and noncognitive effects of multigrade and multiage classes: A best-evidence synthesis. *Review of Educational Research, 65*(4), 319–381.

Vispoel, W. P., & Austin, J. R. (1995). Success and failure in junior high school: A critical incident approach to understanding students' attributional beliefs. *American Educational Research Journal, 32*(2), 377–412.

Washburne, C. (1939). Introduction. In G. Whipple (Ed.), *Child development and the curriculum* (Thirty-eighth Yearbook of the National Society for the Study of Education, Part 1, p. 3). Bloomington, IL: Public School Publishing Co.

Weinreich-Haste, H. (1982). Piaget on morality: A critical perspective. In S. Modgil & C. Modgil (Eds.), *Jean Piaget: Consensus and controversy* (pp. 181–206). New York: Holt, Rinehart & Winston.

Weisskopf, V. E. (1989). *The privilege of being a physicist.* New York: Freeman.

White, M. G. (1977). *The origin of Dewey's instrumentalism.* New York: Octagon Books. (Original work published 1943)

White, V. (1958). *Studying the individual pupil.* New York: Harper & Brothers.

Wilkerson, I. (1989, October 22). Chicago schools try a radical new cure. *New York Times,* p. E3.

Wilson, W. J. (1987). *The truly disadvantaged.* Chicago: University of Chicago Press.

Wirth, A. G. (1980). Socio-technical theory: An alternative paradigm for schools as "good work" places. *Teachers College Record, 82*(1), 1–13.

Wong, K., & Rollow, S. (1989, April). *From mobilization to legislation: A case study of the recent Chicago school reform.* Paper presented at the annual meeting of the Western Political Science Association, Salt Lake City.

Wood, G. H. (1990). Teaching for democracy. *Educational Leadership, 48*(3), 32–37.

Young, E. F. (1902). *Ethics in the school.* Chicago: University of Chicago Press.

Young, E. F. (1906). *Isolation in the school.* Chicago: University of Chicago Press.

Young, E. F. (1916). Democracy and education. *Journal of Education, 84*(1), 7–8.

Youniss, J., & Damon, W. (1994). Social construction in Piaget's theory. In B. Puka (Ed.), *Moral development: A compendium* (pp. 267–286). New York: Garland.

Zevin, J. (1993). World studies in secondary schools and the undermining of ethnocentrism. *The Social Studies, 84*(2), 82–86.

Zumwalt, K. (1989). Beginning professional teachers: The need for a curricular vision. In M.C. Reynolds (Ed.), *Knowledge base for the beginning teacher* (pp. 173–184). Oxford: Pergamon.

Index

About the Author

LAUREL N. TANNER is a professor of education at both the University of Houston and Temple University. Since taking her doctorate in curriculum theory and development from Teachers College in 1967, she has published numerous books, including *Classroom Discipline for Effective Teaching and Learning* and (with Daniel Tanner) *Curriculum Development: Theory into Practice*, the award-winning *History of the School Curriculum*, and *Supervision in Education*.